China's Quest for Military Supremacy

We dedicate this book to our fathers, Robert J. Wuthnow and David Calvin Saunders, and to our sons, Samuel Wuthnow, Thomas Wuthnow, and Miles Campbell Saunders, with respect, admiration, love, and hope for the future.

China's Quest for Military Supremacy

JOEL WUTHNOW

and

PHILLIP C. SAUNDERS

polity

First published in 2025 by Polity Press

Polity Press
65 Bridge Street
Cambridge CB2 1UR, UK

Polity Press
111 River Street
Hoboken, NJ 07030, USA

ISBN-13: 978-1-5095-5693-9 (hardback)
ISBN-13: 978-1-5095-5694-6 (paperback)

A catalogue record for this book is available from the British Library.

Library of Congress Control Number: 2024939676

Typeset in 10 on 13pt Swift
by Cheshire Typesetting Ltd, Cuddington, Cheshire
Printed and bound in Great Britain by CPI Group (UK) Ltd, Croydon

The publisher has used its best endeavors to ensure that the URLs for external websites referred to in this book are correct and active at the time of going to press. However, the publisher has no responsibility for the websites and can make no guarantee that a site will remain live or that the content is or will remain appropriate.

Every effort has been made to trace all copyright holders, but if any have been overlooked the publisher will be pleased to include any necessary credits in any subsequent reprint or edition.

For further information on Polity, visit our website:
politybooks.com

Contents

Maps, Figures, and Tables

Maps

Figures

Tables

Acknowledgments

Students are often the best teachers. This volume grew out of lectures that we designed for a course on the People's Liberation Army (PLA) at the National Defense University in Washington, DC. The goal of the course was to find a way to explain how the PLA – which the Department of Defense has since designated as its "pacing challenge" – operates as an institution, what motivates its leaders, and how to evaluate its capabilities and operations in Asia and beyond. The material needed to be relatable to our students, who were mostly U.S. military officers at the lieutenant colonel/colonel level and senior civilians, while also avoiding the trap of mirror imaging. The PLA has tried to emulate some aspects of a Western military organization but has also remained different in many ways, especially in its Leninist identity and its commitment to defend a particular political party, the Chinese Communist Party. The PLA had also been changing very quickly during the Xi Jinping era, which meant that new teaching materials were needed. Dr. Wuthnow also offered a similar course for master's degree students in Georgetown University's Security Studies Program. More than a hundred students in these courses since 2020 helped us find ways to make knowledge about the PLA more accessible at a time when greater understanding is of the essence, and we tried to incorporate those lessons into this volume. For that, we are in their debt.

Our work is informed by our own research on the PLA and access to China's military that resulted from our participation in various U.S.–China military exchanges. But a general work on the PLA far exceeded our own expertise and required that we draw on insights gleaned from the international PLA studies community, a network of scholars in North America, Europe, and Asia who collectively try to understand the critical features of Chinese military power through open sources despite the PLA's notorious opacity. Presenters and discussants at annual PLA conferences, some of them sponsored by the National Defense University along with our partners at the RAND Corporation, Taiwan's Council of Advanced Policy Studies, and the U.S. Institute of Peace, were especially useful in bringing us up to speed where we lacked subject matter expertise, challenging our assumptions, and improving our own research projects.[1]

Several colleagues went a step further and provided detailed feedback on previous drafts of this volume, either on individual chapters or the full manuscript. They include Kenneth W. Allen, Dennis J. Blasko, Tai Ming Cheung, Bernard D. Cole, Fiona Cunningham, J. Michael Dahm, David Finkelstein, Cristina Garafola, Geoffrey Gresh, Kristen Gunness, Melodie Ha, T.X. Hammes, David Logan, Ryan Martinson, Michael McDevitt, James Siebens, Andrew Taffer, and Jonah Victor. We also received constructive feedback from five anonymous reviewers at the prospectus stage and from two reviewers who read the draft manuscript. Their corrections, suggestions, and insights have made this volume immensely better than what we could have produced without their guidance. Undoubtedly, there will still be errors of fact and judgment in this book and for those we are solely responsible.

Completion of a volume such as this one requires a large and supportive team. At the National Defense University, we were fortunate to receive encouragement from the president, Lt. Gen. Michael T. Plehn, and from recent directors of the Institute for National Strategic Studies, Dr. Laura Junor and Dr. Denise Natali. We also benefited from excellent research assistance from several colleagues – Lauren Edson, Xiang "Sean" Chi, and Bernice Xu – who not only collected data and helped to prepare graphics and figures, but also provided useful comments on the manuscript. Parts of Chapter 5 benefited from research on Chinese nuclear modernization co-authored with David Logan and parts of Chapter 6 benefited from research on military diplomacy co-authored with Melodie Ha and research on China–Russia military relations co-authored with Andrew Taffer. At Polity Press, we thank our editor, Louise Knight, for her vision for a general reader on the Chinese military and for her support at every step of the process, as well as to editorial assistants Inès Boxman and Olivia Jackson, who kept us on track and steered us in the right direction on numerous occasions. Katherine Michaelson provided able proofreading assistance.

Introduction

In August 2022, following a brief visit of then U.S. Speaker of the House Nancy Pelosi to Taipei, Beijing lost its temper. Alongside new economic penalties against Taiwan, China's leaders tasked the People's Liberation Army (PLA) with conducting a bold series of military demonstrations against the island, which China considers a rogue province. The navy held live-fire exercises in seven zones around Taiwan, mimicking the maritime closure areas the island would face in a blockade; air force jets streamed across the midline of the Taiwan Strait, long considered an informal boundary between the two sides; ballistic missiles flew over the island at high altitudes; drones hovered with apparent impunity over Taiwan's offshore islands; and military propagandists attacked reality itself by placing fabricated content on social media, suggesting that PLA units were operating far closer to Taiwan than they really were. International observers worried that Taiwan could be the next victim of great power aggression, following Russia's invasion of Ukraine six months earlier. Some feared that China's leaders would order a full-scale attack by 2027, coinciding with the PLA's centennial anniversary.

Much as the 2008 Olympics marked China's emergence as a global heavyweight, the 2022 military demonstrations against Taiwan symbolized a new era for the PLA. No longer the humble force that former leader Deng Xiaoping had in mind in the 1980s when he urged patience – summed up in his often-quoted quip, "hide our capabilities and bide our time"[1] – the PLA was now more confident, even brazen. Other signs of growing confidence included China's increased use of intimidation tactics in regional territorial disputes, such as those with Japan, Vietnam, the Philippines, and India; the development of new capabilities, including a blue-water navy, stealth aircraft, innovative conventional missile forces, and a major nuclear buildup; a military reorganization launched at the end of 2015 that established a new joint command structure that will be instrumental in China's ability to prepare for and conduct modern wars; and the bold leadership of Chinese President and Chinese Communist Party (CCP) General Secretary Xi Jinping, who exerted firmer control of the PLA than either of his immediate predecessors, Jiang Zemin and Hu Jintao. Xi regularly visited PLA units, urging them to prepare to "fight and win wars," rather than lining their own pockets.

Yet the PLA's new era, unlike Putin's Russia, has not involved large-scale wars against neighboring states. There is a sense of caution that reflects both the party's preoccupation with economic stability at home and a belief that the military might not yet be fully prepared for the type of war China's leaders would seek – one with a "quick victory" all but guaranteed. Although tensions with Taiwan and other neighbors have flared, Beijing has not lost sight of its long-term military modernization goals. In 2020, the CCP approved a new modernization plan with an initial milestone in 2027; other targets were fixed for 2035 and the country's centennial in 2049, by which time the PLA would become "world-class forces," if all went according to plan. The new era is thus defined not only by boldness, but also by a pragmatism that has set China on a different trajectory from its Russian partners and may lead it to field far more lethal and capable military forces in the coming decades.

Purpose of the Book

This book chronicles the development of Chinese military power in the new era. The general aim is to provide national security practitioners, students, and general readers with enough knowledge about how the PLA functions as an institution – its capabilities, structure, and operations – to place recent developments in context, understand how the military instrument supports the strategic goals of the CCP, and more effectively develop and analyze policies and strategies. It thus follows several previous works that provided broad assessments of the PLA in earlier eras.[2] China's increasing military assertiveness, coupled with important changes in PLA hardware and organization under Xi and the general shift in global geopolitics toward an era defined more by great power competition than by cooperation, requires a new look at where the PLA has been, where it is today, and where it might be heading.

A general assessment of China's military power requires consideration of a variety of political, strategic, technical, and operational issues. The book's questions thus include the following: what is the relationship between the PLA and the CCP, and how complete is the party's control of the army? How do China's leaders assess their security environment and what roles and missions does this imply for military power inside China, in Asia, and globally? How has China's military strategy evolved, and what changes has this prompted to the PLA's organizational structure and resourcing approaches? How has the PLA been modernizing the force across the individual warfighting domains, both conventional (land, air, and sea) and strategic (space, cyber, and nuclear)? In what ways are Chinese leaders employing military power to shape the regional environment to their advantage, and what successes and failures have they experienced? How is the PLA preparing for a war with Taiwan and the United States, what might be Beijing's strategic calculus for when and how to use force, and what problems might be encountered? What is the Chinese military's role outside of Asia, and are they poised to challenge the United States as a dominant military power?

The opaque nature of the Chinese system makes these questions difficult to answer. China does periodically publish defense white papers, PLA spokesmen comment on recent events in monthly press conferences, and the Chinese military publishes its own newspapers, though some sources (especially those published in English) are meant more to influence foreign perceptions than to inform. Chinese military pundits, some on active duty, often discuss military matters, but do not represent official views and often cater more to a domestic audience's desire for patriotically charged rhetoric.[3] PLA analysts publish professional articles and books, some of which are accessible, despite growing Chinese restrictions on the availability of sources for foreign researchers. Some of these works have been translated and can be studied by those interested in hearing what the PLA is telling itself.[4] Just one example is the 2020 edition of the PLA's *Science of Military Strategy*, a core text used to educate senior officers in China's military educational system. We have also been fortunate in having had many interactions with PLA analysts and operational commanders in our roles at the U.S. National Defense University, which offered unique glimpses into PLA thinking and progress over the years.

The book also builds on a substantial literature that has been produced on the PLA outside China. At the official level, the U.S. Department of Defense publishes an annual report on China's military power that offers a useful snapshot of PLA capabilities and operations, typically covering events that took place in the previous calendar year; others, including Japan and Taiwan, publish their own assessments. Foreign scholars of the PLA have produced top-notch studies on the individual PLA services and on other topics, such as China's military strategy and technological innovation base.[5] Conferences on the PLA, including those held in the United States, Taiwan, and Singapore, have produced volumes that add to our collective knowledge of how the PLA has been evolving.[6] Nevertheless, information about the PLA remains fragmentary, sometimes conflicting and misleading, and difficult to access, meaning that many of the judgments offered in this book must remain tentative.

General Argument

The main contention in this book is that the PLA is stronger and more confident today than at any point in its history, although it also has intrinsic flaws that neither technology nor money will solve, and that create vulnerabilities should the PLA ever be ordered into combat. Any discussion of the PLA's advantages must begin with a consideration of the direction and leadership provided to the army by the CCP, especially under Xi. The party has launched the country on a path toward the "China dream" of achieving "national rejuvenation" by the middle of the twenty-first century, and has clearly indicated that a strong military is essential if the country is to achieve related goals, including economic security, technological superiority, international influence, and especially "national reunification" with Taiwan. Xi has routinely discussed what he calls the "strong army dream," which he views as part of the "China dream." While he is often described as an "assertive" leader willing to use provocative military displays against neighbors,[7] his pivotal contribution has been in building a stronger peacetime force, most notably carrying out a downsizing and major restructuring of the PLA, beginning in 2015 and continuing into the 2020s.

China's confidence also results from qualitative and quantitative improvements in military hardware. PLA ground forces are equipped with a new generation of fighting vehicles, helicopters, and long-range artillery systems. The air force fields fifth-generation fighters that may be nearly as capable as their U.S. counterparts and has developed new long-range bombers and transport aircraft. The navy is often associated with its growing fleet of aircraft carriers, but its firepower is generated more from advanced surface combatants, such as the *Renhai*-class (Type-055) cruiser, as well as its upgraded diesel-electric attack submarines. China's land-based missiles are among the world's finest and include innovative technologies such as anti-ship ballistic missiles designed to target U.S. aircraft carriers, and long-range missiles fitted with hypersonic glide vehicles meant to evade U.S. missile defenses. China's strategic forces have also been updated. These now include powerful anti-satellite weapons, offensive cyber forces, and most notably a rapidly expanding nuclear deterrent. There is also, to use a cliché, a "quality in quantity." China's military remains the world's largest in terms of manpower. Its growing inventory of fighters, large-tonnage naval and Coast Guard ships (buttressed by the world's largest shipbuilding industry), and missile forces are often displayed against those unable to muster similar numbers.

A third advantage is money. China's official defense budget has surpassed $200 billion, though the actual figure is significantly higher, since several categories of defense expenditures, including research and development and paramilitary forces, are not included in the official numbers. Chinese defense spending outpaces that of all other Asian countries. It remains less than the roughly $800 billion the United States spends on its military, but PLA budgets support activities mostly confined to Asia, while U.S. budgets are stretched to fund operations globally. Maintaining steady budget growth over the last two decades has allowed the PLA to recruit and cultivate higher quality personnel, maintain equipment, conduct training, and procure modern capabilities – and the prospects for continued budget growth are bright. Indeed, China is still spending only a tiny fraction of its gross domestic product on the military (roughly 2%). This is far less than the Soviet Union spent in the late Cold War, when Moscow exhausted its treasury to compete with the West, and less than war-weary Russia, and even the United States today. Beijing has ample room to continue to fund the PLA even as China's economic growth rates slow.

A final source of Chinese strength is what we might call strategic discipline. Chinese diplomats often comment that China has not gone to war since 1979, whereas the United States has been engaged in a near-continuous series of conflicts for much of the same period. Beijing has also avoided signing military alliances that could entangle it in others' wars. These features of restraint are not a reflection of a benign foreign policy, but rather a result of the party's commitment to amassing national strength, including capable military forces, in peacetime. Military expenses are manageable because the party does not need to pay the immense costs of mobilizing for and conducting a war. Even Xi Jinping has carefully sought to keep conflicts with territorial rivals and the United States below the level of lethal violence, instead pursuing military modernization as part of the party's long-term aspirations to achieve "national rejuvenation." As Oriana Mastro has argued, the origins of China's successes can be traced to the strategic focus of a "stealth superpower."[8]

Nevertheless, the PLA suffers from deep-rooted flaws, most of which cannot be fixed by building new capabilities or spending more money. The most fundamental problem is a lack of trust between the Chinese Communist Party and the army. Civilian autocrats throughout modern history have worried about how to build a military strong enough to protect the nation, but not so powerful that it adopts policies against the regime. Military coups in Romania (1989) and the Soviet Union (1991) are well known to Beijing; in China itself, leaders can remember the abortive coup that Lin Biao staged against Mao in 1971, as well as the 1989 Tiananmen movement, in which some in the PLA refused to obey orders to use force against student protesters. The concern today is not a coup, although this possibility can never be ruled out, but the challenge of managing a force that enjoys a high degree of autonomy. Xi has become the strongest leader of the PLA since Mao but has struggled with accountability among his senior officers. The limits on his control became clear in late 2023 when he fired his defense minister and the leaders of the strategic missile force under clouds of corruption – a turn of events that came a decade after Xi launched a massive anti-corruption campaign in the PLA and across the party-state. Questions about the reliability of his senior officers, and about the quality of the equipment they purchased, could reduce the party's confidence in the PLA's warfighting abilities.

Problems of accountability among PLA officers are worsened by doubts about their professional competence. Xi and other Chinese leaders have frequently lamented the poor technical and leadership abilities of those who would lead troops into battle. These officers are said to be afflicted with a "peace disease"

– the idea that commanders without combat experience cannot imagine the difficulties they would face in war, and thus cannot effectively prepare for it. Xi has encouraged the PLA to cope with this problem through more realistic training, but this is at best a partial solution. Beyond these critiques, China's military does not provide its officers with the same experiences that help build the leadership skills of their U.S. counterparts. Few PLA leaders have experience commanding troops outside their own service, weakening their ability to prepare for modern joint warfare. Even fewer have gained experience outside their own professional specialties; it is rare for a commander, for instance, to have served a tour in a logistics billet. Almost none of them have served for any length of time overseas or alongside foreign colleagues. This system promotes a rigidity of thought and institutional myopia that is not well suited to the rigors of command on a dynamic modern battlefield.

The PLA's organizational culture also creates hindrances to quick and effective decision-making. Based on the party's need to maintain control over the army, the PLA has retained important vestiges of the Leninist system it borrowed from the Soviets a century ago. This includes political commissars who function as co-equals at every echelon of the PLA down to the company level and party committees that adjudicate major decisions for units down to the battalion level. Compounding the problem is the tendency of the Central Military Commission (CMC) to micromanage decisions, and the dominant role played by Xi as its chairman. The conflux of consensus-based and centralized decision-making weakens the ability of individual commanders to make bold choices and adapt quickly to new or challenging situations without extensive consultations, a system completely at odds with the tendency of the U.S. and other Western militaries to empower lower-level officers through a principle sometimes referred to as "mission command."[9]

A fourth limitation is the PLA's modest global presence. China's military strategy, organization, and resources are all oriented toward regional missions, especially operations against Taiwan and U.S. forces in Asia. There has been much less attention on projecting combat power far beyond China's own neighborhood. Overseas operations are small in scale and typically only involve a single service, such as the navy's deployment of ships to conduct anti-piracy patrols in the Gulf of Aden. There is no network of large overseas bases from which to conduct major combat operations, although the navy has begun establishing a more modest string of small bases and has access to civilian ports; and there is no joint command structure that would handle planning, training for, and leading more complex overseas operations. Despite warming relations with partners such as Russia and Pakistan, China cannot count on the military support of foreign nations for any war it might undertake. These limitations reduce China's ability to coerce opponents far afield and would reduce its ability to prevail in an escalating global conflict with the United States. By contrast, the United States, for the foreseeable future, will leverage its alliances and forward presence to remain the world's single remaining global military power.

The last disadvantage for the PLA, paradoxically, is strategic discipline. Refraining from wars after the end of the Cold War allowed China to become a "stealth superpower," but also reflected Beijing's desire to avoid serious risks to other interests. Protecting the economy from the consequences of war was not only necessary to further PLA modernization, but also to sustain growth, raise living standards, and deliver better governance. The party's performance in meeting these goals was key to its legitimacy among the people and ultimately to its own survival. The development and use of China's military tools has thus been carefully weighed against other priorities, some of which could be more vital to the party than even its own aspirations for "national reunification." Based on these calculations, Beijing has hesitated to fully exploit the new capabilities at its disposal. It has intimidated Taiwan, regional rivals, and the United States, but has steered away from lethal violence and deescalated some crises, as it did after a melee involving Chinese and Indian troops in June 2020 that involved fatalities on both sides. External security goals remain unfulfilled, and, from a military perspective, the PLA has been unable to gain the combat experience it would need to overcome the "peace disease."

In the years ahead, China could be tempted to go far beyond the August 2022 demonstrations after Speaker Pelosi's visit and use lethal force against Taiwan. In some cases, such as a formal declaration of independence, Beijing might feel it has no choice. But lingering weaknesses and vulnerabilities limit the PLA's prospects for a "quick victory" and create opportunities for China's adversaries. For the United States and its allies, this means developing the agile forces, operational concepts, and skilled leadership necessary to deter and, if necessary, defeat aggression. In other regional disputes, bold Chinese ambitions, increasing budgets, "world-class forces," and continued technological innovation will give the PLA greater confidence and options to intimidate its opponents. Outside Asia, much of the world faces a PLA with limited capabilities that is often employed more for positive publicity than for coercive purposes. In the foreseeable future, United States will remain the world's leader in terms of ability to project combat power, but over the long run, new capabilities and changes in the strategic landscape could chart a different course for a PLA that has been, thus far, mainly concerned with problems found much closer to home.

Chapter Outline

The remainder of the volume is organized into eight chapters. Chapter 1 considers the PLA's status as a pillar of the CCP, and the limits of the party's ability to exercise control over the military. It provides an overview of the history and current structure of party control, as exercised through the political commissar and party committee systems. It then argues that the party's need to grant the PLA sufficient autonomy to professionalize set the stage for corruption, poor coordination between the PLA and other bureaucracies, and continuing questions about the ideological commitment of some PLA officers to the party's values. Xi Jinping has sought to strengthen the party's role in the military, and consolidate his own power in the process, by being more involved in the PLA than either Jiang or Hu, controlling key appointments, increasing power to internal watchdogs such as financial auditors, carrying out a widespread anti-corruption campaign, and trumpeting the need for ideological orthodoxy. But the limits of these reforms became clear when, a decade into his tenure, Xi was forced to fire numerous senior officers due to suspected corruption. Strains between the party and its army are likely to continue and could grow into more serious threats to the regime.

Chapter 2 describes the strategic worldview of Chinese leaders. It argues that the PLA is not simply reacting to perceived slights by others but is an important tool for the party to advance its vision of "national rejuvenation" by addressing problems at the domestic, regional, and global levels. Internally, the PLA and its paramilitary cousin, the People's Armed Police, are the ultimate backstop to regime survival and ensure control over parts of the country prone to unrest, especially Tibet and Xinjiang. Regionally, concerns that Taiwan is slipping toward independence dictate that the PLA deter independence and increase its ability to compel unification talks or seize the island. China's periphery contains varied other problems, ranging from hotly contested territorial claims in the South and East China seas, and across the Sino–Indian border, to potential conflict on the Korean Peninsula. The military thus needs to enforce Chinese sovereignty claims and prepare for other contingencies. Moreover, in the PLA's mindset, the United States remains the pivotal strategic challenger, whose military forces may intervene to support Taiwan or a regional ally. Countering U.S. influence in the region and preparing to oppose U.S. intervention are therefore important PLA missions. Globally, the party worries about threats to critical imports, the safety of Chinese citizens, and maintaining a positive image for China. This creates an expectation that the PLA must be able to operate overseas, even if its main attention is focused domestically and on China's periphery.

Chapter 3 explains the evolution of China's military strategy from the Cold War to the present and the resulting implications for the PLA's organization and approaches to resourcing and innovation. The current strategy requires the PLA to focus on Taiwan while also preparing to respond to domestic emergencies, conduct other regional operations, and go abroad when needed. The main form of operations for the PLA has shifted from large-scale ground combat to "integrated joint operations" involving close collaboration among the services and across the warfighting domains. One of Xi's main contributions was overseeing a restructuring of the PLA to become more joint – a new command structure was fashioned whose main duties include planning, training for, and conducting joint operations. These reforms ultimately improved the PLA's effectiveness by allowing forces to operate with greater cohesiveness and to transition more quickly from peacetime to wartime. At the same time, increasing budgets have allowed the PLA to purchase the advanced hardware and recruit the technically literate personnel it will need to conduct its most important missions. The procurement system has also been adjusted to reduce reliance on foreign arms imports, strengthen China's defense industrial base, and foster closer cooperation between the military and civilian firms, which have been on the leading edge in developing artificial intelligence, quantum computing, and other technologies the PLA will need in the "intelligentized" wars of the future.

China's military strategy has guided the modernization of conventional and strategic forces. Chapter 4 considers modernization across the land, air, and sea domains. The ground forces have lost manpower but remain politically influential and conduct important missions in border security, as the land force in a Taiwan invasion, and in preparing for conflicts on the Korean Peninsula or with India. In addition, the People's Armed Police has undergone reforms to handle internal security and augment the PLA in wartime. The air force has styled itself as a "strategic" service whose missions have grown beyond territorial air defense to encompass long-range strike and power projection. The navy is no less "strategic," blossoming in a few decades from a coastal defense force to a "blue water" force that has sailed past the first island chain, and into the Indian Ocean and beyond, while coordinating with the Coast Guard and maritime militias in managing regional disputes closer to home. All three services have produced "world-class" equipment and increased the quality of their personnel. Yet, as with most modern militaries, the PLA also suffers from interservice competition for prestige, influence, and resources that limits progress toward a capable, and cooperative, joint force.

Chapter 5 turns to the modernization of China's strategic forces in the nuclear, space, and cyber domains. Chinese strategists view dominance in the information domain, which includes space, cyberspace, and electronic warfare, as critical for modern warfare. The PLA has invested heavily in offensive cyber and counterspace capabilities to exploit U.S. military vulnerabilities, but its efforts to harness space and cyberspace to support joint operations have also created new vulnerabilities. A future conflict will almost certainly involve warfare in space and cyberspace; the question is whether it will also affect critical civilian infrastructure and nuclear-related command and control systems. The Rocket Force operates China's ground-based conventional and nuclear missiles, which give the PLA long-range precision-strike capabilities and are the linchpin of China's nuclear deterrent. China has embarked on an unprecedented buildup of its nuclear forces, including the creation of a nuclear triad, and appears to be rethinking the political and military utility of nuclear weapons. One important goal may be to provide a "nuclear shield" that would give China the freedom of action to initiate a conventional conflict against Taiwan while reducing the risk of U.S. intervention or nuclear escalation. A larger Chinese nuclear arsenal will have important implications for regional security, strategic stability, and the global arms control regime.

Chapter 6 considers how a modernized PLA has sought to shape the regional environment in China's favor. This has followed a dual-track approach, combining military diplomacy to win "hearts and minds" with coercive diplomacy. On one track, the PLA engages with foreign militaries through senior-level visits, bilateral and multilateral security dialogues, military exercises, ports calls, and functional exchanges. It also conducts non-traditional security cooperation to demonstrate that a stronger PLA can make contributions to regional security. PLA exercises with foreign militaries mostly focus on non-traditional security, but its exercises with Russia, the Shanghai Cooperation Organization, and Pakistan have been more combat-focused, including Sino–Russian bomber and maritime patrols in Northeast Asia. On another track, the PLA has used intimidation tactics to shape adversary decision-making, including military construction in disputed areas, aggressive enforcement of territorial claims, dangerous intercepts of U.S. and allied military operations near China, and disinformation campaigns. PLA coercion has undercut efforts to portray China as a peaceful power and led regional countries to improve their diplomatic and security ties with the United States, the European Union, and major powers such as Japan, India, and Australia. The PLA has thus succeeded in shaping the regional security environment, but not in the manner party leaders desired.

Chapter 7 covers China's preparations for war with Taiwan. It argues that Beijing has several options short of war to exert greater pressure on Taipei, including a quarantine of the island using its numerically superior maritime forces. However, Beijing faces complex economic, military, and political trade-offs in any strategic decision to implement any of its major military campaigns against Taiwan, including missile bombardments, blockades, or a full-scale invasion. Among the most important factors is Beijing's perception of the likelihood and effectiveness of U.S. intervention on Taiwan's behalf. This would create a much larger and less predictable conflict than the narrower fight the PLA prefers, and so Chinese planners have devoted much attention to the ways in which they can counter U.S. intervention. One of those is leveraging China's growing strategic arsenal to intimidate Washington, mirroring the apparent success that Putin had in brandishing his powerful nuclear capabilities to minimize NATO's role on the Ukraine battlefield. Rising confidence that the PLA can fight the war it wants, however, must be balanced against recent adaptations that Taiwan is making to improve its own defenses, and adjustments in U.S. strategy to operate in a contested environment.

The final chapter widens the aperture to consider the PLA's role outside Asia. Based on the imperatives of China's military strategy to focus on deterrence and warfighting in the immediate periphery, there has been far less attention on global roles and missions. Over the last few decades, the PLA's overseas presence has mostly been confined to UN peacekeeping missions, anti-piracy patrols near the Horn of Africa, and a few non-combatant evacuations. The opening of a naval base in Djibouti in 2017 and Chinese ownership and management of civilian ports across the Indian Ocean region and beyond marked a new effort to develop the logistics infrastructure needed to support PLA operations abroad. However, several constraints remain, including the absence of an overseas joint command structure and lack of military allies. Future changes to the PLA's overseas role will be shaped by changes in the security environment. Resolution of the Taiwan issue on China's terms, for instance, could free up resources for China to undertake a far more ambitious military presence abroad. Absent such changes, it remains doubtful that the PLA will be able to compete with the United States as a global military power.

1

The Party's Army

The People's Liberation Army (PLA) is on its way toward fielding "world-class forces" by mid-century, but the price of that transformation is incomplete control by the Chinese Communist Party (CCP) and its civilian leadership. Founding leader Mao Zedong sought a symbiotic relationship between the party and the army but understood that to modernize it needed some autonomy to manage its own affairs. In the later 1970s, Deng Xiaoping expanded the PLA's latitude to pursue modernization and allowed it to go into business to compensate for tight budgets. This helped build the PLA into a more competent professional force but had negative repercussions such as excessive military secrecy, widespread corruption, and a perceived drift away from strict obedience to party values and priorities. His successors, Jiang Zemin and Hu Jintao, made attempts to rein in the army, but with limited success.

Sensing a military slipping from the party's grasp, Xi Jinping made serious efforts to restore party control. Some of the tools he used include strengthening his own status as chairman of the Central Military Commission (CMC), appointing trusted allies into senior roles, reinforcing Marxist political indoctrination (as well as promoting "Xi Jinping Thought") within the PLA, breaking up patronage networks and rotating senior officers, and increasing the authority of the PLA's internal watchdogs: auditors, anti-corruption inspectors, and military courts. Xi's goal is for the PLA to become both more "red" (politically reliable) and more "expert" at fighting wars.

However, Xi's push for total control of the military has yielded mixed results. Xi has become the strongest leader of the PLA since Mao and used his strong influence to push through historic reforms and pursue a cleaner and more professional officer corps. Yet even after Xi's attempts to enforce tighter party supervision, the PLA is still a largely self-governed force with limited opportunities for civilian oversight and intervention. Moreover, powerful fiefdoms continue to exist in the PLA, and its degree of acceptance of Marxist virtues of selfless sacrifice, especially among a senior leadership awash with growing defense budgets, is dubious at best. The limits of party control became strikingly clear in late 2023 when Xi fired his defense minister and the leadership of his strategic missile force under a cloud of corruption. Given incomplete political control, CCP civilian leaders will continue to be wary that the army is pursuing its own agenda; "absolute" loyalty to the party will never be taken for granted.

This chapter explores the relationship between the CCP and the PLA in five sections. The first discusses how Chinese leaders since Mao sought to maintain political control over the PLA while pursuing modernization. It also provides an overview of the political work system instrumental to the party's control over the army. The second argues that excessive autonomy granted to the PLA under Deng led to management and supervision problems that his successors had to grapple with even as they promoted military professionalization. The third section explains how Xi pursued a multipronged political strategy to strengthen the party's (and his own) control. The fourth analyzes the results of Xi's strategy and suggests that internal governance remains a key challenge for China's military. The conclusion argues that the party will have to navigate a balance between an army that is both "red" and "expert."

Political Control and the PLA

The central dilemma of civil–military relations is how to build an army strong enough to defend the nation, but not so independent that it threatens the political status quo.[1] In mature democracies, the problem is alleviated by a military code of values that includes acceptance of the principle of civilian control, aided by external monitoring mechanisms such as legislative oversight, the rule of law, and a free press. Under these circumstances, militaries can serve as an effective warfighting force but have little interest in interfering in domestic politics.

In China, by contrast, the army serves as the armed wing of the CCP. This is captured in Mao's famous dictum that "political power grows out of the barrel of a gun. Our principle is that the party commands the gun, and the gun must never be allowed to command the party."[2] Mao's general view was that the military should be closely aligned with the party's Marxist–Leninist values and revolutionary agenda. This accorded with the PLA's origins as a body of "revolutionary soldiers" – founded on August 1, 1927, at the outset of the Civil War between the CCP and the ruling Nationalist party – who saw themselves as instrumental in carrying out the party's utopian vision. The wartime relationship between civilian political cadres responsible for recruiting, motivating, and directing soldiers to achieve CCP political objectives and soldiers fighting under the party's direction to achieve a revolutionary victory produced close ties between CCP civilians and PLA personnel. These ties endured even when CCP civilians turned their attention to building the People's Republic of China (PRC) into a powerful socialist state.

During much of the Mao era (1949–1976), the boundaries between civilian and military spheres were blurred because China's senior CCP leaders had extensive military experience and connections gained through service in the war against Japan and the Chinese Civil War. CCP civilians made key strategic decisions, including to intervene against United Nations forces in the Korean War and to pursue nuclear weapons. After launching the Cultural Revolution in 1966 to secure his position against perceived rivals inside the CCP civilian leadership, Mao ultimately called the PLA out from the barracks to restore order and govern society at the grassroots level.

Party control over the PLA was reinforced by a system of political control based on the organizational practices of the Soviet Red Army, which had been established during the Bolshevik Revolution a decade earlier. Soviet leaders, especially Leon Trotsky, understood that party control could not be taken for granted based on common values, but must be actively enforced through close supervision at all levels.[3] Mao and his colleagues embraced this opinion, as did his successors, who ensured that most of this system of control survived through the present. At the pinnacle, the CMC serves as the nexus between the party's most senior civilian official and the military brass. Technically an organ of the CCP Central Committee, the commission is responsible for high-level decision-making, weighing in on subjects such as organizational structure, military strategy, acquisition, and leadership issues. The commission is typically chaired by the top civilian leader who serves concurrently as party general-secretary. This system channels contacts between PLA leaders and the CCP civilian leadership through the civilian CMC chairman and prevents senior PLA officers from lobbying individual members of the Politburo Standing Committee.

At lower tiers of the PLA, party control is the remit of political commissars and party committees. Under the "dual-leadership" system, the PLA officers who serve as political commissars occupy equal authority with military commanders in units down to the company level. The two officers routinely consult with each other, though in practice there is a division of labor whereby commanders focus on professional military issues such as training and planning, while commissars are responsible for morale, personnel management, and political indoctrination. Political commissars are in a specialized career track, although many began their careers as commanders and they receive similar training (thus enabling them to scrutinize commanders' judgments and provide input on military decisions). In the view of Mao and his successors, "dual leadership" was so critical to party control that the PLA retained the system permanently. The Soviets, by contrast, found that it damaged battlefield efficiency and downgraded commissars to become members of the commander's staff during World War II.

Party control is also exercised through party committees at all units of the PLA down to the battalion level. Companies have similar arrangements called party branches. Under the Leninist principle of collective decision-making, party committees – composed of political commissars (who serve as the secretary), commanders (who serve as deputy secretary), their deputies, and a few others – are supposed to have the final say in major decisions in peacetime. One of their most important functions is selecting candidates for promotion. They also transmit high-level party guidance down to the units. Only during emergencies can the normal functioning of party committees be suspended, though even in these cases commanders and political commissars are supposed to consult with each other and promptly report their decisions to their committee. Party committees are in turn responsible to committees at the next higher level, all the way up to the highest-level party committee: the CMC. The commissar and party committee apparatus is administratively guided by the Political Work Department, whose director sits on the CMC. This department is the successor to the General Political Department (GPD), whose roots can be traced back to 1930.[4]

Even PLA personnel outside the political work system are intimately involved in party affairs. All PLA personnel take an oath of loyalty to the party, rather than to a constitutional order as in the Western system:

> I am a member of the People's Liberation Army. I promise that I will follow the leadership of the Communist Party of China, serve the people wholeheartedly, obey orders, strictly observe discipline, fight heroically, fear no sacrifice, loyally discharge my duties, work hard, practice hard to master combat skills, and resolutely fulfill my missions. Under no circumstances will I betray the Motherland or desert the army.[5]

The overwhelming majority of PLA officers are party members in good standing; they need to attend periodic party meetings, have a grounding in party dogma and history, study the party leadership's positions on contemporary issues, and follow party rules related to personal conduct, such as those prohibiting accepting bribes, engaging in for-profit business activities, practicing religion, traveling without permission, or criticizing the party. Many non-commissioned officers and some conscripts are also party members. Officers and enlisted personnel, including those who choose not to become party members, are also subject to regular party indoctrination through study sessions (and in the modern day, study programs that can be completed online). Some accounts suggest that political indoctrination accounts for about 40 percent of basic training and about 20 percent to 30 percent of a soldier's time once they have joined a unit.[6]

At various times, however, the pursuit of party control has conflicted with the military's need to carve out a separate sphere in which to become a professional warfighting force. In the mid-1950s, Marshal Peng Dehuai, who led Chinese forces in the Korean War, sought to build the PLA into a more modern force by means such as differentiated uniforms and ranks, professional military education, and modern military doctrine stressing combined-arms operations.[7] Peng also advocated following the Soviets in abandoning the "dual leadership" system, but failed to convince Mao and was eventually purged for questioning

Mao's decision to launch the Great Leap Forward. During the 1960s, Deng Xiaoping and Liu Shaoqi advocated the PLA becoming both "red" and "expert." This call for increased focus on building military expertise faced opposition as Mao sought to keep the army's focus on social revolution. Indeed, the Cultural Revolution (1966–1976) constitutes a lost decade for PLA modernization as the army became deeply involved in politics, maintaining domestic order, and local governance.

Following Mao's death in 1976, Deng encouraged PLA leaders to focus on building military skills rather than politics and granted the PLA more autonomy to pursue this goal.[8] Getting the PLA "back into the barracks" was not difficult because most officers, especially among the younger generations, had little interest in governing society. Military representation in key CCP decision-making organs decreased over time, so that the military now holds only about 20 percent of the seats on the party Central Committee, and the PLA lost its final representative on the Politburo Standing Committee in 1997. Senior PLA officers, including the CMC vice chairmen who remained on the lower-level Politburo, increasingly confined their contributions to the military sphere.[9] The CMC insulated the PLA from civilian intervention while limiting the PLA's ability to pursue its own institutional interests by exploiting potential splits in the CCP leadership. The result was a PLA leadership focused on improving military capability that made significant progress on modernization and reform during the Deng era and into the 1990s.

Unlike Peng Dehuai, however, Deng did not seek reduced party influence within the army. As in civilian governance, top CCP leaders relied on both the political values of loyal party members (including the duty to obey decisions made by senior party leaders) and monitoring mechanisms to ensure compliance and exercise control over the military. Deng advocated a professional military ethos that blended technical competence with political subordination. PLA officers cultivated martial virtues such as leadership, courage, loyalty, and self-sacrifice but did not develop a code of professional ethics independent of the CCP.[10] The PLA remained a party–army, party membership was still required of officers, and political work continued and even increased after the 1989 Tiananmen crisis, when some PLA units did not obey orders.

Excessive Autonomy

While the expansion of a distinct military sphere in the 1980s succeeded in keeping the PLA in its "bureaucratic lane in the road," the ways in which Deng promoted military autonomy produced negative consequences for party control that Xi Jinping ultimately needed to address thirty years later. Unlike militaries in mature democracies, there were no credible external constraints, such as legislative or judicial oversight. The fact that a large share of PLA revenue came from off-budget commercial activities, which Deng tolerated to compensate the military for low official budgets in the 1980s, reduced the effectiveness of budgets as a tool of civilian oversight (although the PLA *did* gradually become more dependent on state funding approved by the National People's Congress as extra-budgetary revenue declined in the 1990s). This new party–army bargain, which James Mulvenon has referred to as "conditional compliance," was like that in other communist countries in which coercive forces and other "strategic groups" were compensated for their political acquiescence.[11]

There was also no attempt to create additional civilian control such as a secretary of defense-equivalent within the military. The party general-secretary, in his role as CMC chairman, provided the sole link between the civilian party elite and the PLA.[12] As a result, civilian control rested on the authority and effectiveness of the CMC chairman. While Deng wielded strong influence due to his decades of military experience and extensive network of military contacts, his successors, Jiang Zemin and Hu Jintao, came into office with no military experience or close ties to the PLA. Both had to curry favor among senior officers to consolidate their authority, including by tolerating corruption. Senior PLA officers often took advantage of this situation through illicit business empires or corrupt promotion schemes. Jiang's continuing efforts to exert power and influence from retirement also enhanced the military's leverage at Hu's expense. Jiang stayed on as CMC chairman for two years after Hu's accession as CCP general-secretary and the former's hand-picked choices of Guo Boxiong and Xu Caihou as CMC vice chairmen undercut Hu's authority even after Jiang stepped down in 2004.[13] Guo and Xu effectively administered the PLA throughout Hu's tenure, preserving the façade that they were acting under Hu's direction but likely appealing quietly to Jiang for support when necessary.

Deng also failed to institute effective self-policing within the PLA. Many scholars have noted that control of military activities in authoritarian states requires infiltration and surveillance by secret police or other party agents. In China, this function was performed by military officers operating within the political work system, consisting of political commissars, party committees, and discipline inspectors. This created ambiguity about whether the ultimate loyalty of uniformed political commissars and discipline inspectors was to the CCP or to the military. Moreover, during and after the Deng era, those political control mechanisms resided within a single bureaucracy in the PLA – the GPD. This single point of failure gave corrupt senior GPD officers the ability to protect corrupt actors in the PLA from senior civilian party officials.[14] These problems produced three negative consequences for party–army relations: military secrecy, corruption, and ideological divergence.

The first problem concerns excessive secrecy between the PLA, civilian party leaders, and other parts of the Chinese bureaucracy, especially the diplomatic corps. Limited civilian insight into PLA finances, research and development activities, and even some operational decisions meant that military and civilian activities were often not well coordinated. Two examples are the negative international response to the January 2007 test of an anti-satellite weapon, which appeared to catch Hu Jintao off guard, and the January 2011 flight test of a J-20 stealth fighter, which led to a diplomatic embarrassment as it coincided with the visit of U.S. Secretary of Defense Robert Gates to Beijing.[15] Scholars have argued that Hu was not kept abreast of the specific operational details of the tests.[16] This does not mean that the PLA had gone "rogue" by disobeying orders or acting without authorization, but that it sometimes acted in an aggressive and uncoordinated manner without informing the leadership or coordinating with other agencies. Scholars have noted that control over internal military information is an important source of bureaucratic power for the PLA.

This problem was exacerbated by the PLA's reluctance to participate in a cohesive interagency process. One of the drivers for Chinese proposals to institute a body like the U.S. National Security Council was the perception of ineffective responses to incidents such as the May 1999 accidental NATO bombing of the PRC Embassy in Belgrade and the April 2001 collision of U.S. and Chinese military aircraft in the South China Sea. The PLA's resistance to sharing information with civilians, however, meant that a National Security Council-like structure could not take root. To be sure, the military was represented on the National Security Leading Small Group, a Jiang-era invention intended to facilitate bureaucratic coordination during crises, but this was an ad-hoc arrangement with no ability to compel the PLA to share information or respond to requests from civilian agencies.

A second problem is the rise of prolific corruption and cronyism in the PLA. The full scale of PLA corruption is unknown, but some indications are provided in the anti-corruption campaign launched in early 2012 and expanded when Xi became CMC chairman in November 2012. Military cases involve purges from the party of high-ranking cadres such as former CMC vice chairmen Xu Caihou and Guo Boxiong, and former General Logistics Department deputy director Gu Junshan, who were all accused of selling military posts. However, corruption was found at many levels of the PLA, and in more mundane areas. Typical examples of malfeasance included unlawful privatization of military housing, disobeying traffic regulations, extravagant travel, and abuse of retirement benefits. Such activities often represented violations of party rules and norms that officers, as party members, were supposed to follow. PLA-run businesses, such as military hospitals, were also frequent targets of corruption allegations.

Widespread corruption may have had positive value in the early stages of China's economic transition by giving CCP officials personal incentives to support market reforms, but it had several negative consequences for the

PLA's development. First was that party leaders may not have been able to rely on the PLA as an effective warfighting instrument. No military is optimized for combat when senior officers gained their positions through bribes. Second was military resistance to reform. As early as 1998, PLA Chief of the General Staff Fu Quanyou warned that substantial reforms to the PLA's size and structure would be difficult because they would "inevitably involve the immediate interests of numerous units and individual officers," and run into the problem of "selfish departmentalism."[17] Graft-prone parts of the PLA, such as the political work and logistics systems, were likely especially averse to restructuring. Third were the negative effects corruption had on morale among those personnel who were genuinely interested in serving the party's, rather than their own, interests.

The final problem is concerns among party elites about the ideological reliability of PLA personnel. Questions about whether the army can be fully trusted date to the early part of the reform era. The lessons of the Soviet Union and Romania, when armies turned against communist leaders, and the failure of some PLA units to obey orders during the Tiananmen crisis (notably Beijing-based units who refused to carry out orders to fire on citizens from their own hometown), were never far out of mind.[18] The latter problem was blamed on unnamed Western conspirators, as well as on ousted party general-secretary Zhao Ziyang and his agents in the PLA, whose alleged support for the "nationalization" and "depoliticization" of the army was said to have weakened party control. These terms refer to the idea that the PLA might transition from a "party–army," whose main purpose is defending the party's interests, to an army subordinate to the state and ultimately to the people. There was thus a resurgence of political indoctrination highlighting the "absolute leadership" of the party over the military after 1989.

Even long after Tiananmen, similar themes could still be found in the PLA's internal propaganda. This reflected continuing discussions in the PLA about one day transitioning into a national army.[19] In 2007, for instance, CMC vice chairman Cao Gangchuan argued that "some hostile forces" had made it their goal to "separate the military from the Party leadership," while in 2011 CMC member Li Jinai blamed "domestic and foreign hostile forces" for spreading similar ideas. A 2014 essay in the party's flagship journal *Qiushi* explained that the idea of rebranding the PLA as a national army has blurred the understanding of "some officers and men" about the principle of the party's "absolute leadership" over the military. The author stated that "some" have also "blindly admired" Western models of civil–military relations, in which armies serve national goals and not those of political parties. If those ideas gained prominence, the PLA would "lose its soul" and thus its ability to defend the party.[20] Even in the absence of active plotting by the army against the party, civilian leaders learned from Tiananmen that they could not take enduring political support by military members for granted.

The Party Strikes Back

When Xi Jinping was appointed CMC chairman in November 2012, he inherited the consequences of the excessive autonomy granted to the PLA under Deng. Moreover, his tenure as a civilian vice chairman of the CMC from 2010 to 2012 exposed him to the degree to which the CMC military vice chairmen had usurped Hu's authority and the extent of secrecy, corruption, and ideological laxity within the PLA. As in other aspects of governance, Xi focused on re-establishing the role of the party, and his own role as party general-secretary, within the military. Xi's strategy thus represented a rebalancing toward tighter party control, placing him more in line with Mao than with his immediate predecessors.

Xi's efforts to strengthen control over the PLA were facilitated by outgoing leader Hu Jintao. Instead of attempting to follow the precedent established by Deng and Jiang, Hu voluntarily gave up his position as CMC chair in November 2012 along with his other party and state positions. Retired PLA officers have privately stated that Xi was able to shape the composition of the incoming CMC, including the choice of vice chairmen Fan Changlong and Xu Qiliang. Hu formally handed authority over to Xi in an enlarged CMC meeting on November 16, 2012, when both the incoming and outgoing CMC chairman addressed the senior PLA leadership.

Xi's strategy to establish his bona fides and reassert party control was wide-ranging and multifaceted. The first leg of the strategy involved bolstering his own status in the military, which he needed to do since his own military background was confined to a few brief years as a military aide-de-camp to the defense minister in the early 1980s. A main theme of the propaganda surrounding Xi's efforts to enhance his authority in the PLA has been on the "CMC chairmanship responsibility system." The concept itself was enshrined in the 1982 PRC Constitution, but under Jiang and Hu, significant authority devolved to the uniformed CMC vice chairmen, with the chairman taking a more passive role. Hu approved revisions of the "Working Rules of the Central Military Commission" in October 2012 that stressed the authority of the CMC chairman under the "CMC chairmanship responsibility system." As evidenced by the investigations into Xu and Guo, delegating too much authority to professional officers exacerbated corruption problems. By emphasizing his status as chairman, Xi signaled a return to control by the civilian party elite.

The time and attention Xi devoted to military affairs early in his tenure helped him burnish his reputation in the PLA. In his first three years as CMC chairman, from 2012 to 2015, Xi made 53 publicized appearances at military events. During the equivalent period from 2004 to 2007, Hu made only 36 appearances. In a landmark 2014 speech at Gutian, site of the 1929 party congress that decided conclusively that the purpose of military power "was chiefly for the service of political ends," Xi referenced the need for a "new military leadership system of absolute party leadership of the military." Xi was also personally associated with major PLA reforms undertaken during his tenure: he announced the first details on the reforms at a military parade in Beijing in September 2015 and chaired the CMC meeting that adopted a more detailed reform plan. Similarly, Xi led updates to China's military strategy in 2014 and 2019. The latter identified "Xi Jinping Military Thought" as the strategy's core guiding principle. This put Xi on the same level as Mao and Deng, who each had their own "thoughts" personally connected with China's military strategy (for more details, see Chapter 3).

The creation of the Central National Security Commission at the 18th Party Congress's third plenum in late 2013 also enhanced Xi's authority in the party's larger security apparatus. Although the plenum's report was vague about the nature of this organization, the Politburo soon clarified that it would be a party organ under the Central Committee led by Xi. The two vice chairmen were the second and third-ranking civilian party members. Although focused more on internal than external challenges, the commission was designed to improve information sharing and coordination between the PLA and civilian agencies – a necessary institutional arrangement for strategic planning and crisis response that neither Jiang nor Hu was able to achieve. The organization would do this by maintaining a permanent structure with a staff, unlike the former National Security Leading Small Group, and by including PLA representation at both the senior and staff level.

The second part of Xi's strategy involved personnel assignments. Xi himself was more engaged in personnel selection than his predecessors, reportedly interviewing candidates for senior military positions down to the level of group army commander. His appointments included officers well known to him – the new slate of CMC members announced at the 20th Party Congress in 2022, for instance, comprised close Xi affiliates, including keeping former childhood friend Zhang Youxia on as vice chairman, past the typical retirement age of 68. Since Xi could not be personally involved in all aspects of military management, he installed trusted aides to ensure that his instructions were followed. One such individual was Lieutenant General Qin Shengxiang, who served as director of the CMC General Office – which manages the flow of information from the CMC to the rest of the PLA – from December 2012 until September 2017, prior to his appointment as the PLA Navy's political commissar. Another was Lieutenant General Zhong Shaojun, who was a senior civilian aide to Xi during his time as Zhejiang party secretary. When Xi became CMC chairman, Zhong was given a military rank of senior colonel and designated as CMC General Office deputy director and director of Xi's personal office in the CMC. Zhong was later promoted to replace Qin as director of the CMC General Office. His close association with Xi and responsibilities in this sensitive role likely gave him strong influence despite his relatively low formal rank when he was first appointed to the PLA.

Xi's personnel appointments were not only aimed at consolidating his personal control, but also at cleaning up corruption throughout the officer corps. Almost as soon as he arrived as CMC chairman, Xi took charge of an expansive anti-corruption campaign within the military that resulted in the punishment of more than 100 PLA officers above the Corps Leader-level (major generals), including former Chief of the General Staff Fang Fenghui and former GPD director Zhang Yang. Xi also pointed to former CMC vice chairmen Xu Caihou and Guo Boxiong, who had also been targeted in the anti-corruption investigations, as cautionary examples for would-be rule-breakers, discussing these cases at the 2014 Gutian conference and elsewhere.

Xi also took steps to ensure that new patterns of corruption would not take root. A key change involved rotating senior officers to reduce the risk of collusion between commanders and political commissars and to break up existing patronage networks that might facilitate corruption. Rotation of senior officers is a traditional means of preventing officers from developing their own local political networks that might challenge civilian control.[21] Under Xi's initial organizational reforms, the assignment pattern of commanders and political commissars varied at different levels. At the level of the Theater Commands, four of the five commanders were previously assigned to other military regions, while all five of the political commissars were local (for more on the organizational structure of the PLA, see Chapter 3). At the Theater Command Army component level, four of the five commanders were local, while the political commissars rotated from other military regions. At the group army level, almost all of the commanders of the group armies were transferred from other military regions, while most of the political commissars were from the local area.

These rotations meant that commanders and political commissars usually did not have an existing personal relationship and were less likely to trust each other and engage in corrupt behavior. They also meant that if a theater commander contemplated ordering subordinate ground units to engage in unauthorized activity, the operational chain of command included a Theater Command Army commander and group army commanders that he did not know well. This pattern of senior officer assignments enhanced party control provided by the political commissar system, but likely at a cost to operational effectiveness because the theater commander, political commissar, and subordinate commanders were unfamiliar with each other.

The third leg of Xi's political strategy focused on party work and indoctrination in the PLA. At the 18th Party Congress in November 2012, the CMC reiterated that the PLA must "unswervingly uphold the absolute leadership of the party over the army," guarantee "absolute loyalty and reliability," and support a new generation of party officials. Xi made the same argument at the November 2014 Gutian conference and elsewhere. At the same time, the CMC highlighted the need for "reliable" party cadres in the army, defined in one document as those who have "resolute" political views, carry out orders "without hesitation," and resist "incorrect ideological trends."[22] Senior PLA officers were also required to *biaotai*, or publicly pledge their dedication to the party. Xi's military writings and speeches also became standard reading for PLA officers. Along with this effort, Xi lauded the role of political commissars, who take charge of indoctrination across the PLA. Instead of downgrading their role, as the Soviets had done decades earlier, Xi believed they must be empowered if the PLA is to be "absolutely loyal" to the party.

Xi's emphasis on party loyalty is consistent with a pattern of periodic political campaigns deemed necessary to ensure that party control does not waver. A January 2015 CMC instruction on political work reaffirmed the need to "forge the soul" of the army to follow party commands, requiring continued ideological education at all levels, but "especially in the upper echelons." Hence, even as officer training and promotion criteria increasingly stressed operational capabilities, the need for party education and political bona fides remained central to the PLA's personnel system. Indeed, one PLA officer suggested that political loyalty had become the most important factor in promotions during the Xi era.

Xi-era political education also emphasized a renewed commitment to Marxist principles. Speaking at the November 2014 Gutian political work conference, Xi said that the most fundamental political problems were ideological, including those related to "ideals and beliefs," "party spirit," and "revolutionary spirit." A *PLA Daily* commentary published shortly thereafter stated that the root of the ideological malaise was the clash of competing value systems, in which the ideas of PLA members are becoming "more independent, more selective, more changeable, and more diversified."[23] This critique supported Xi's larger contention that the West was insidiously supporting "color revolutions" that would threaten the "political security" of the party and its leadership. The CMC thus required that the army be educated with the "important theories of communism and socialism with Chinese characteristics," in addition to the specific principles exhorted by Xi. This led to an emphasis on socialist norms such as austerity, intra-party democracy, service to the people, criticism and self-criticism, and upright actions. The goal was to instill values that counteract more self-interested impulses which give rise to materialism and ultimately to corruption.

A final prong of Xi's strategy was strengthening the institutional and regulatory monitoring mechanisms in the PLA. An initial change came in October 2014, when the PLA Audit Office was returned to the CMC from the General Logistics Department (GLD), where it had resided since 1992. The office's director explained that the transfer was meant to enhance "independence, authority, and effectiveness" of auditors within the military, allowing for greater supervision of "high-level leading organs and cadres."[24] A *PLA Daily* report noted that, between 2013 and 2015, the Audit Office had audited 4,024 cadres at or above the Regiment Leader level, resulting in 21 dismissals, hundreds of demotions and other penalties, and recovery of 12.1 billion RMB in losses due to waste and mismanagement.[25]

More important was the wholesale reorganization of the CMC bureaucracy announced in January 2016. Specifically, the party replaced the four general departments, including the scandal-prone GPD, with fifteen smaller offices, departments, and commissions that would report directly to the CMC chairman (Figure 1.1). This change was needed because the general departments had become powerful enough to limit the CMC's ability to exercise "unified command" over the military. The result was that information on matters such as finances, operations, and personnel that once would have gone through the general departments (and was thus subject to manipulation) would now be able to reach the party general-secretary more directly.

A centerpiece of this reorganization was the transfer of the Discipline Inspection Commission, responsible for anti-corruption investigations, from the former GPD to the CMC. Underscoring its influence in internal governance, the CMC announced that roving teams of discipline inspectors would investigate party members across the PLA. CMC vice chairman Xu Qiliang encouraged inspectors to "take advantage of their new standing" within the PLA to verify "officers' political loyalty, power, and responsibility." Hotlines were established so that personnel could anonymously report party violations to the Discipline Inspection Commission. In November 2017, Discipline Inspection Commission secretary general Zhang Shengmin was elevated to the status of a CMC member, becoming one of the PLA's top six uniformed officers. In January 2018, the PLA issued a new CMC Inspection Work Regulation governing the discipline inspection process and specifying the responsibilities of the CMC Inspection Work Leading Small Group, its subsidiary inspection groups, and similar bodies established in the services and the People's Armed Police. Forming a separate chain of control, the reorganization also transferred the Political and Legal Affairs Commission, responsible for military courts and prosecutors, from the GPD to direct CMC control.

Taken together, these reforms extricated oversight functions from the general departments and gave investigators, judges, and auditors greater autonomy from those they were supposed to be supervising. The Audit Office, Discipline Inspection Commission, and Political and Legal Affairs Commission would complement the oversight roles played by the political commissars and party committees. This would improve the center's ability to identify, investigate, prevent, and punish corruption at higher levels, critical to the success of the anti-corruption campaign. Xi could also rely on information being provided through these separate channels to make personnel decisions, while avoiding overreliance on any single source of information.

Strengthening the supervisory mechanisms complemented new restrictions on the PLA's remaining commercial activities, such as accepting civilian patients

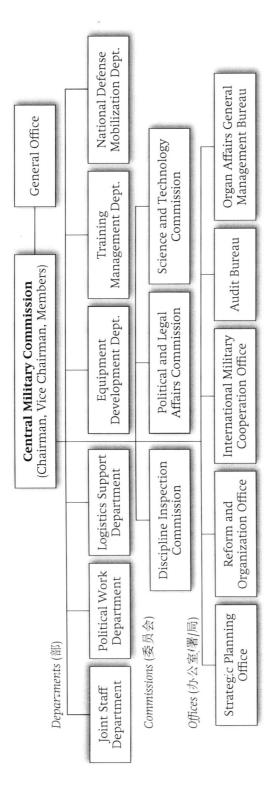

Figure 1.1 Revised CMC Organization

Source: Joel Wuthnow and Phillip C. Saunders, *Chinese Military Reforms in the Age of Xi Jinping*, China Strategic Perspectives 10 (2017), 11.

in PLA hospitals, leasing warehouses, and contracting out military construction units. These policies helped to close loopholes that had allowed the PLA to stay in business long after earlier restrictions from the Jiang era. In addition, rules promulgated early in Xu's tenure aimed to prevent garish displays by PLA officers, such as use of military license plates to avoid traffic laws, use of luxury cars, opulent banquets, and excessive foreign travel. Nevertheless, concerns remained about the efficacy of such laws. Xu Qiliang noted that "We need to correct the phenomenon of having law but not enforcing it, not enforcing the law strictly, and not pursuing those who break the law."[26]

"Absolute" Party Loyalty?

Xi's political strategy was a response to the problems created by excessive autonomy granted to the PLA under Deng, which produced military secrecy, corruption, and ideological drift. The results, however, were mixed. Strengthening his own authority within the PLA and steps to improve internal oversight and governance put the military in a weaker position to resist party intervention. Consequently, Xi was better prepared than Jiang or Hu to enact sweeping structural reforms to the PLA, which began in late 2015. For instance, the ground forces could not effectively oppose large manpower cuts, and the services had to cede operational control to joint commanders at the national and theater levels (see Chapter 3 for details). It is probably also the case that the PLA was less overtly corrupt under Xi than at any point in the preceding three decades. Rotating commanders and political commissars at different levels helped to reduce collusion and avoid an overconcentration of power in the PLA. Breaking up the general departments reduced bureaucratic obfuscation and created independent reporting chains through which Xi could monitor and control military activities. Stressing party values ensured that PLA officers at least are aware what the CCP's priorities are, even if they do not always share them.

Nevertheless, even after Xi attempted to rein in the military, "absolute loyalty" to the party's leadership remained elusive. One reason is that the nexus between the civilian CCP leadership and the PLA was still confined to a single individual – the party general-secretary. This means that past problems could resurface if that person becomes distracted by other responsibilities or is politically weak (a possibility for Xi's successor). Moreover, the reforms did not increase the role of senior party civilians in the army or enhance external legislative or judicial oversight.[27] While strengthening supervisory mechanisms could be useful in rooting out malfeasance, the PLA remains a self-policing organization with uniformed political commissars responsible for ensuring CCP control. To the extent that the army is systemically corrupt, bureaucratic changes within the PLA will be of little help.

While Xi achieved some success in dismantling the general departments, large power bases remain within the PLA. Those include the successor organizations to the general departments: the CMC Joint Staff, Political Work, Logistics Support, and Equipment Development departments. Even the CMC Discipline Inspection Commission, responsible for rooting out graft within the PLA, is itself a powerful bureaucracy led by a CMC member. The party general-secretary might attempt to control these organizations by installing trusted aides and controlling personnel appointments, but the lack of a comprehensive way of managing these organizations, similar to U.S. political appointments, means that there are there are still ample opportunities for corruption and bureaucratic resistance. The top leader must pick the officers he judges to be most loyal and honest from within a system where most are corrupt.

At the same time, the PLA has been loath to cede control of military intelligence and information on Chinese military capabilities and operations and can decide what information to share with civilians. The Central National Security Commission was intended to compel the PLA to become more transparent and cooperative in the Chinese system. However, if it does not function well, problems of interagency coordination could persist. While details on this organization's functioning have been sparse, it is telling that, since its creation in 2013, it has not been credited with playing a decisive role in any major crisis, including the 2020 Covid pandemic, and it apparently failed to prevent a February 2023 incident that saw China's diplomatic arm caught off-guard when a Chinese spy balloon flew over U.S. territory before Secretary of State Antony Blinken's planned visit to Beijing. One explanation is that the military has dug in its heels to protect its key bureaucratic advantage: control of sensitive information.

In terms of ideological affinity, political education to rekindle PLA officers' commitment to Marxist values may have fallen on deaf ears. Senior PLA officers have been willing to say the correct slogans and swear their loyalty to the party and to its top leadership. But formal compliance is not the same thing as genuine belief. Moreover, the hypocrisy of CCP leaders pursuing an anticorruption campaign when their own family members have amassed fortunes by trading on their political connections will undermine efforts to produce cleaner governance.[28] The appeal of Marxism in Chinese society has waned since the 1980s. This is no less true in the PLA, as illustrated in the extreme in cases of self-aggrandizement such as those of Xu Caihou and Gu Junshan. PLA members might vocalize support for Marxism on cue, but it is unclear that those values are being re-internalized to any significant degree.

The combination of poor external oversight, bureaucratic parochialism, and questionable internalization of Marxist values on the part of PLA officers came to the fore in the dismissal of several senior generals in late 2023. The purges included the commander and political commissar of the PLA Rocket

Force, which is responsible for the land-based nuclear deterrent force; defense minister Li Shangfu, who held a seat on the CMC and previously headed the Equipment Development Department; and the head of the military court. Several other generals associated with the Rocket Force and the procurement system lost their seats in the National People's Congress soon after. The party did not announce the reasons, but commentary generally suggested that the dismissals centered on graft in the acquisition system.[29] These firings were notable because they involved individuals in sensitive positions who had presumably undergone strenuous vetting and had been appointed by Xi himself in 2022. Xi's ability to corral the army was manifestly not "absolute."

Conclusion

Striking a balance between "red" and "expert" has long been a challenge that CCP leaders have faced in controlling the PLA. Lin Biao, who served as Mao's top commander from 1959–1971, is remembered for his attempts to reassert party control within the military but did so while allowing the PLA space to modernize. When some PLA units refused to follow party orders in 1989, Deng ordered a renewed political campaign to stress Mao's dictum that the "party commands the gun." Yet Deng also prioritized a high degree of autonomy that the PLA needed to modernize. Facing the deleterious consequences of that autonomy, Xi has encouraged a reassertion of party control while also requiring the PLA to be able to "fight and win wars."

Despite Xi's ambitions and limited successes, it is doubtful that he and his successors can recreate the symbiotic party–army relationship that existed under Mao. Future party leaders are unlikely to have served in the PLA and may find it politically expedient to allow the military to keep some degree of autonomy – especially to win support and allies at the outset of their tenures. Professionally, modern warfare requires officers with specialized professional skills, advanced weapons and platforms, and expertly designed strategies. This argues in favor of allowing the PLA freedom to run its own affairs, rather than being scrutinized by civilian party cadres without the relevant knowledge. A final reason why party–army relations will remain distant is that military officers themselves have little appetite to return to the role played by their predecessors under Mao in running the country's domestic affairs.

Some level of friction between the party and the army will likely persist, but whether more serious tensions erupt that could destabilize the party itself remains to be seen. One scenario would be a succession crisis where no single civilian party leader commands the respect of the army. A contest between two or more civilian elites could bring in the military as a "kingmaker," or different civilian "candidates" could lobby different PLA generals for support. Such a campaign would reflect the PLA's intrinsic ability to wield physical force and its status as a bloc of votes in the party Central Committee, where it holds approximately 20 percent of the seats.

Another scenario is military opposition to a CCP leader seen as weak on the international stage. One way the CCP justifies its rule is by identifying itself as a vehicle for Chinese nationalism and insisting that it is the only political force that can build China into a rich and powerful country. However, the CCP's claim to be the only legitimate authority rests on its performance in achieving these goals, allowing military officers and others to reach their own judgments on party legitimacy. It is not hard to imagine deep resentment within the PLA toward leaders viewed as soft on China's perceived enemies and even talk about ineffectual party leaders as national "traitors."[30] That does not mean that a nationalist coup is likely as in the Soviet Union in 1991, but it does mean that party leaders need to be mindful about how policies might be viewed among hardliners in the military, and to a lesser degree, the public.

A third scenario is a domestic crisis that puts the party and the Chinese people at odds. While the oath that PLA personnel take requires them first to obey the directions of the CCP, the second line submits that they will "serve the people wholeheartedly." The precedent is the 1989 Tiananmen crisis, in which some soldiers sided with the people. The CCP's insistence on reiterating the principle of "absolute loyalty" to the party suggests that CCP leaders themselves are not fully confident about the PLA's willingness to carry out unsavory orders, such as using force against Han Chinese (including those on Taiwan). Indeed, the PLA itself was likely glad that many of its domestic security missions were transferred to the People's Armed Police during the reform era, meaning that the PLA itself will probably not be put in a position where soldiers have to decide whether they will be a party army, or the people's army.

Absent an escalation of tensions between the party and the army, the PLA will continue to focus on its daily responsibilities of defending Chinese interests and its longer-term assignment to be better prepared for modern warfare. These responsibilities are governed by the tasks the party has handed to the military, based on the leadership's view of the strategic environment. Chapter 2 describes the party's strategic outlook and the PLA's resulting roles and missions at the domestic, regional, and global levels. Chapter 3 then considers the ways in which military strategy, organization, and resourcing approaches have evolved in recent years based on the party's directives. Given the complicated security environment they must navigate as they seek to remain in charge and achieve "national rejuvenation" by mid-century, party leaders, like Xi and those before him, will depend on a PLA that is both "red" and "expert."

Yet, herein lies a paradox for the PLA. The pursuit of party control implies certain organizational practices and structures that could reduce the military's mandate to professionalize and prepare for future conflict. Every hour spent on political indoctrination is one hour less spent on professional military training and education. Quality officers may fail to be promoted because they are deemed ideologically "impure." Micromanagement from the center, expressed most recently through Xi's dominant role under the "CMC chairman responsibility system," combined with consensus decision-making through party committees and the supervisory role played by political commissars, could hinder the PLA's ability to reach quick and effective decisions, especially at lower levels, in wartime. Such complications are the price of being a party–army in the twenty-first century.

Further Reading

Benson, Jeff W. and Zi Yang, *Party on the Bridge: Political Commissars in the Chinese Navy* (Washington, DC: Center for Strategic and International Studies, 2020).

Clemens, Morgan and Benjamin Rosen, "The Impact of Reform on the PLA's Political Work System," in Roy Kamphausen, ed., *The People of the PLA 2.0* (Carlisle, PA: U.S. Army War College, 2021), 1–39.

Jost, Tyler, *Bureaucracies at War: The Institutional Origins of Miscalculation* (Cambridge: Cambridge University Press, 2024).

Mattingly, Daniel C., "How the Party Commands the Gun: The Foreign–Domestic Threat Dilemma in China," *American Journal of Political Science* 68 (2024): 227–242.

Saunders, Phillip C. and Andrew Scobell, eds. *PLA Influence on China's National Security Policymaking* (Stanford: Stanford University Press, 2015).

Shambaugh, David, "The Soldier and the State in China: The Political Work System in the People's Liberation Army," *China Quarterly* 127 (1991): 527–568.

Xi Jinping, "Report to the 20th National Congress of the Communist Party of China," October 25, 2022, https://www.fmprc.gov.cn/mfa_eng/zxxx_662805/202210/t20221025_10791908.html.

2

Threat Perceptions

The development of China's military is rooted in the strategic outlook of the leaders of the Chinese Communist Party (CCP). Those perspectives have evolved since the founding of the People's Republic of China in 1949, partly influenced by shifts in the party's priorities, and partly by changes in the security environment. During the Cold War, military forces were essential for deterring or pushing back a possible attack by a superpower rival and thus were necessary for pursuing the CCP's agenda of radical social and economic transformation of the country. In the era of "reform and opening," harnessing military power took a back seat to an emphasis on economic construction; this was possible due to a rapprochement with the United States and the decline and eventual elimination of the Soviet threat. A "period of strategic opportunity" for development persisted in the first two decades of the post-Cold War era, although a booming economy now supported more expansive military modernization. Under Xi Jinping, the party has pursued an ambitious vision of "national rejuvenation," but one clouded by escalating tensions with the United States and the perception that security threats could be found almost everywhere.

This chapter begins with a discussion of the party's basic platform from the Mao era through the present. This is necessary to frame the Chinese leadership as not obsessed with security for its own sake, but because of the need to create a favorable environment for the achievement of larger strategic aims, though these goals have changed significantly since the Cold War. The next section introduces the array of security challenges confronting the country and the party, focusing on the expansion of the concept of "national security" in the years since Xi took office. The perception is that the "period of strategic opportunity" which allowed the party to focus on economic development in the past has begun to close; resistance to China's rise must be expected and conflict is perceived to be closer at hand.

The following sections describe recent CCP assessments of the security environment that are relevant to the PLA's roles and missions. This is organized into a discussion of challenges in several concentric rings of security, beginning with threats to the regime itself and to the territorial integrity of the Chinese mainland. The second covers a contentious region. Most important is a deteriorating situation across the Taiwan Strait; the party not only needs to deter Taiwan independence but also faces the possibility that "peaceful reunification" may be impossible. There are also challenges from regional rivals such as Japan and India and in maintaining a stable periphery. Next is the view of the United States as China's most important strategic challenger, which Beijing assesses is plotting to carry out full-scale "subversion and containment" of China, aided by its network of allies and partners. The outermost ring is the challenge of protecting China's interests beyond Asia. These include defending sea lanes crucial to Chinese energy imports and trade, and protecting Chinese nationals overseas. The conclusion identifies dilemmas that this array of challenges creates for military planning.

The Party's Vision

It is tempting to reduce the motives of the CCP to a basic impulse for survival, akin to how an organized crime syndicate seeks self-preservation to continue its illicit schemes. The party's leaders of course seek their own survival, and many have benefited from ill-gotten gains, especially as the economy has soared in recent decades. But this narrow interpretation loses sight of the party's larger vision for social and economic governance and its quest for international prestige and influence, both of which have evolved considerably from 1949 to the present. Mao Zedong, who led the country from 1949–1976, was a Marxist revolutionary who navigated a place for China between the superpowers during the Cold War. His successor, Deng Xiaoping (1978–1989), pursued a policy of "reform and opening" while keeping the party firmly in charge. Deng's successors, Jiang Zemin (1989–2004) and Hu Jintao (2004–2012) followed a similar path of economic modernization without political liberalization. Xi Jinping's arrival in 2012 heralded a "new era" of increasingly centralized power but with a familiar vision of "national rejuvenation."[1]

From the early days of the party's founding in 1921, and throughout his tenure as leader of the party and chairman of the new republic, Mao sought expansive social and economic transformation. He was a Marxist but with an emphasis on changing the structure of power in the countryside to advantage agricultural workers, whose mobilization he saw as instrumental to the success of the revolution, and who formed the core of the "peasant army" that became known as the PLA, when it was founded in 1927.[2] Encapsulating his worldview, he wrote in 1927 that "revolution is not a dinner party . . . A revolution is an insurrection, an act of violence by which one class overthrows another."[3] The revolution continued in many ways after 1949; Mao's first priorities were land reforms that saw communes established, an Anti-Rightist campaign that targeted officials deemed to be ideologically impure, and a radical but misguided agricultural experiment known as the Great Leap Forward, which resulted in a devastating famine from 1959 to 1961. The Cultural Revolution (1966–1976) saw Mao mobilizing China's youth against CCP rivals whom he viewed as counterrevolutionaries to preserve his own power.

Mao's foreign policies were a study in contrasts. He favored economic and social revolution but accepted Soviet advisors in the 1950s to help build the machinery of a modern bureaucratic state. He also allied with Stalin against his primary enemy, the United States, in the 1950s, before souring on Khruschev – who he saw as a revisionist – in 1960 and eventually pivoting toward a cautious rapprochement with Washington against the Soviet Union. Mao supported domestic self-sufficiency and set severe restrictions on the presence of foreigners in China but also pursued membership in the United Nations and postured China as a leader of the Non-Aligned Movement, championing the interests of what he called the Third World. He dispatched his premier, Zhou Enlai, to the Bandung Conference in 1955 to trumpet the "Five Principles of Peaceful Coexistence," which included respect for sovereignty and territorial integrity, but sponsored communist guerilla movements in Southeast Asia and Africa.[4] He also sent Chinese troops across borders in major campaigns in Korea (1950) and India (1962).

Deng Xiaoping was one of the pragmatists purged by Mao during the Cultural Revolution but made his return in 1978.[5] At the pivotal third plenum of the 11th Central Committee that December, Deng launched what would become known as "reform and opening." This shift was a response to the poor social and economic conditions afflicting the country at the end of the Cultural Revolution, and a return to a focus on national modernization – of seeking "wealth and power" – that can be traced to the "self-strengthening movement" at the end of the nineteenth century.[6] Deng era reforms included dismantling the communes, reintroducing market principles, and professionalizing the bureaucracy (including the military). Yet Deng, like Mao, remained a committed Leninist. Unlike Mikhail Gorbachev's *glasnost* reforms in the contemporary Soviet Union, Deng opposed political liberalization that could have included space for citizens to question the regime. This commitment to authoritarian rule led by the party center came into specific focus during the 1989 Tiananmen Square demonstrations that culminated with the massacre of thousands of civilians.

The "opening" portion of Deng's agenda had several dimensions. Diplomatically, he pursued a policy of "independence and self-determination," but leaned toward the United States and against the Soviet Union. He realized that China's technological backwardness required support from the international community, which led him to promote foreign investment, joint ventures between Chinese and foreign companies, the import of high-tech products from the West, and sending Chinese students to pursue advanced degrees abroad. He also commenced negotiations that resulted in China's entrance into the World Trade Organization in 2001. Mao had secured China's seat in the United Nations in 1971, but Deng showed a greater embrace of the international system, such as contributing troops to UN peacekeeping missions and joining international arms-control treaties. More broadly, Deng preferred to avoid military confrontations after China's brief invasion of Vietnam in 1979, so that the country could focus on economic recovery first, followed by the modernization of the PLA, a policy that has come to be summed up in the axiom, "hide our capabilities and bide our time."

The party remained committed to Deng's reform and opening policy for the next three and a half decades. Jiang Zemin was a charismatic Shanghainese bureaucrat who pursued further economic reforms, including to the country's lethargic state-owned enterprises, the real estate sector, banking, and foreign exchanges. He also encouraged Chinese businesses to "go out" looking for new markets – which resulted in a proliferation of Chinese citizens and firms operating across the developing world. His successor, Hu Jintao, was a technocratic manager who had previously served as party secretary of Tibet. His "scientific outlook on development" combined a push for balanced economic growth and a higher standard of living for ordinary citizens, implicitly pushing back against the rapid growth pursued under Deng and Jiang, which favored wealthy coastal elites. Internationally, Hu is credited with a successful 2008 Beijing Olympics, but also an assertive turn in maritime territorial disputes and international negotiations that gathered steam after the 2008 global financial crisis.[7]

Xi Jinping, the son of a revolutionary veteran and a former senior official in Fujian, Zhejiang, and Shanghai, emerged as Hu's successor in 2012. A propaganda campaign launched at the 19th Party Congress in 2017 defined Xi's rule as a "new era" – the next stage in China's development after Mao and the reform era of Deng, Jiang, and Hu. The power consolidation around Xi marked a pivot from his immediate predecessors. Deng had opposed a centralization of authority in the hands of a single person, which he had assessed as a cause of Mao's excesses, instead encouraging collective decision-making by elites in the party's Politburo and its Standing Committee. He also granted more authorities to the State Council (the country's national government, as distinct from the party). Xi's analysis was that to achieve an ambitious agenda of national progress, the party needed to re-exert its control, with himself labeled as its "core." This also meant further restricting civil society and popular discourse.

While decision-making under Xi changed, there was a high degree of consistency in his platform for national modernization. His signature phrase, "socialism with Chinese characteristics," dated to the Deng era and echoed Hu's message that growth should be more equitable. At the 20th Party Congress in 2022, the party agreed on a roadmap in which per capita GDP would be elevated to the status of a "mid-level developed country" by 2035. Other populist goals, which aligned well with Hu's prescriptions, included improving the quality of governance, raising standards of living in rural areas, and reducing carbon emissions. Xi also identified a grandiose, if ambiguous, set of goals for the party to pursue after 2035. As his report to the 20th Party Congress report noted, "We will continue to work hard and build China into a great modern socialist country that leads the world in terms of composite national strength and international influence by the middle of the century."[8] Xi's vision for what he calls "national rejuvenation" thus lies in the same vein of nation building that originated in the nineteenth century and was resurrected by Deng in the 1980s.

Xi's focus on domestic revitalization complemented a bold foreign policy. Many observers have identified Xi as crucial to an "assertive" Chinese foreign policy, although some elements of a more strident position – especially in maritime disputes – can be traced to the latter part of the Hu era. U.S. scholar Rush Doshi, for instance, argues that a more assertive diplomatic stance stemmed from CCP perceptions of rising national power and U.S. decline following the 2008 global financial crisis.[9] Other elements, including the rise of hawkish "wolf warrior" diplomats, expansive land reclamation in the South China Sea, and an uptick in military coercion across the Taiwan Strait unfolded during Xi's era. The tone and practice of China's policies have become more bellicose; no longer can Beijing be said to be pursuing a "hide and bide" strategy. Nevertheless, Xi has retained his predecessors' caution in crossing the threshold of lethal violence, placing him in contrast to his contemporary, the more militaristic Vladimir Putin in Russia. He has instead tried to balance an ambitious pursuit of China's sovereignty interests with the deployment of economic carrots (and sticks), and diplomatic offensives to maintain regional stability – which remains a precondition for the country's economic growth.

A Complex Security Environment

China's leaders have all needed to pursue their distinct policy visions within a contentious security environment, though perspectives on security challenges have evolved since 1949. Mao kept the country on a war footing for most of his tenure due to poor relations with the superpowers and the need to use the possibility of war to mobilize the people for mass movements such as the Great Leap Forward.[10] By the 1980s, Deng Xiaoping concluded that a major conflict was not likely. This was a result of rapprochement with the United States, waning tensions with the Soviet Union, and Deng's prioritization of market reform and economic opening. In 1985, he announced that "peace and development" had become the "keynotes of the times" and in 1987 declared that China was already well into a 70-year "period of international peace" (1980–2050). This judgment meant that defense spending could be kept to low levels and that national defense could safely be placed as the last of Deng's "four modernizations."[11] His successors confirmed that China was in a "period of strategic opportunity," permitting continued focus on reform and opening.[12]

However, party officials were never under the illusion that they could ignore challenges in the security realm. These problems are illuminated in a series of biennial defense white papers that Beijing initiated in the late 1990s, which offer an authoritative view on major security challenges, as depicted in Table 2.1 below.[13] These present a dialectical perspective that while "peace and development" remain as the main trend, there are also factors of instability that demand the party's attention. The first white paper, in 1998, listed "hegemonism," "enlargement of military blocs," regional ethnic and religious conflicts, and transnational issues such as terrorism, proliferation, and smuggling, among those factors. Subsequent white papers pointed to an even broader array of challenges at home and abroad, such as "separatism" in Tibet and Xinjiang, Taiwan independence activism, instability on the Korean Peninsula, India–Pakistan nuclear tensions, South and East China sea disputes, and perceived U.S. and Japanese "militarism." Diverse challenges meant that the PLA would have to be prepared for many missions in multiple theaters.

While Deng, Jiang, and Hu maintained a distinction between development and security, with the latter subordinated to the former, Xi Jinping's tenure

Table 2.1 Security Challenges Listed in China's Defense White Papers, 1998–2019

	South Asia Instability	Afghanistan Instability	U.S. Alliances Strengthening	Korean Peninsula Instability	Taiwan Independence	Uighur/Tibetan Independence	Diaoyu/Senkakus Infringement	Japan Militarization	South China Sea Infringement	Australia Strengthening Alliances
1998	✗									
2000			✗	✗	✗			✗	✗	
2002	✗	✗	✗	✗	✗					
2004			✗	✗	✗			✗		
2006		✗	✗	✗	✗			✗		
2008			✗		✗	✗				
2010		✗	✗	✗	✗	✗				
2013			✗		✗	✗	✗			
2015			✗	✗	✗	✗		✗	✗	
2019			✗	✗	✗	✗		✗		✗

Source: Authors' table based on data from China Defense White Papers, 1998–2019.

saw an increasing blurring of the two. In 2014, Xi proposed a "holistic national security concept" premised on the idea that both "internal and external factors" of instability are "more complex than at any time in history."[14] He outlined eleven areas of security that would demand the party's attention: political, homeland, military, economic, cultural, social, technological, informational, ecological, resource, and nuclear. Political security was notably listed first in Xi's comments and in later party discussions, reflecting an orientation that problems occurring in many areas of governance, if left unchecked by the party, could ultimately coalesce into broader threats to the regime. The massive protests that erupted in China in 1989, and the decline and fall of the Soviet Union two years later, underpinned this analysis.

Xi's "holistic security concept" was the ideational core of a larger "national security system" that he developed to help the party avoid a similar fate.[15] Accompanying the concept was an institutional innovation in the form of a Central National Security Commission, led by Xi and composed of senior party members and representatives of the security services, diplomats, and others responsible for "security," broadly defined, who would conduct strategic planning and oversee bureaucratic coordination. Meanwhile, more than twenty laws related to national security, including the Hong Kong National Security Law, Counter-Espionage Law, and new legislation on cybersecurity, civil society, and counterterrorism, were passed. These laws were used to justify higher degrees of security control in areas ranging from Hong Kong to the activities of foreigners in China. Foreign analysts assessed the "national security system," with its conceptual, institutional, and legal faces, as amounting to nothing less than the securitization of the country, driven by the party's (and Xi's) profound sense of *insecurity*.

As Xi approached his second decade in power, the accumulation of internal and external crises only deepened the party's preoccupation with security. These included the 2014 and 2019 student movements in Hong Kong that challenged the city's Beijing-approved leaders; the 2020 Covid pandemic, which precipitated a nearly three-year lockdown of society that contributed to economic slowdown and mass discontent; the re-election of Tsai Ing-wen as Taiwan's independence-leaning president in 2020; an intensification of strategic competition with the United States during the Trump and Biden administrations; and Russia's 2022 invasion of Ukraine, which threatened to destabilize a part of the world vital to Chinese economic interests. At the 20th Party Congress in October 2022, Xi notably failed to repeat previous party statements that the "period of strategic opportunity" remained open, instead telling party members that:

> Our country has entered a period of development in which strategic opportunities, risks, and challenges are concurrent and uncertainties and unforeseen factors are rising. Various "black swan" and "gray rhino" events may occur at any time. We must therefore be more mindful of

potential dangers, be prepared to deal with worst-case scenarios, and be ready to withstand high winds, choppy waters, and even dangerous storms.[16]

To understand the range of security challenges influencing the party's outlook – and laying the foundation for the set of missions that the PLA needs to be prepared to conduct – it is useful to analyze the security environment as a series of layers (or what some Western analysts refer to as concentric rings or circles).[17] These include threats from within the party itself and among the larger population, combined with the prevalence of natural disasters and humanitarian emergencies; a complex regional picture involving tense cross-Strait relations as well as frictions between China and its neighbors and continuing transnational dangers; acceleration of strategic rivalry with the United States, which has increased pressure on China on many fronts; and the appearance of global risks, such as threats to critical sea lanes and personnel involved in overseas economic activities. The following sections detail each of these layers.

Trouble at Home

Looking at the security environment from the perspective of Chinese leaders sitting in Zhongnanhai, the party's main compound next to the Forbidden City in Beijing, the most immediate threats can be found virtually outside the window. Coup attempts might not appear likely given the image of solidarity at party congresses, but cannot be ruled out. Some may remember the attempt by former defense minister Lin Biao and his allies within the PLA to stage a coup against Mao in 1971, before fleeing to Mongolia where his plane mysteriously crashed. They may also recall the abortive August 1991 insurrection by Soviet military elements dissatisfied with Gorbachev's reformist policies, or the Romanian military's sacking of the Ceausescus two years earlier. At a minimum, party leaders need to consolidate their power so that they and their agendas are not undermined by other elites, much as Xi dispatched political rivals such as Bo Xilai and Zhou Yongkang and then strengthened his position by abolishing terms limits on the country's president. As discussed in Chapter 1, they must also work to ensure that the army remains committed to CCP leadership, even if "absolute loyalty" is not guaranteed.

Chinese leaders must also attend to challenges against party leadership from various constituencies. The western third of the country consists of two large autonomous regions, Tibet and Xinjiang, populated by ethnic minorities, many of whom prefer greater autonomy or even independence. Tensions in both regions have periodically erupted into violence against the regime or against Han Chinese citizens, most recently in protests that swept the Tibetan plateau in 2008 and riots in the Xinjiang capital Urumqi in 2009.

There are also transnational dimensions, including concerns about support for Uighur independence from co-ethnic groups in Central Asia (especially the Turkistan Islamic Party) and international support for the Dalai Lama and Tibet's government-in-exile in India. Party documents regularly use the phrase "three evils" (separatism, extremism, and terrorism) to describe security problems in western China.

The party has designed a multifaceted strategy to strengthen control in Tibet and Xinjiang. This includes encouraging migration of Han Chinese into minority areas, restricting the use of minority languages in public settings, tightly controlling religious practices, increasing use of surveillance technology to monitor social activities in cities such as Urumqi and Lhasa, and placing some Uighurs in long-term detention and political reeducation camps – or what Chinese authorities call "vocational education and training centers" – with no legal basis.[18] It also includes law enforcement and intelligence cooperation with countries such as Pakistan and the Central Asian republics against Uighur activists and diplomatic attempts to vilify exiled leaders such as the Dalai Lama and former World Uighur Congress leader Rebiya Kadeer. Nevertheless, the PLA and the party's paramilitary wing, the People's Armed Police, maintain large contingents in Tibet and Xinjiang as a deterrent and an insurance policy against a future uprising.

Another concern is that social and economic grievances among the larger Han Chinese population might evolve into a regime-threatening movement. There are frequent "mass incidents" in China from individuals and groups dissatisfied with various issues, such as forced land requisition, banking scandals, unregulated pollution, and even veterans' complaints. Official tallies noted that incidents, which could involve anywhere from a few to thousands of people, rose from 8,700 in 1993 to more than 87,000 in 2005, the last year figures were released. Most incidents are transient and low-profile although some have posed serious governance challenges. Examples include 2011 riots in the southern village of Wukan that resulted in party officials being expelled over illegal land seizures, the 2019 student movement in Hong Kong, in which hundreds of thousands of citizens demonstrated against perceived government overreach, and protests that broke out in several Chinese cities in November 2022 against draconian pandemic policies, during which some citizens even called for the overthrow of Xi Jinping.

The problem for the party is keeping isolated "mass incidents" from growing into broader movements against the regime. In the 1989 Tiananmen protests, various grievances, many of them linked to inflation and corruption, merged into a single campaign for political reform. The party has tried to reduce the prospects for a similar incident by claiming to support accountability (including "letters and visits" offices through which citizens can petition the government), finding scapegoats at the provincial and local levels to alleviate pressure against senior officials, media propaganda portraying top leaders as in touch with the grassroots, regulating civil society groups (both domestic and foreign-linked, some of which have been banned outright), and exercising control over social media narratives.[19] Local law enforcement has also become better trained and equipped for internal security, including carrying guns on patrol since 2014. As in western China, the People's Armed Police and the military are on call in case all else fails.

China's exposure to natural and humanitarian disasters also occupies significant party attention. As in other parts of the world, mudslides, hurricanes, wildfires, and other natural disasters are becoming more intense due to the impact of climate change, evidenced by epic flooding that inundated the central city of Zhengzhou in 2021 and killed 400 people. China has also experienced some of the world's deadliest earthquakes (including the 2008 Sichuan earthquake that killed nearly 70,000) and has periodically suffered from pandemics such as SARS and Covid as well as industrial accidents such as massive explosions at the port of Tianjin in 2015. In 2018, the party instituted a bureaucratic reform that strengthened the civilian emergency response system, but the PLA and People's Armed Police are still frontline actors in large-scale disasters throughout the country and must prepare for those contingencies. A failure to prioritize disaster prevention and response not only implies humanitarian consequences but also potential challenges to the regime if citizens are left dissatisfied – just one way, as reflected in the "holistic security concept," that governance and security are interrelated.

Taiwan and the Neighborhood

While party leaders look first to problems at home, their gaze is never far removed from the Taiwan Strait. The party's objective of gaining control over Taiwan is the product of the Chinese Civil War, in which the losing side (the Kuomintang, or KMT) fled the mainland to Taiwan and established a de facto government that claimed to be the legitimate authority of both Taiwan and the mainland. The intervention of the U.S. 7th Fleet in the Taiwan Strait, which took place after Chinese troops entered the Korean War in 1950, meant that Mao could not realize plans to invade the island. Two military crises erupted in the 1950s focused on Taiwan's outlying islands, but U.S. support and nuclear threats deterred a wider conflict. The problem became more complex in the late Cold War when Deng Xiaoping redefined China's approach to Taiwan as one of "peaceful reunification," guided by an offer that was later extended to Hong Kong – known as "one country, two systems" – marked by the promise of autonomy in return for acknowledgment of the CCP as the legitimate authority of "one China" spanning both sides. Such a deal, never attractive on its face, became even less plausible in the 1990s as Taiwan became more democratic, and those who perceived themselves as

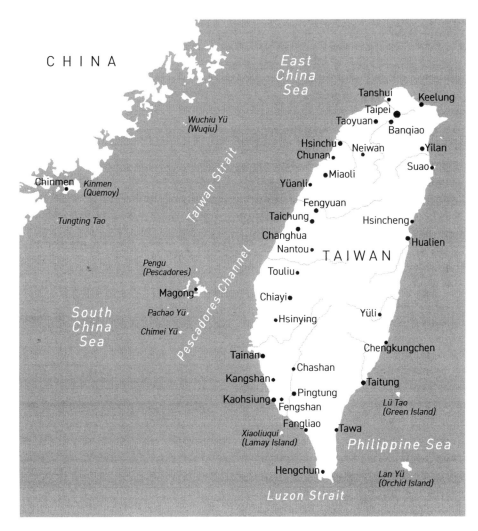

Map 2.1 The Taiwan Strait
Source: Joel Wuthnow et al., eds., *Crossing the Strait: China's Military Prepares for War with Taiwan* (Washington, DC: NDU Press, 2022), xiii.

more distinctly Taiwanese than Chinese gained political influence on the island.

Progress toward unification faded into the background as the challenge of deterring what Beijing believed to be steps toward Taiwan independence came to the forefront. The multifaceted strategy that emerged consisted of trying to build links with those groups on Taiwan who generally opposed independence while isolating and attacking others, who were labeled as "secessionists." Tensions came to a head in June 1995 when Taiwan's leader, Lee Teng-hui, visited the United States (long considered a taboo, except when "transiting" to other countries) and delivered a fiery speech in preparation for Taiwan's first fully democratic presidential election the next year. To warn Lee not to push for independence, China conducted two sets of large military exercises and fired missiles near Taiwan's major ports, leading to a political crisis that culminated in the deployment of two U.S. aircraft carriers in March 1996. These events contributed to greater attention by the PLA on how to counter U.S. intervention in a future crisis, which was the key requirement driving its pursuit of "anti-access/area denial" capabilities. Tensions continued in the administration of Chen Shui-bian (2000–2008), from the pro-independence Democratic Progressive Party (DPP), who had supported a vision of "one country on each side" of the Strait. In 2005, China's legislature passed an Anti-Secession Law that authorized the use of force to prevent Taiwan independence.

While cross-Strait ties warmed under KMT president Ma Ying-jeou (2008–2016), tensions increased with a return to DPP leadership under Tsai Ing-wen in 2016. Beijing was incensed when Tsai, upon inauguration, refused to accept the "1992 Consensus," by which the CCP and the KMT had agreed to a position that there is "one China," albeit with different interpretations. At the same time, Beijing became concerned about a perceived shift in U.S. policy. Whereas U.S. officials had discouraged Lee and Chen from pursuing legal independence, Beijing saw Washington encouraging Taiwan independence as part of a broader strategy to permanently separate the mainland from Taiwan. This perceived change, combined with historically low support for unification in Taiwan (which plummeted after China's 2019 crackdown in Hong Kong), led to a growing sense that "peaceful reunification" might be out of reach. The PLA, as discussed in Chapter 7, could no longer focus simply on deterring independence, but might be called on to solve the cross-Strait impasse through force. Xi Jinping gave the military a 2027 deadline to build the capability to accomplish that goal.

Nevertheless, Chinese leaders could not focus myopically on Taiwan. They also needed to manage a complex regional environment in which maintaining positive relations with neighboring countries had to be pursued alongside preparations for potential crises and the prosecution of China's expansive territorial claims.[20] Compared to the United States, which has benefited from a favorable geostrategic situation defined by two oceans and friendly relations with its two neighbors, China shares land borders with fourteen countries and sea borders with six countries and Taiwan. These include some friends, such as Russia, Laos, Cambodia, and Pakistan, several combustible or conflict-prone regimes (North Korea, Myanmar, and Afghanistan), a handful of U.S. allies (Japan, South Korea, Thailand, and the Philippines), and several countries with whom China remains locked in territorial disputes (India, Bhutan, Japan, Vietnam, the Philippines, Malaysia, and Brunei, plus Taiwan), even though it managed to successfully negotiate other border disputes in the 1990s.[21] A brief

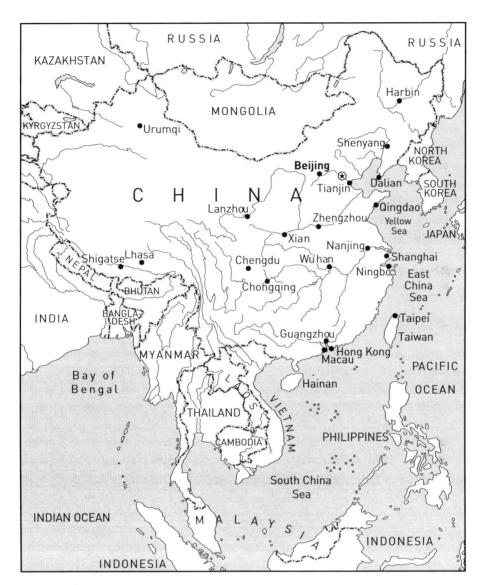

Map 2.2 China's Regional Environment

tour of China's periphery illustrates the range of regional challenges facing the party.

Starting in the Northeast, China shares a border with North Korea. The two countries were close allies during the Cold War, evidenced by Mao's decision to send Chinese troops to assist Pyongyang against the United States during the Korean War (1950–1953) and the signing of a formal defense treaty in 1961 but, since the 1990s, Beijing has had to wrestle with two realities.[22] First is South Korea's economic dynamism and the resulting need for China to balance relations between the two Koreas. Second is the North's pursuit of nuclear weapons and delivery systems, which China has opposed in principle but never strongly resisted due to its competing desire not to weaken the regime – which remains an important strategic buffer between China's northeast and a U.S. ally. Under Kim Jong-un, the North remains a tinderbox with resulting military implications. The PLA has therefore needed to train for several contingencies, including securing "loose nukes," responding to what could become a humanitarian catastrophe if the North Korean regime were to collapse, and preparing to intervene in a future military conflict on the peninsula.

Proceeding to the south, Sino–Japanese relations have been a source of tension for decades, with memories of Japan's occupation of mainland China in the 1930s and 1940s still fresh. Modern relations have been strained under the weight of rising nationalism on both sides and an unresolved territorial dispute.[23] The contested area covers the Senkaku Islands (which the Chinese refer to as the Diaoyus, and Taiwan calls the Diaoyutai), which are a group of rocky islets in the East China Sea – intrinsically insignificant but legally consequential since ownership could confer the right to exploit energy resources in a 200nm Exclusive Economic Zone, as defined in the UN Convention on the Law of the Sea, which both states have ratified. Tensions exploded in 2012 when, in an ironic twist, Japan's central government purchased three of the islands from a private owner to defuse tensions with China after the nationalistic governor of Tokyo sought to acquire them himself. Nevertheless, Beijing was incensed and deployed the Coast Guard to assert its own territorial claims. Relations continued to sour as Japan relaxed constraints on its postwar peace constitution, cultivated a tighter military alliance with the United States, and deepened its unofficial ties with Taiwan. Yet China has had to balance its nationalistic impulses with the pragmatic need to manage relations with a country that ranks as one of its top trading and investment partners.

Another, even more complex, set of territorial disputes remains in the South China Sea. Beijing has long asserted vast, yet ambiguous, claims within a sea stretching more than 1.3 million square miles from southern China toward the Indonesian archipelago and the Strait of Malacca. Those claims reside within China's so-called "nine-dash line," which covers most of the sea, including land features in the Paracels, Spratlys, and Scarborough Shoal. Other countries have asserted overlapping claims, the most extensive of which are from Vietnam and the Philippines, followed by Malaysia and Brunei.[24] China consolidated its control over the Paracels in 1974 when it defeated South Vietnam in a short naval battle but has not achieved total control elsewhere. China's enforcement of its claims became more active in the twenty-first century as protection of critical sea lanes and exploitation of fisheries and hydrocarbon resources in the sea were regarded as essential to the country's economic development.[25] A major campaign to build artificial islands in the

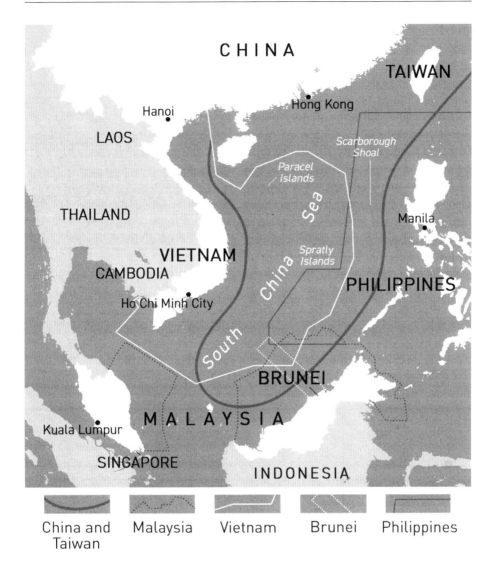

Map 2.3 Overlapping South China Sea Claims

Spratlys commenced in 2013, which facilitated new military bases and a more enduring presence for the Chinese air force, navy, and Coast Guard. A ruling by a United Nations arbitral tribunal in July 2016 that invalidated Beijing's claims was no deterrent to expanded and sometimes aggressive enforcement patrols. Nevertheless, as in other disputes, Beijing avoided the use of lethal force, preferring to gradually expand its effective control of contested areas while maintaining stability in its relations with Southeast Asian rivals.

Turning to the southwest, China has entered a strategic rivalry with India, focused on the unresolved border dispute.[26] New Delhi and Beijing sharply disagree on the proper demarcation of a frontier extending more than 2000 miles, with specific disagreements in two main sectors – Aksai Chin, located to the west and effectively controlled by China, and Arunachal Pradesh to the east, effectively controlled by India. (China also has a separate Himalayan border dispute with tiny Bhutan, which was previously an Indian protectorate.) Both sides have dispatched large numbers of troops to patrol near the unofficial Line of Actual Control, occasionally resulting in minor skirmishes.[27] Other sources of Sino–Indian tension include China's "all-weather" partnership with Pakistan, India's hosting of the Dalai Lama since 1959, the growing presence of the Chinese navy in the Indian Ocean, which India has long considered its strategic backyard, and India's growing alignment with the West through the Quadrilateral Security Dialogue and closer military cooperation with the United States. The two sides, however, have tried to prevent tensions from escalating into armed conflict. Not only are both nuclear powers, but both are also trying to manage a mutually beneficial economic relationship bilaterally and through multilateral arrangements such as the BRICS organization.

Farther west and to the north, China shares a narrow border with Afghanistan and longer frontiers with Tajikistan, Kyrgyzstan, Kazakhstan, and Mongolia. The pressing issue across the Central Asian landscape is maintaining secure borders in remote regions, across which China has faced an influx of narcotics (specifically from Afghanistan), as well as the infiltration of Uighur fighters into Xinjiang and the possibility of terrorists aligned with groups such as the Islamic State and al Qaeda. In 1996, China established a group that eventually became known as the Shanghai Cooperation Organization (SCO) to coordinate counterterrorism policies with its three Central Asian neighbors and Russia; China engaged in military exercises through the SCO and bilaterally with its neighbors. To promote a more proactive approach to border security, the People's Armed Police established an outpost inside Tajikistan in the 2010s and conducted joint counterterrorism patrols.[28] Security cooperation complemented economic and diplomatic outreach through the Belt and Road Initiative, though Beijing continued to face challenges, most notably the collapse of the Afghan government and its replacement by the Taliban in 2021.

Russia occupies the last segment of China's periphery. Sino–Russian relations have evolved from a strategic alignment against the United States in the 1950s, to outright animosity from 1960 through the 1980s, to a strategic partnership with the new Russian Federation beginning in 1991. The two sides have often adopted coordinated positions when their interests align, including rhetoric railing against the perceived excesses of U.S.-led military interventionism and its support for "color revolutions."[29] Militarily, as discussed in Chapter 6, the two countries conduct frequent exercises, some of them involving thousands of troops and advanced equipment. Also solidifying relations are China's purchases of Russian arms and energy, and its status as Russia's largest trade partner. Yet the two countries are not allies and continue to suffer from mistrust due to historical antagonism, Russian concerns about Chinse encroachment in its sparsely populated Far East and Central Asia, and divergent interests on some issues (for instance, Russia has been a key arms supplier to India and Vietnam). Russia's 2022 invasion of Ukraine created a new dilemma for Beijing, which was caught between support for Moscow and the need to maintain stable ties with the European Union and avoid Western sanctions.

A Strong Adversary

Domestic and regional troubles are intensified, from a Chinese perspective, by strategic challenges from the United States. During the Cold War, Sino–U.S. relations were more straightforward than they have been recently. The two maintained no diplomatic or economic relations following the Chinese Civil War, with simmering hostilities punctuated by direct combat in the Korean War (1950–1953) and a PLA role in assisting North Vietnam in its war against the United States. Following Mao's decision to intervene in Korea, Washington decided to establish a "defensive perimeter" around China through military alliances and deployments along the first island chain (in Japan, South Korea, the Philippines, and Taiwan), and alliances farther afield with Thailand, Australia, and New Zealand. China formed its own alliance with the Soviet Union against the United States in 1950 and prepared military forces to defend against anticipated U.S. attacks on the mainland, while laying the groundwork for nuclear and ballistic missile programs designed to counter U.S. nuclear threats.

The Sino–Soviet split in 1960, followed by the Soviet military buildup under Leonid Brezhnev and military clashes along a contested border that reached a peak in 1969, created the political conditions in which the United States could explore rapprochement with China. Henry Kissinger's secret visit in 1971 set the stage for formal recognition based on a joint communique signed between Mao Zedong and Richard Nixon in Shanghai in 1972; two more communiques were signed by their successors in 1979 and 1982. These became the basis for normalized relations, which required the United States to withdraw its military forces from Taiwan and sever formal diplomatic ties with the island, though the Taiwan Relations Act passed by Congress in 1979 provided a framework for unofficial relations and required the administration to "provide arms of a defensive character" to Taiwan. In the face of a common Soviet foe, Washington and Beijing fostered military and intelligence cooperation in the late 1970s and 1980s. Driven by China's market reforms and U.S. demand for Chinese imports, they also built the foundation for economic ties that lasted into the post-Cold War period.

The collapse of the Soviet Union and the 1989 Tiananmen crackdown marked the end of expansive Sino–U.S. strategic coordination. Beginning with the George H.W. Bush administration, U.S. presidents generally pursued a dual track approach, sometimes called "hedging": building U.S. military influence in Asia as a deterrent to Chinese aggression while also seeking access to China's growing market and encouraging Beijing to integrate itself more firmly into the international community. The Clinton administration rebuilt the waning U.S. alliance with Japan while supporting most-favored-nation trading status for China and encouraging its entrance into the World Trade Organization. George W. Bush took office in 2001 with a more hawkish view on China, but the 9/11 terrorist attacks required him to shift U.S. attention to the Middle East. The end of that administration saw the beginnings of a return to Asia, including an upgraded U.S. partnership with India. The Obama administration built on this policy by announcing a strategic "pivot to Asia" in 2011 that sought to enhance U.S. economic and military influence in the region while coordinating with China on global challenges such as North Korean and Iranian nuclear proliferation and climate change.[30]

U.S. strategy during the Trump and Biden administrations shifted to a more explicit focus on strategic competition with China. The 2017 *National Security Strategy* reflected the Trump campaign's emphasis on combatting "malign" Chinese economic activities, including intellectual property theft, state intervention in the market that violated China's World Trade Organization pledges to uphold fair trade, and "cyber-enabled economic warfare." A trade war quickly ensued as the United States imposed tariffs on Chinese products, and Beijing retaliated with reduced market access for U.S. firms. Trump's strategy eventually expanded to include military and diplomatic instruments as well,[31] though critics argued that this approach was undercut by Trump's abandonment of the Trans-Pacific Partnership, which President Obama had negotiated to preserve U.S. influence in the region, and by disputes on burden-sharing with U.S. allies.[32]

In its own *National Security Strategy*, the Biden administration lodged a similar complaint that China "is the only competitor with both the intent to reshape the international order and, increasingly, the economic, diplomatic, military, and technological power to do it."[33] This implied a whole-of-government effort to compete through stronger bilateral military alliances with Japan, Korea, Australia, and the Philippines, cooperation through multilateral arrangements such as the Quadrilateral Security Dialogue (the "Quad") and the Australia–U.K.–U.S. partnership (AUKUS), and restrictions on China's access to advanced technology. However, Biden's strategy also recognized that Washington and Beijing would have to cooperate on select issues where they had common interests, such as climate change. Biden also prioritized the need for "guardrails," including renewed military crisis communications channels with the PLA, to prevent competition from spiralling into open hostilities.

Chinese officials saw the competitive turn in U.S. strategy as concerning on many levels. Filtered through China's Cold War experience, U.S. military alliances were seen as emboldening countries such as Japan and the Philippines to press their own territorial claims, making the South and East China sea disputes harder to resolve. The Quad and AUKUS appeared as incipient Asian versions of NATO, even if they remained loose diplomatic fora and not formal security institutions. Growing U.S. support for Taiwan was seen in China as encouraging pro-independence activists and closing the door to peaceful unification. U.S. military exercises and reconnaissance operations near China were considered an affront. The 2019 student movement in Hong Kong was alleged to be further evidence of U.S. support for a "color revolution" targeting the CCP. U.S. narratives of China's "malign" economic activities and "exploitative" Belt and Road Initiative put Beijing on the defensive diplomatically. Technology restrictions were viewed as threatening a basis of China's economic growth and national competitiveness.[34] Speaking in early 2023, Xi Jinping complained that "Western countries led by the United States have implemented comprehensive containment, encirclement and suppression against us, bringing unprecedentedly severe challenges to our country's development."[35]

Chinese perceptions of growing strategic pressure from the United States have led to new considerations for the PLA. As noted above, countering potential U.S. intervention in a Taiwan conflict has only increased in relevance. This resulted in decisions to field more advanced long-range missile forces to hold U.S. forces at risk and developing a larger strategic arsenal to resist U.S. nuclear coercion and offer Beijing tools to deter U.S. intervention. The PLA has also needed to balance coercive activities against neighbors with larger considerations of U.S. alliance commitments and a strategic imperative to drive wedges between these countries and the United States, which sometimes meant emphasizing cooperation ahead of differences. Strategic rivalry has also promoted solidarity between the Chinese and Russian militaries, though avoiding Western sanctions led Beijing to limit the degree of direct military support for Russia after its 2022 invasion of Ukraine. U.S. restrictions on high-tech exports to China have incentivized the PLA to improve its own capacity for innovation and onshore critical supply chains.

On the other hand, Chinese leaders also needed to consider how to manage military interactions with the United States. A desire to avoid miscalculations or accidents led both sides to approve hotlines and other confidence-building measures after the 1995–1996 Taiwan Strait crisis. Reflecting a desire to work with China on common global challenges, there were even more ambitious agendas for cooperation in areas such as anti-piracy and disaster relief in the 2000s.[36] At the outset of his tenure, Xi Jinping called for a "new-type military-to-military relationship" with the United States that would inject stability into bilateral relations. In practice, however, intensifying competitive dynamics and strategic distrust have narrowed the appetite for cooperation. Washington has become concerned that contacts with the PLA legitimize coercive Chinese policies while delivering few tangible benefits, and Beijing perceives that political incentives to stand up to the United States – by refusing to speak in moments of tension or by dangerous intercepts of U.S. air and naval operations in the region – often outweigh the risks of escalation. Effective crisis communications are also limited by China's centralized command structure, in which lower-level officials do not feel empowered to make decisions in an unfolding crisis and must first seek out guidance from the party leadership.[37]

Global Risks

Beyond the Indo-Pacific region, China faces a variety of threats with military dimensions. The most serious strategic issue is sea lane protection. According to the U.S. government, China procures more than 70 percent of its oil from overseas, most of which travels through the Strait of Malacca. Beijing has also sought to expand maritime-based trade with Europe as part of a strategy of diversifying away from the U.S. market, but that trade must pass through maritime chokepoints such as the Strait of Malacca and the Suez Canal. One challenge is that seaborne trade has been exposed to piracy in places like the Horn of Africa and Southeast Asia. The greater risk has been that China lacks a significant overseas naval presence to defend those sea lanes, yielding that responsibility to the U.S. Navy and others. Yet reliance on a strategic rival to defend one's sea lanes creates vulnerability to coercion or to an actual blockade during a conflict in Asia. Hu Jintao referred to this problem as the "Malacca Dilemma."[38]

Beijing has tried to resolve this dilemma in several ways. One is by reducing reliance on maritime trade through the Malacca Strait. This includes greater reliance on rail links between Europe and Asia, higher levels of imports of natural gas and oil through pipelines, and the construction of the China–Pakistan Economic Corridor, which is intended to facilitate the flow of oil through Pakistan, avoiding shipments through the narrow chokepoints of Southeast Asia. China also maintains a strategic petroleum reserve with locations across the country, designed in the mid-2000s to provide 90 days of supplies but which has likely expanded to provide additional capacity. The most ambitious leg of the strategy has been building a blue water navy composed of large surface combatants, submarines, and port facilities stretching across the Indian Ocean. These forces have actively conducted anti-piracy operations off the Horn of Africa since December 2008 and, along with the air force, have trained for higher end contingencies, including countering foreign blockades far from China's coasts.

Global economic activity has also created new vulnerabilities that Chinese leaders have needed to address. Encouraging Chinese enterprises to go abroad in search of new markets since the turn of the century has resulted in more than ten million Chinese citizens living abroad and more than 150 million annual outbound trips for tourism, study abroad, and other purposes. Monitoring and, in exigent circumstances, protecting these individuals has thus been unavoidable for Beijing. The relative importance of overseas protection increased with the advent of the Belt and Road Initiative in 2013. The BRI consisted of thousands of individual investments and construction projects, some that had begun under previous Chinese leaders and others started under Xi.[39] This initiative was designed to find markets for excess industrial capacity left over from China's response to the 2008 global financial crisis, generate stronger trade linkages between China and its partners, and provide access to strategic locations and resources.[40] The core of the BRI was six economic corridors stretching from China across Central Asia, the Middle East, and into Europe, creating stronger long term trade connections with these regions, though projects also proliferated beyond Eurasia, into Africa, Latin America, and even the polar regions.

Chinese strategists understood the risks inherent in a greater overseas presence. As one major general from the PLA's Academy of Military Sciences put it, the BRI route "passes through many geopolitically fragile areas, with complex historical issues, intense ethnic and religious contradictions, and frequent armed conflict."[41] Among the specific challenges described by Chinese security analysts are hostage-taking and assassinations by terrorist groups such as the Islamic State and al Qaeda, attacks by militants opposed to the presence of Chinese workers, which have occurred in Pakistan and some African countries, Chineze citizens caught up in civil wars and regional conflicts, including the outbreak of violence in Yemen in 2014 and the Sudan civil war in 2023, and natural or humanitarian disasters.[42] These challenges implied a need for stronger intelligence, law enforcement, and counter-terrorism cooperation with host countries, but as discussed in Chapter 8, the PLA has also needed to be able to protect Chinese citizens in distress when other options are not available.

Challenges to China's material interests accompanied more diffuse threats to China's image and ideational interests. Since the reform and opening period began in 1978, China's leaders have sought to fashion a more favorable reputation for their country and greater influence in international forums and discourse. This diplomatic priority was based on a desire for status and recognition as a major player, as a necessary condition for expansion of access to foreign markets, as a way of containing the spread of liberal norms that put pressure on authoritarian regimes, and as a source of diplomatic support for China's positions on controversial issues such as cross-Strait relations, China's claims in the South China Sea, and policies in Xinjiang. The challenge, from China's perspective, is that the United States, its allies, and anti-China activists are working to undermine China's reputation and foster global opposition to its rise. U.S.-sponsored discourse on the BRI as a strategic ploy or opportunistic gambit out of touch with local interests is only one manifestation of this concern.

Promoting China's image – or what Chinese officials often call "telling China's story well" – is thus a diplomatic goal for Beijing. This has involved traditional diplomacy, attempts to shape social media discourse in China's favor, attempts to shape the agenda in regional and international institutions, proliferation of Chinese state-sponsored media outlets in foreign countries, educational programs such as Confucius Institutes, cultivation of ties with foreign civil society groups and elites seen to be favorable to the CCP through "United Front" work, and simultaneous efforts to suppress voices seen as hostile to China's interests. There is also a military dimension to the process of burnishing China's reputation. As discussed in Chapters 6 and 8, many activities in which the PLA is engaged, such as dialogues between senior military officials, anti-piracy and peacekeeping operations, and port visits are focused on enhancing China's image and receptivity toward its rise in the developing world.

Conclusion

A difficult geostrategic context has been a hindrance to Chinese leaders pursuing their distinct visions since Mao. In a "new era" in which threats to the party, and its quest for "national rejuvenation," come in many forms and from many directions, China's leadership construes most areas of governance as related to "national security." For example, continued economic growth, pandemic prevention and control, anti-corruption campaigns to silence political rivals and burnish the party's reputation, restrictions on the free expression of ideas, limitations on civil society, draconian social control measures in western China, and diplomats charged with "telling China's story well" to audiences abroad all fit within the loose boundaries of "national security" in China today. This broad definition means that there is a much wider cast of security actors across the bureaucratic landscape than in the United States or elsewhere.[43] These include Internet monitors, health authorities, financial regulators, civil affairs personnel, and party officials at all levels. The armed forces are only one bright star in this constellation.

Nevertheless, amid a complex security environment, the PLA and the People's Armed Police have a wide set of responsibilities. Beginning with the innermost ring of security, they must ensure the safety of senior officials, maintain order in Tibet and Xinjiang, respond to "mass incidents" that exceed the capacity of local law enforcement, and contribute to the management of natural disasters. Within the region, the primary missions are deterring Taiwan independence and preparing to provide options to the party to compel reunification through force, though the armed forces also need to enforce China's extensive territorial claims within the first island chain and across the Sino–Indian border, prepare to handle instability on the Korean Peninsula, safeguard China's extensive land borders, and conduct military diplomacy to shape the security environment. Countering U.S. intervention and shaping a favorable environment in light of a perceived competition from the United States also requires sharper military tools and new concepts. Beyond Asia, the PLA's more limited functions include safeguarding critical sea lanes and conducting non-traditional security operations.

This diverse set of roles and missions, combined with finite resources, implies a series of tradeoffs that Chinese strategists must consider. First, for the party center, there are choices, not so much between "guns" and "butter," as sometimes discussed in the West, but between different forms of security. Funding for the military needs to be balanced against items such as infrastructure construction, financial stimulus, and subsidies for state owned enterprises, which can be characterized as security spending, since economic complaints, if left unattended, can evolve into threats to the regime; and to support expensive foreign ventures, such as the BRI, which influence China's ability to compete with the United States in the developing world. Similarly, there are also tradeoffs between funding for the coercive instruments of *domestic* control, such as the Ministry of Public Security (which oversees the local police) and the People's Armed Police, and *external* security, which focuses on the PLA, the Ministry of State Security (China's intelligence service), and the diplomatic corps.

Second, choices need to be made about how to design and distribute forces. The PLA's signature mission might involve a cross-Strait conflict, but the litany of other domestic, border, coastal, and global contingencies require forces postured for crises that may break out in other theaters. (Moreover, even in a cross-Strait scenario, the PLA perceives a potential "chain reaction" of conflicts elsewhere, meaning that forces would have to be on high alert across China's vast periphery, not just in the southeast.) While some forces, such as advanced fighter aircraft, are relatively flexible, there is also a need for competency in specialized areas such as mountain or jungle warfare, small island seizure, or countering weapons of mass destruction, that imply investments in narrowly tailored military hardware and training. Some missions are more relevant to some services than others, meaning that choices need to be made between them – cuts to the ground forces, for instance, can provide resources for larger naval and air forces.

Third, different time horizons require different considerations. There are persistent near-term requirements, such as patrolling in disputed areas and maintaining a steady drumbeat of major exercises to maintain readiness, which put pressure on training and maintenance accounts. Simply staffing the PLA also requires burdensome manpower expenses, especially for technically literate recruits who are difficult to attract and retain in military service. However, those near-term expenses must be weighed against the long-term acquisition of systems which will allow the PLA to compete on the future battlefield. A related choice is deciding how much to invest in the next genera-tion of existing weapons and platforms, such as a new aircraft carrier, versus how much to invest in different kinds of technologies, such as uncrewed systems or artificial intelligence, which could be game changers in the future.

Such tensions – between different forms of security spending, different force models, and near- and long-term spending – must be adjudicated at the highest reaches of the CCP and in the CMC, which is the party's highest organ for military decision-making. The next chapter considers how these dilemmas translate into strategic choices in three respects. First is the adoption and evolution of a formal military strategy that prioritizes missions and defines operational approaches. Second is the adaptation of the military's structure to enable it to achieve those missions. Third are changes in the approach to resourcing in terms of the budgets, personnel, and technology needed to implement the strategy. All of these choices are implications of the difficult security environment that the party has had to navigate as it pursues its long-term agenda.

Further Reading

Bush, Richard C., *Difficult Choices: Taiwan's Quest for Security and the Good Life* (Washington, DC: Brookings Institution Press, 2021) .

deLisle, Jacques and Avery Goldstein, eds., *After Engagement: Dilemmas in U.S.–China Security Relations* (Washington, DC: Brookings Institution Press, 2021).

Economy, Elizabeth C., *The World According to China* (London: Polity, 2022).

Gill, Bates, *Daring to Struggle: China's Global Ambitions Under Xi Jinping* (Oxford: Oxford University Press, 2022).

Medeiros, Evan S., ed., *Cold Rivals: The New Era of US-China Strategic Competition* (Washington, DC: Georgetown University Press, 2023).

Pei, Minxin, *The Sentinel State: Surveillance and the Survival of Dictatorship in China* (Cambridge: Harvard University Press, 2024).

Shirk, Susan L., *Overreach: How China Derailed Its Peaceful Rise* (New York: Oxford University Press, 2022).

Ye, Min, *The Belt Road and Beyond: State-Mobilized Globalization in China: 1998–2018* (Cambridge: Cambridge University Press, 2020).

White Paper, *China's National Defense in the New Era* (Beijing: State Council Information Office, 2019).

3

Strategy, Organization, and Resources

Strategy is a way to match goals with finite resources. China's complex geo-strategic situation has long required leaders to think carefully about how military capabilities – scarce in the past and still limited today, despite China's rapid economic growth – should be developed and employed. Against which adversaries should the PLA train to fight? Where should forces be deployed? What operations should they be able to conduct? In the PLA's early years, Mao Zedong and his commanders had to develop concepts for how a struggling guerilla force could win against larger and better equipped armies (the Japanese and the Nationalists). After 1949, they needed to decide how a standing army could protect a new nation's interests while also guaranteeing the party's survival. As the Cold War came to an end, the task was to build a modern force that could not only defend the Chinese homeland but also accomplish more complex missions abroad. At each step, they revisited the basic questions of military strategy and at times made bold changes.

Changes in military strategy have implications for two areas of military planning. One is organization and force structure. During Mao's time, China's military objectives could mostly be attained through a large ground force, supplemented by a small nuclear deterrent. Beginning in the 1990s, the focus shifted to the ambitious tasks of deterring Taiwan independence while preparing to invade the island if called on by the party. This required power projected beyond the Chinese mainland and the use of land, air, sea, and missile forces in concert. The stunning U.S. victory in the 1991 Gulf War offered the PLA lessons on how joint operations, combined with modern technology, could be used to subdue weaker opponents. A new strategy led to a new organization as the army's share of the force diminished and, in the Xi era, fundamental reforms to the command structure were made to promote the PLA's ability to conduct modern warfare. Nevertheless, problems in other theaters continued to worry China's leaders. This required that Chinese forces be distributed around the periphery and prepare for other contingencies.

The second implication concerns resources and modernization priorities. The party has had to decide how much revenue should be funneled to the military, how to develop a modern officer corps, and how to acquire the weapons and equipment it would need to deter opponents and fight wars. These questions came to the fore after the Cold War as the PLA shifted from a strategy based on mass to one based on quality. Increasing growth created opportunities for rapid modernization, but leaders needed to choose how much of the budget to allocate to long-term acquisition, how much toward personnel expenses, and how much on operations and maintenance. Isolated during much of the Cold War, China also began to acquire advanced weapons from foreign countries while laying the foundation for a defense industrial base that could produce capabilities on a par with the West – what Xi has referred to as "world-class forces."

China's current military strategy requires the PLA to defeat regional opponents in what are envisioned to be short, high-intensity campaigns. Both the PLA's organizational structure and the approaches to resources and modernization have become better aligned with that objective. The question is whether and under what circumstances the strategy could evolve once again. The PLA is not currently required to undertake combat missions beyond Asia, nor has it prepared for a protracted war with the United States. Whether it will move in these directions will depend on how the situation across the Taiwan Strait plays out, strategic competition between China and the United States, and China's internal political and economic situation. Yet even now, the PLA is analyzing lessons from Russia's military campaign in Ukraine for clues about the kinds of conflicts it will need to prepare for next. The answer could be a war of greater duration and scale than they previously anticipated.

This chapter begins with a discussion of how China's military strategy has evolved through history. The focus is on the transition from the Cold War to the strategy that developed thereafter and remains mostly intact today. It notes that while preparing for a high-end conflict with Taiwan has long been the priority, the strategy has also changed in practice to encompass a greater overseas peacetime role for the PLA, the adoption of low-tech "gray zone" tactics in regional territorial disputes, and, most recently, an expansion of China's nuclear deterrent. It then outlines the pillars of the PLA's organization and chronicles the decisive structural reforms undertaken in the Xi era. This section also notes organizational issues that could complicate the PLA's effectiveness, including army dominance in the leadership and the tightening of party control. This is followed by a review of how the PLA has harnessed resources, in terms of money, people, and technology, to modernize to meet its strategic aims. The conclusion considers the conditions under which Chinese strategy could move in a new direction.

A Military Strategy for a New Era

The origins of China's contemporary military strategy can be traced to ancient times with the compilation of the seminal treatise *The Art of War*. The volume, written by the apocryphal author Sunzi in the fifth century BCE, contained a series of maxims that military leaders should consider before waging campaigns. Its most famous maxim, widely quoted today, is that the most successful general can "win without fighting" by assembling such dominant forces that the enemy has no choice but to capitulate before the battle begins. Yet Sunzi also realized that less powerful forces may not have this option. For weaker armies, deception, cunning, and even strategic retreat are among the favored tools. The *Art of War* and other ancient texts were canonized during the eleventh-century Song Dynasty into the "seven military classics," which Harvard professor Alastair Iain Johnston argues produced a "parabellum paradigm" – the idea that to achieve peace, leaders must continually prepare for war.[1]

Ancient ideas infused modern military thinking as the PLA fought its early campaigns from the 1920s to the 1940s. Mao looked back to the *Art of War* for inspiration on how to use his own forces, which were the weaker side in manpower and equipment against both the Japanese invaders and the Nationalists (Kuomintang) during the Civil War. Consistent with Sunzi's emphasis on cunning, he relied on guerilla warfare – luring the enemy deep into hostile territory, attacking their supply lines rather than their main forces, and blending in with local populations sympathetic to Communist goals, calling this approach "people's war." He also conducted strategic retreats when needed, most famously during the 1934–1935 Long March, in which his army traveled from the vulnerable southeast to a remote base at Yan'an, in central China. He adopted a conventional approach only after his forces had become strong enough to make direct conflict tenable.

Mao's strategy also incorporated Marxist concepts about the purpose of military power. Contrasting his mission with the Western imperialists, he argued that military forces should be used defensively to avoid "national subjugation," rather than offensively to seize foreign territory and colonize others. However, within a defensive strategy, Mao argued that forces should be used dynamically, maneuvering to find the enemy's weak spots and conducting surprise attacks when possible. He did not approve of the type of static trench warfare that had proved futile in World War I. In a 1936 essay, written not long after his army arrived in Yan'an, he outlined the principles of "active defense":

> Active defense is also known as offensive defense, or defense through decisive engagements. Passive defense is also known as purely defensive defense or pure defense. Passive defense is actually a spurious kind of defense, and the only real defense is active defense, defense for the purpose of counterattacking and taking the offensive. As far as I know, there is no military manual of value nor any sensible military expert, ancient or modern, Chinese or foreign, that does not oppose passive defense, whether in strategy or tactics. Only a complete fool or a madman would cherish passive defense as a talisman. However, there

are people in this world who do such things. That is an error in war, a manifestation of conservatism in military matters, which we must resolutely oppose.[2]

After the People's Republic of China (PRC) was founded in 1949, Mao and his successors had to consider the role of military power in their new regime. The essence remained the principle of "active defense," a concept that survived Mao's time and remains in use to the present. Under this concept, the use of force is always construed in self-defensive terms. The primary goals of military power are to deter adversaries, and to fight and win wars against those who threaten China's vital interests. Even when the PLA crossed borders to fight its enemies abroad, as they did in Korea (1950–1953), India (1962), and Vietnam (1979), those incursions were justified as necessary responses to strategic threats posed by others.[3] In other words, "active defense" does *not* mean that China will wait to attack before being attacked – it may strike first but will justify those actions as defensive in nature.

Military strategy starts with the need to describe the purpose of military power but must also explain how finite resources should be harnessed. Adopting a more formal approach to strategy after 1949, Mao and the Central Military Commission (CMC) unveiled a series of "military strategic guidelines" that answered the most fundamental strategic questions: where, against whom, and how should the PLA be prepared to fight. The first strategy was approved in 1956, followed by another nine over the next six decades, as outlined in Table 3.1 below. In 2019, Xi promulgated the latest strategy, known as the "military strategic guidelines for the new era." These judgments changed over the years, based on two factors. First was changes in the strategic landscape that required the PLA to deter or fight wars against new adversaries and sometimes in different theaters. Second were changes in the character of war, including new operational forms and technologies that the PLA would need to incorporate into its own planning.

A basic distinction can be made between China's military strategies during and after the Cold War. From the 1950s until his death in 1976, Mao was preoccupied with a general conflict against the superpowers. U.S. and Chinese forces fought bloody campaigns against each other on the Korean Peninsula between 1950 and 1953, but Mao's larger concern was preparing for an anticipated attack on the mainland. The first military strategy thus directed the PLA to withstand a U.S. incursion in northeastern China, which Mao called the "main strategic direction." The rupture of Sino–Soviet relations in 1960, combined with Brezhnev's military buildup and the outbreak of military conflict along the border in the late 1960s, shifted his attention to the northern frontier. The Soviet Union was formally declared China's "primary opponent" in a 1977 update to the military strategy. The approach to the superpowers was to lure in their forces after they had invaded, extend their supply lines

Table 3.1 China's Military Strategies, 1956–2019

Year	Name	Primary Opponent	Primary Direction	Basis of Preparations for Military Struggle	Main Form of Operations
1956	Defending the motherland	US	Northeast	US amphibious assault	Positional defense, mobile offense
1960	Resist in the north, open in the south	US	Northeast	US amphibious assault	Positional defense, mobile offense
1964	Luring the enemy in deep	US	None specified	US amphibious assault	Mobile, guerilla warfare
1977	Active defense, luring the enemy in deep	USSR	North-central	Soviet armored/ airborne assault	Mobile, guerilla warfare
1980	Active defense	USSR	North-central	Soviet armored/ airborne assault	Positional warfare or fixed defense
1988	Dealing with local wars and military conflicts		None specified		
1993	Local wars under high tech conditions	Taiwan	Southeast	Warfare under high-tech conditions	Joint operations
2004	Local wars under informationized conditions	Taiwan/US	Southeast	Warfare under informationized conditions	Integrated joint operations
2014	Informationized local wars	Taiwan/US	Southeast and maritime	Informationized warfare	Integrated joint operations
2019	Informationized local wars	Taiwan/US	Southeast and maritime	Informationized warfare	Integrated joint operations

Sources: Authors' table based on data from M. Taylor Fravel, "Shifts in Warfare and Party Unity: Explaining Changes in China's Military Strategy," *International Security* 42: 3 (2018): 50–51; M. Taylor Fravel and Joel Wuthnow, "China's Military Strategy for a 'New Era': Some Change, More Continuity, and Tantalizing Hints," *Journal of Strategic Studies* 46: 6–7 (2023): 1149–1184.

through hostile territory, and then exhaust them through protracted struggle, as the PLA had done in the past.

The Cold War strategy focused on the superpowers but in practice the PLA had to be used in other ways. Two conflicts that the PLA fought were not in theaters then labeled the "main strategic direction" – the 1962 border war with India and the 1979 Vietnam war. In the first case, Chinese troops swept across the frontier in response to Indian prime minister Jawaharlal Nehru's policy of establishing forward posts closer to Chinese territory. The result was a Chinese victory as Indian forces returned to their previous positions.[4] In the second case, the PLA conducted a three-week campaign to "teach a lesson" to Vietnam after Hanoi's 1978 invasion of Cambodia, China's close ally. The short-lived campaign was frustrated by fierce Vietnamese resistance and because of China's desire not to invite escalation with Vietnam's ally, the Soviet Union. Although the PLA soon withdrew, a series of border clashes with Vietnam continued into the 1980s.[5] During the Cultural Revolution, Mao used the PLA for a different purpose: governing the country after Red Guards had destroyed the bureaucracy.

The end of the Cold War marked a turning point for China's military strategy for three reasons. First, Beijing's rapprochement with Moscow during the 1980s diminished prospects of a superpower clash. By 1985, Deng Xiaoping had reached the judgment that "peace and development," rather than large-scale war, was the dominant strategic trend. Conflicts, if they were to occur, would only be "local wars" of limited scope and duration, rather than the "general wars" that Mao feared. This provided China with a "period of strategic opportunity" during which it could rebuild the economy after the calamity of the Cultural Revolution. Deng realized that China could not become wealthy and powerful without a strong military, which he directed to return to its barracks and focus on professionalization (with the exception being his orders for it to crack down on protesters during the 1989 Tiananmen movement). Nevertheless, he placed military modernization last in his "four modernizations" – a sign that agricultural, industrial, and technological progress must come first.

Second were developments on Taiwan. Mao's plans to land troops on the island after Nationalist forces under Chiang Kai-shek fled there in 1949 were frustrated when the United States sent the 7th Fleet into the Taiwan Strait in response to China's intervention in the Korean War. With no viable options to invade, China could only shell Taiwan's offshore islands in the 1950s and broadcast propaganda for the rest of the Cold War. By the 1980s, Deng hoped to convince Taiwan's leader, by then Chiang's son, Chiang Ching-kuo, to form a political union under the "one country, two systems" formula. This was plausible given the official view on both sides that there was only "one China" and growing cross-strait economic links. However, Taiwan's democratization and the rise of a distinct Taiwan identity created a problem that Deng's successor,

Jiang Zemin, had to address: deterring Taiwan from formally declaring independence. A 1993 update to the military strategic guidelines shifted the "main strategic direction" to the southeast opposite Taiwan. This meant greater attention to that theater and new deterrent tools such as a large short-range ballistic missile arsenal arrayed along the coast.[6]

The U.S. factor made the Taiwan problem more complex. The Cold War alliance between Washington and Taipei ended with the normalization of U.S.–China relations in 1979, but the Taiwan Relations Act passed that year by Congress required Washington to help Taiwan meet its defense needs. This led to the George H.W. Bush administration's unprecedented sale of 150 F-16s to Taiwan in 1992, drawing Beijing's ire. Subsequent administrations continued to sell arms and undertook other activities deemed objectionable to China's leaders. The Clinton administration angered China with its role in the 1995–1996 Taiwan Strait crisis – approving a rare visit to the United States by Taiwan leader Lee Teng-hui and then dispatching two aircraft carriers to the area in response to PLA missile tests designed to influence Taiwan's first presidential election in March 1996. This was followed by the accidental U.S. bombing of the Chinese embassy in Belgrade during the 1999 Kosovo war, which Beijing viewed as a deliberate act to intimidate China.[7] These events led PLA planners to conclude that any war with Taiwan would inevitably include the United States, and that the PLA needed to concentrate on finding ways to deter or defeat U.S. intervention.

Challenges at other points along China's extensive land and coastal borders, however, meant that the PLA could not focus exclusively on Taiwan. Old problems such as the Sino–Indian border dispute persisted and new ones appeared, such as North Korea's illicit nuclear weapons program in the 1990s and concerns about a collapse of that regime. There was also a view within Chinese strategic circles that other rivals like India, Japan, or Vietnam would try to stir up trouble if a conflict were ever to break out in the Taiwan Strait. Chinese strategists referred to this as "chain reaction warfare." Such concerns meant that the PLA would need to develop specialized forces for missions such as mountain warfare or countering WMD with little relevance for a Taiwan contingency. As discussed below, they also meant that Chinese forces would have to prepare to conduct a large-scale campaign while deterring opponents elsewhere.

Third were lessons derived from the 1991 Gulf War. China's leaders were stunned by the rapid success of U.S.-led coalition forces against Iraq, which fielded the world's fourth largest conventional army at the time. Liu Huaqing, then vice chairman of the CMC, recalled that during the conflict, "high-tech weapons displayed their effective role, putting the multinational forces in an overwhelmingly dominant position."[8] China's military thus needed to adapt. This meant less attention to wars of attrition and more on short, high-intensity campaigns conducted across all domains. Central to this was what

China's military strategists called "system destruction warfare" – wars that would be won by whoever could more effectively destroy the opposing side's war machine, which in the modern context entailed attacks on critical targets such as sensors, command, control, and communications networks, and logistics hubs.[9] These requirements led the PLA to focus on joint operations and had tangible effects on force structure, including procurement of the same kinds of long-range strike weapons that had been displayed in the Gulf and other conflicts in the 1990s.

Changes to China's formal military strategy after 1993 amounted to incremental adjustments in the same basic direction. Geographically, the focus remained on the southeast although the advent of ultra-long-range weapons meant that the PLA also needed to be able to operate farther into the western Pacific to target distant U.S. bases and platforms. The revolution in information technology allowed for more efficient and resilient command, control, and communications systems and technical improvements in areas ranging from sensors to logistics. Hence, the PLA would still focus on "local wars," but these would be carried out "under informationized conditions." Such advancements also meant that the PLA could aspire to a higher level of "jointness," in which the different services would not merely coordinate with each other – which had been the goal in the early 1990s – but develop and carry out highly integrated operations.

The focus of China's military strategy has largely persisted in the Xi era. In updates to the military strategic guidelines in 2014 and 2019, the southeast was still labeled the "main strategic direction," integrated joint operations remained the "basic form of operations," and planners had to prepare for "informationized local wars." Chinese military theorists also saw the character of war shifting to what they called "intelligentization," referring to the integration of artificial intelligence and other cutting-edge technologies, although these new features were said to still be "on the horizon" in 2019.[10] The important change under Xi was not the strategy itself but the urgency with which it needed to be implemented. The reason was changing perceptions of the security environment. Xi viewed the "period of strategic opportunity" as closing, the activities of Taiwan independence forces as increasingly pernicious, and the United States, which in 2017 unveiled a new national security strategy focused on competition with China, as more hostile than ever. He thus urged the PLA to be more ready for a cross-Strait campaign while deterring or defeating U.S. intervention, rather than pivoting in a new direction.

Updates to the military strategy after the Cold War set the PLA on a clear path but do not offer a complete picture of how China's military has developed in practice. Three other developments need to be mentioned. First are the PLA's overseas responsibilities, as discussed further in chapter 8. The strategy prioritizes regional deterrence and warfighting, but China's expanding overseas interests meant that military power would also need to be used farther afield. In 2004, Hu Jintao handed the PLA what he called its "new historic missions," including the protection of maritime interests in the South and East China Seas and critical sea lanes across the Indian Ocean. Four years later, the navy began its participation in anti-piracy patrols off the Horn of Africa. Overseas responsibilities gained further prominence in 2011 when the PLA needed to coordinate the rescue of more than 30,000 Chinese nationals from Libya during its civil war.[11] Xi's Belt and Road Initiative further expanded the places where the PLA might have to act to protect Chinese citizens or property.

Second is the development of hybrid warfare tactics. China's warfighting doctrine focuses on high-end joint operations and the application of advanced technology in battle, but Chinese forces are often used in less sophisticated ways to coerce opponents. Assertive military and paramilitary actions increased in the latter part of the Hu era, reflecting his focus on securing China's maritime rights and interests, and based on a view of diminished U.S. capabilities after the 2008 global financial crisis. This also reflected the significant growth of China's conventional forces over the previous decade. The air force, navy, and Coast Guard had all become the region's largest, offering China's leaders new means with which to enforce territorial claims and nudge rival claimants from contested areas. But these activities almost always remained below the level of lethal violence to maintain a generally stable regional environment, perceived as necessary for China's continued economic growth.

As explored further in Chapter 6, hybrid warfare, also sometimes known as "gray zone" coercion, came in several varieties. Some tactics involved the use of individual platforms or units from a single service to intimidate foreign opponents (as when fighter jets are dispatched to intercept U.S. military flights in international airspace near China). Others involved larger numbers of low-end capabilities, such as Coast Guard vessels or armed fishing boats under local maritime militia forces, to establish presence in a contested region. The PLA also built infrastructure in disputed areas to assert its rights and enable larger-scale operations, including in the Himalayan border region and in the South China Sea, site of China's massive land reclamation program in the 2010s. Even cyber warfare, carried out by PLA hacking units set up in the 1990s to conduct cyber-espionage and manipulate information in foreign societies, falls within this category. In a way, these activities represented the continuation of Mao's emphasis on guerilla warfare, albeit in new domains and with the application of new technology.

Third was the development of China's nuclear strategy. Although outside the formal bounds of the military strategic guidelines (which focus on conventional strategy), China has built up its nuclear forces since the Mao era. Perceived U.S. aggression and nuclear threats in the 1950s prompted Mao to initiate China's nuclear and intercontinental ballistic missile programs, which were carried out domestically after the Soviet Union refused to supply assistance. This led to China's first nuclear test in 1964. The core of the doctrine was what scholars refer to as "minimum deterrence" – a no-first-use pledge combined with a small nuclear arsenal just large enough to survive a first strike and retaliate. In the 1990s, China's military strategists established a new concept of "integrated strategic deterrence" in which nuclear weapons would be used alongside other military tools, such as cyber and counter-space, and broader elements of national power to shape the choices of China's adversaries, implying in part that major powers would not be able to use nuclear coercion against Beijing.[12]

Beginning in the Xi era, significant changes to China's nuclear forces began to appear. As elaborated in Chapter 5, this included an expansion in the number of nuclear-armed missiles, fielding of dual-capable bombers, and the revelation that China's nuclear ballistic missile submarines were conducting operational patrols in the South China Sea. There were also signs that China was conducting research on the viability of low-yield nuclear weapons, which might be used on the battlefield rather than for strategic-level deterrence. The PLA was also investing in a larger network of early warning satellites that could be used to support a "launch on warning" posture – going beyond a doctrine of attacking only after being attacked first with nuclear weapons. As the second decade of Xi's tenure began, foreign observers started to see signs that China's doctrine might be evolving from the limited goals of Mao and his successors to a more ambitious nuclear posture.

Organizational Adaptation

In principle, there should be an alignment between strategy and military organization and force structure. China's Cold War military strategy was relatively well aligned with its structure: mobile and guerilla warfare against a putative U.S. or Soviet invasion of China, or smaller cross-border campaigns such as those with India or on the Korean Peninsula, put a premium on land warfare. The organizational structure that the PLA borrowed from the Soviet Union was suited to that end. The leadership was dominated by army officers, the ground forces were organized into massive formations (group armies, divisions, and regiments) that could lure enemies deep into Chinese territory or sweep across land borders, and the small air force and navy only needed to be able to defend China's territorial airspace and coastal waters.

The disconnect came later. China's military strategy shifted toward high-intensity joint operations across the Taiwan Strait and in other offshore scenarios in the early 1990s, but the PLA's force structure and capabilities were still not well aligned with that objective when Xi took office in 2012. The ground forces remained by far the PLA's largest service – accounting for nearly

70 percent of the PLA as late as 2015 – and nominally "joint" commanders in the military regions only had peacetime control over army units, with naval and air force units reporting to their service headquarters. This arrangement reflected the legacies of the PLA's past but was ill-suited to its future because it didn't prioritize power projection capabilities and because service-centrism meant that the PLA would have been hard pressed to plan, train for, and conduct joint operations, including the pinnacle of all operations – a full-scale amphibious invasion of Taiwan.

To be sure, the PLA had taken some modest steps forward prior to Xi's arrival. A series of downsizings reduced the armed forces from three million troops in 1987 to 2.3 million in 2015, with cuts targeting lower-readiness army units. In 1996, fourteen mobile divisions were transferred from the PLA to the People's Armed Police, where they were reoriented toward a domestic security mission. Cutting manpower reflected a shift from a military focused on "quantity" to one based on "quality," as Jiang Zemin put it, though some troops merely changed uniforms and became members of the People's Armed Police – China's internal security force – in the 1990s. The PLA also consolidated its sprawling logistics enterprise, reducing inefficiency by placing general purpose supplies under new military region "joint logistics departments."[13] When Hu Jintao was appointed CMC chairman in 2004, he was joined by the air force, navy, and missile force chiefs, who had never sat on the CMC, in a symbolic display of "jointness." Under Hu, the air force and navy were handed new mission statements that required them to operate farther from China's land and coastal borders.

More ambitious reform plans circulating within the PLA, however, failed to materialize. This reflected the power of the bureaucracy to resist changes that would have threatened their vested interests. It also reflected the political weaknesses of Jiang and Hu, neither of whom had deep ties to the PLA and who thus struggled to rein in corruption or force the military to accept changes to its structure and lines of authority. Compounding matters was the interregnum period of 2002–2004, when Jiang and Hu vied for leadership, putting the military in a favorable position to avoid supervision. The result was a twenty-year lag between the adoption of the pivotal 1993 military strategy and the unfolding of a broader structural overhaul at the end of 2015. Xi's ability to convince and cajole the bureaucracy to cooperate was a testament to his greater influence in the military and, as discussed in Chapter 1, a successful political strategy combining both coercive tools such as the anti-corruption campaign and concessions to military leaders.

The product of Xi's reform efforts was a military better structured for modern warfare.[14] Leading his reforms was a 300,000-person manpower reduction, which once again concentrated on the bloated ground forces. Many of the affected were mid-career officers in non-combat roles such as headquarters staff. Central authorities softened the blow by requiring local governments and state-owned enterprises to approve lateral transfers, creating frictions as the civilian sphere struggled to absorb former soliders, but they did not repeat the previous maneuver of converting demobilized soldiers into People's Armed Police. This effort brought the PLA down to two million active-duty troops by 2018 – leaner than before, although still the world's largest. It also meant that the army declined as a share of the PLA to just under half, while the other services increased in relative terms (but not in absolute terms).

As a matter of organization, Xi-era reforms affected all the major components of the PLA: the CMC, the services, and the theaters. The CMC sits at the highest echelon, led by the civilian leader who typically serves concurrently as the leader of the Chinese Communist Party. He is assisted by a small cadre of senior uniformed officers. At times there has also been a civilian vice chairman (a role that Xi served in from 2010 to 2012 when he was preparing for the top spot). The commission does not decide *whether* China should go to war – such decisions would be reached by the civilian party elite in the Politburo Standing Committee – but it would have the final say in *how* such a war would be waged. It thus plays a pivotal role in formulating China's military strategy and makes decisions on other key military issues such as force structure and the contours of military reform.

Under Xi, the CMC has been a small executive body composed of himself and just six senior officers. The important change was to the massive bureaucracy directly underneath it. Prior to his arrival, the commission sat atop four general departments, which had evolved over many decades into semi-autonomous fiefdoms with responsibility for operations, political work, equipment, and logistics. They also served collectively as a national headquarters for the ground forces. This system created challenges for modernization because of widespread corruption (for instance, the former General Political Department oversaw a notorious pay-for-promotion scheme), because their leaders were so powerful that they could resist necessary reforms, and because their responsibilities for army affairs meant that they could never fully focus on joint operations.

It was thus a bold and surprising development when the four general departments were disbanded in early 2016. They were replaced by fifteen smaller departments, commissions, and offices organized by function (see Figure 3.1 opposite). Importantly, supervisory functions such as anti-corruption investigators, auditors, and military prosecutors were placed in separate organizational bins, meaning that they would have fewer opportunities to collude. They also served as distinct reporting chains, improving the ability of Xi and his CMC colleagues to monitor the bureaucracy. Other entities had an operational focus: the Joint Staff Department became a national-level joint operational command, a Training and Management Department focused on joint training and education, and a National Defense Mobilization Department would conduct mobilization preparations.

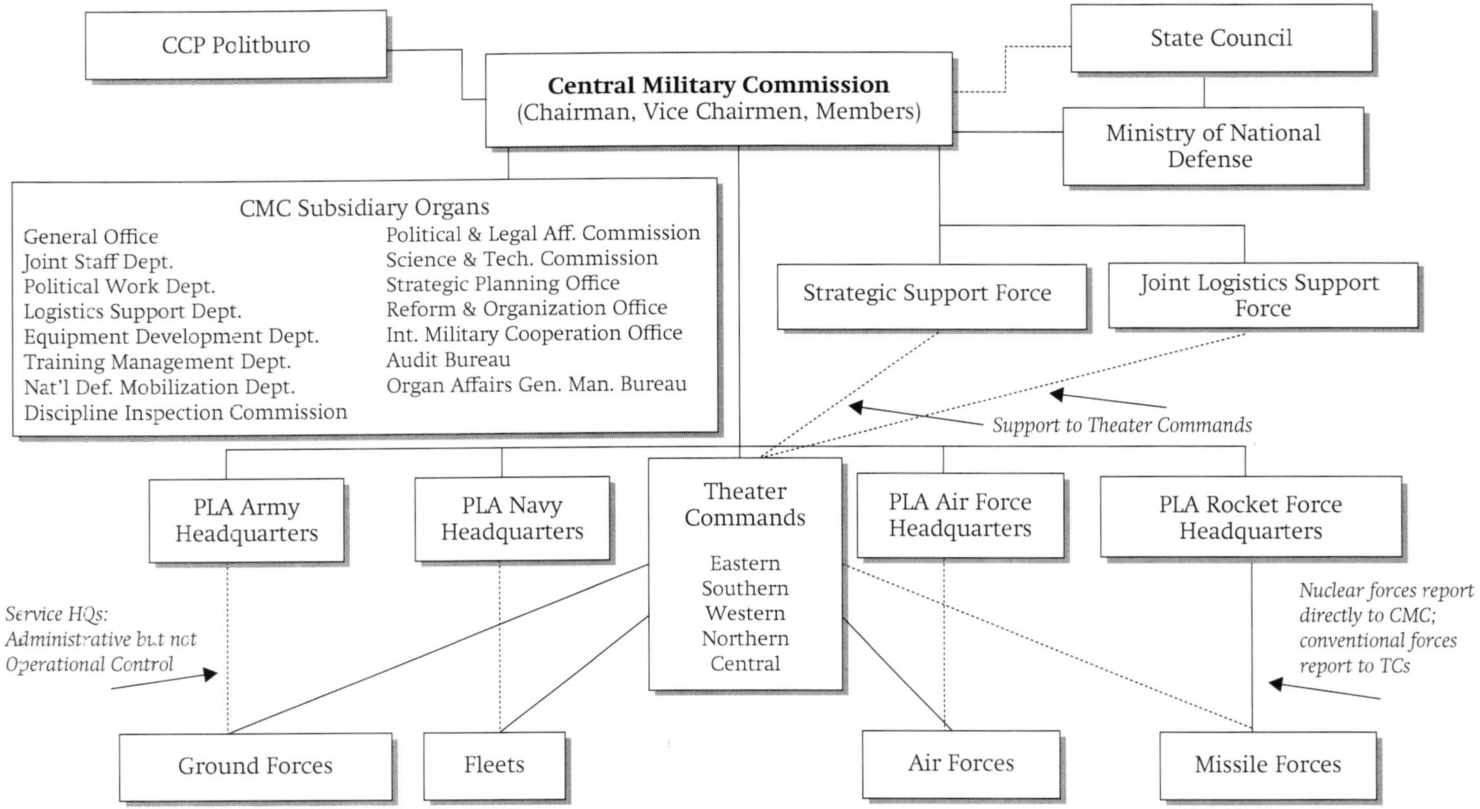
CCP Politburo
Central Military Commission
(Chairman, Vice Chairmen, Members)
State Council
Ministry of National Defense
CMC Subsidiary Organs
General Office
Joint Staff Dept.
Political Work Dept.
Logistics Support Dept.
Equipment Development Dept.
Training Management Dept.
Nat'l Def. Mobilization Dept.
Discipline Inspection Commission
Political & Legal Aff. Commission
Science & Tech. Commission
Strategic Planning Office
Reform & Organization Office
Int. Military Cooperation Office
Audit Bureau
Organ Affairs Gen. Man. Bureau
Strategic Support Force
Joint Logistics Support Force
Support to Theater Commands
PLA Army Headquarters
PLA Navy Headquarters
Theater Commands
Eastern
Southern
Western
Northern
Central
PLA Air Force Headquarters
PLA Rocket Force Headquarters
Service HQs:
Administrative but not Operational Control
Nuclear forces report directly to CMC; conventional forces report to TCs
Ground Forces
Fleets
Air Forces
Missile Forces

Figure 3.1 PLA Postreform Organization
Source: Authors' figure adapted from Phillip C. Saunders and Joel Wuthnow, "China's Goldwater-Nichols? Assessing PLA Organizational Reforms," *Joint Force Quarterly* 82 (2016): 70.

The PLA retained an army, air force, and navy, and added the Rocket Force as a full service. (The Rocket Force, responsible for the country's land-based conventional and nuclear missile arsenal, was previously called the Second Artillery Force with the status of an independent branch of the army). Of these, the army experienced the most sweeping changes. The reforms for the first time created a national army headquarters, which freed up other CMC departments to focus on joint operations. In addition, the army in 2017 underwent a "below-the-neck" reform that resulted in the loss of five of its eighteen group armies and the conversion of most of its remaining divisions into smaller and more mobile brigades. Because of its sacrifices, the army has been called the "biggest loser" of the reforms.[15] The navy and air force experienced fewer changes to their internal structure, though in 2017 the service chiefs were removed from the CMC. They would now have to compete against each other for resources and none would have a de facto veto over the priorities of any other. Although technically not a service, the reforms also brought the People's Armed Police, which is mainly responsible for internal security but would also support the PLA in wartime, under the full control of the CMC.

Just as important was the creation of new support forces. The Joint Logistic Support Force was constituted from the former military region joint logistics departments. The innovation was the creation of a national headquarters that could exercise greater management of military resources and logistics services, such as repair and maintenance. The new force proved its value in early 2020 when it was mobilized to respond to a virus of unknown origin – later identified as Covid-19 – in the central city of Wuhan, ironically the site of the Joint Logistic Support Force's headquarters.[16] In this case, the force summoned mobilized transportation and construction units, military doctors, and medical supplies to conduct a relief operation but, in wartime, it would be responsible for managing the flow of munitions, oil, and other critical resources to joint commanders from across a nationwide storage and distribution network.

Second, in 2016 the PLA created a Strategic Support Force that was intended to handle responsibilities for operations in the information domain, including space, cyber, and network security. In April 2024, the force was dissolved and replaced by three forces directly underneath the CMC: the Information Support Force, the Cyberspace Force, and the Aerospace Force. They are responsible for network defense, offensive cyber and electronic warfare, and space and counter-space operations, respectively. These three support forces, as with the Joint Logistic Support Force, are national assets that could support theater commanders during a contingency or conduct independent operations.

Operationally, most PLA combat forces are arrayed within five theater commands (see Map 3.1 below). These replaced the pre-reform military regions but serve the same general purpose: preparing for domestic and regional

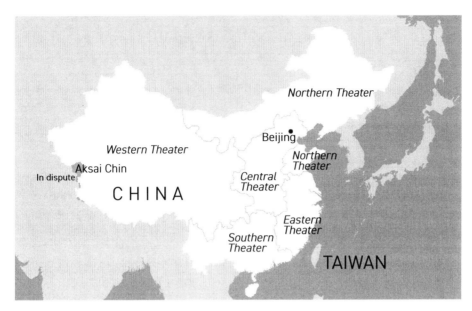

Map 3.1 Theater Commands
Source: U.S. Department of Defense, *China Military Power Report* (2016), 2.

contingencies. The Eastern Theater is always listed first in protocol order, reflecting its status as the theater responsible for the "main strategic direction" – operations across the Taiwan Strait. It also takes charge of the East China Sea, site of the disputed Senkaku/Diaoyu Islands. The following three theaters focus on "secondary strategic directions:" the Southern Theater's purview stretches across China's Southeast Asian land borders and into the maritime expanse of the South China Sea claimed by China; the Western Theater maintains order in Xinjiang and Tibet, and patrols the contested land border with India; and the Northern Theater prepares for a humanitarian disaster or conflict on the Korean Peninsula. The Central Theater functions as a strategic reserve and provides security for the capital.

The important shift was not in function but in lines of authority. The stove-piped military region system was ill-suited to modern joint operations because nominally "joint" commanders had little expertise when employing the air, naval, and missile forces that would be needed to execute "integrated joint operations." In a contingency, PLA doctrine called for a temporary joint "war zone" to be established, whose geographic boundaries and commanders may or may not have been based on the military regions (for instance, in the 1995–1996 Taiwan Strait crisis, a "war zone" was established for exercise and deterrent purposes, but its staff members were flown in from Beijing). Chinese strategists thus worried that a transition from peacetime to wartime operations could be slowed by the need to adjust the command structure and realign authorities.

Today's PLA has largely fixed those problems. A fully joint operational chain of command stretches down from national authorities in Beijing to the five theater commanders, who have full operational control over land, air, naval, and conventional missile forces in their regions. They each have a Joint Operations Command Center that offers a real-time operational picture and strengthens coordination up the hierarchy, culminating in a central Joint Operations Command Center in Beijing, and between units from different services. A highly redundant communications network known as the Integrated Command Platform forms the backbone for coordination between and across those echelons. In peacetime, the theaters carry out responsibilities such as joint training, routine patrols (including in disputed territories of the South and East China seas, and in contested Himalayan border regions), ad-hoc operations such as search and rescue or disaster relief, and preparation of wartime contingency plans.

The chain of command then proceeds down to theater service components – with names such as the Eastern Theater Navy or the Northern Theater Air Force – and to individual units. It largely bypasses the service headquarters, who have been formally assigned the administrative function of recruiting, training, and outfitting forces, although as discussed in Chapter 4, service chiefs continue to exercise oversight of some national assets (for instance, the marine corps falls under navy headquarters and the Airborne Corps falls under the air force). The theaters also have a coordinating relationship with the support forces and other national assets. The system that would prosecute a war is thus mostly in place at the theater level.

The creation of a modern command structure also promotes confidence in operations short of war. The military regions' weak control over naval and air forces reduced their ability to conduct coordinated provocations against China's neighbors (or what PLA strategists refer to as "deterrence operations"). The updated system not only improves coordination, but also offers Beijing reassurance that those forces will operate as intended and that any escalation to higher levels of conflict can be managed. Organizational restructuring thus set the stage for an increase in assertive activities in recent years. One example is the unprecedented number of air, naval, and missile assets working together to signal China's displeasure after then-U.S. Speaker of the House Nancy Pelosi's visit to Taiwan in August 2022. Such moves, discussed in greater depth in Chapter 6, would have been far more difficult to coordinate in the past.

Despite its strengths, however, there are several persistent challenges in China's military structure. First, there is no organizational basis for global combat operations. The system is designed to support the priorities of China's military strategy, which are to safeguard the homeland and prepare for a high-end regional contingency. The strategy requires the PLA to handle a diverse set of overseas missions, such as sea lane protection and international

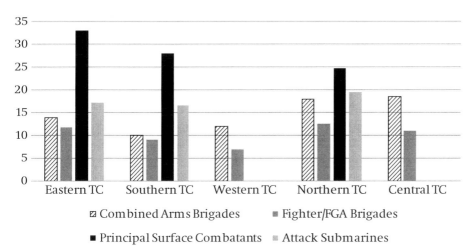

Figure 3.2 Force Distribution Across Theaters, Average from 2017 to 2023
Source: Authors' figure based on data from IISS *Military Balance*, 2017–2023.

peacekeeping, but does not task the PLA to be able to win wars far from home. Thus, PLA operations overseas tend to remain service-centric – for instance, the navy continues to conduct anti-piracy operations off the Horn of Africa. There is no joint command structure for large overseas operations nor is there a well-developed logistics structure centered on large bases.[17]

Second, the PLA faces tradeoffs in distributing forces across the region. While China's military strategy prioritizes a Taiwan contingency, there is an inherent tension in simultaneously deterring regional rivals and foreign intervention in other theaters. Indeed, Chinese strategists worry that any war with Taiwan could precipitate a "chain reaction" of conflicts elsewhere, as others act opportunistically to harm China's interests. Organizationally, the PLA has therefore chosen to stress all-around readiness. This has meant relatively even distribution in the quality and quantity of combat forces; all the theaters have some of the latest equipment, even if advanced platforms like the J-20 stealth fighter sometimes make their debut in the Eastern Theater, and a roughly equal number of large combat units.[18] Such decisions may enhance regional deterrence but come at the expense of the PLA's ability to focus on combat with Taiwan.

Third are the continuing influences of army dominance. Most senior PLA commanders – the individuals who have been tasked with leading the Joint Staff Department and theater commands – are drawn from the ground force. This is the result of the large pool of army officers who had been waiting in line for promotion prior to the reforms. Moreover, their careers have not emphasized joint expertise: they rose through the ranks based on solid performance within combat units and few had opportunities to excel in staff positions or lead troops from the other services. In recent years, the PLA has made some efforts to train joint commanders and staff officers, including through revised training and educational programs, and the selection of a few high-caliber naval and air force officers in leading roles, but an outsized role for the army could slow the PLA's transition into a modern joint force.[19]

The final challenge is how the PLA balances organizational reform with the enduring influence of Leninism. Features such as political commissars and party committees, as described in Chapter 1, not only persist but have been strengthened in the Xi era – not a surprise, given his general belief that organizations cannot be well managed without a firm role for the party. However, there is an inherent tension, which even some Chinese strategists recognize, between the imperative of modern command to enable lower-level commanders to make rapid decisions on the battlefield and exercise their own judgment in the absence of higher-level direction, and the Leninist preference for decisions to be made by the smallest group at the highest level. Whether junior commanders feel able to make tough calls in the absence of direction from the CMC, which serves as the highest-level party committee in the PLA, or from the party general-secretary, remains in doubt.

Resources and Innovation

Implementing military strategy requires not only an effective organization but also adequate resources: money, equipment, and people. During the 1980s, Deng Xiaoping encouraged the PLA to modernize but could provide only limited funding, a product of the underdeveloped state of China's economy as well as Deng's other priorities. To make ends meet, he allowed the PLA to operate profit-making enterprises. Some of these grew into conglomerates with concerns far outside the military sphere, such as stock brokerages, auto imports, and theaters.[20] Steady economic growth in the 1990s allowed Deng's successors to funnel more funds into the military; for a time, annual budget growth exceeded ten percent, but by 2015 growth rates had settled at around seven percent. Jiang Zemin had success in closing many of the PLA's businesses in the late 1990s. Xi Jinping took steps to close the remaining ones after he took office, which aligned with his focus on preparing the PLA to "fight and win wars" – rather than lining its own pockets.

By the early 2020s, China's official military budget had topped $200 billion. This represented the highest level of military spending in Asia and was the world's second highest, behind the United States (which spends more than $800 billion annually). By comparison, the world's third and fourth ranking countries, Russia and India, spent less than $90 billion each. Thus, the PLA had unparalleled resources as a *regional* military but was still relatively far from the level needed to fund a truly *global* force. China's announced budget does not include several categories of defense-related spending, including foreign weapons purchases, paramilitary forces, and some research and development expenses. World Bank estimates, which include these additional categories, are depicted in Figure 3.3 below. Foreign analysts have estimated that these charges amount to about $60 billion. China was narrowing the gap between on- and off-budget expenses from the 1990s through the 2010s, but larger research and development spending in recent years has meant that the gap has begun to widen again.[21]

Nevertheless, in a sign of fiscal discipline, it was also the case that the PLA was not spending itself into the ground. China has spent only a small fraction of its GDP (roughly 2%) on the military, even after accounting for off-budget expenses. Defense spending is also only a small fraction of central government expenditures (5–6%). By contrast, both superpowers spent far more of their national treasuries on military spending during the Cold War, especially after arms racing took off and the Soviet Union struggled to compete. After its 2022 invasion of Ukraine, Russia has become once again mired in unsustainable defense spending, which accounted for about a third of its government revenue. China was able to afford an ambitious modernization program because it opted not to accept the high costs of war. Most likely, PLA budgets will be sustainable in an era of slowing growth rates, precisely because Chinese leaders have kept spending low relative to the size of the economy, and will be able to shift resources from other priorities as needed.

Changing requirements have led to some adjustments in how the PLA has allocated its budgets. Historically, China has reported a roughly even distribution of funding across three categories – personnel, training and maintenance, and acquisition. Under Xi, the share of acquisitions increased to more than 40 percent of the budget in 2017 before a slight drop to 37 percent three years later, but it remains the largest category. This is a sign of the PLA's commitment to developing the high-end weapons systems that it perceives as critical to becoming a "world-class" military by mid-century. In the future, however, acquisition expenses will be constrained by rising maintenance costs – an inevitable outcome of the PLA fielding a large inventory of conventional forces – and by the need to attract and retain expensive high-caliber talent. Indeed, despite the downsizing of the PLA under Xi, military expenditure per soldier nearly doubled during his first decade in office. This was due to large pay increases, housing subsidies, and bonuses for personnel with technical skills and those assigned to remote locations such as Xinjiang and Tibet.

The second major resource is the people of the PLA themselves. The two-million-person active-duty force is composed of about three-quarters enlisted personnel and one-quarter officers, who are supplemented by an expanding cadre of contract-based "civilian personnel," who do not count against end strength and are similar to U.S. Department of Defense civilians, who perform mostly non-combat duties.[22] The PLA has also had a separate category of

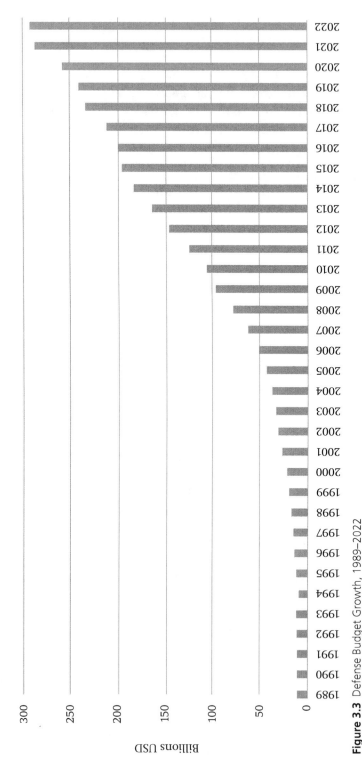

Figure 3.3 Defense Budget Growth, 1989–2022

Source: Authors' figure based on data from The World Bank. Figures shown in 2023 U.S. dollars.

"civilian cadres," who do count toward end strength, but most of these personnel have been demobilized or converted into "civilian personnel."

Formally, a conscription system remains in place, with strict quotas requiring that two-thirds of conscripts come from rural areas and one-third from urban areas.[23] Nevertheless, in practice most PLA enlisted members are volunteers, some of them graduates of two-year colleges, with only relatively small percentages being true conscripts. Despite its low birthrate and aging population, China does not appear to have had much trouble finding volunteers, and the size of the PLA relative to China's large population base means that it would have little trouble filling the ranks if recruitment of volunteers faltered.[24] Nevertheless, there are questions about the quality of incoming recruits, as Chinese leaders, including Xi, have complained about their physical condition and political reliability. Previously, there was one conscription cycle per year, but this increased to two in 2021 to promote more even readiness throughout the year. Some conscripts remain in the PLA to become NCOs or even officers, although most return to their homes, where some of them continue service in the reserves or local militias.

As in other militaries, non-commissioned officers (NCOs) form a backbone of the force. While the PLA has long had senior enlisted members, it only developed a formal NCO corps in 1999. This meant establishing NCO ranks and career paths. As part of Xi's reforms, the NCO corps underwent further reforms, including dividing them into management and technical career fields. The PLA has also instituted a "master chief" program to give senior NCOs more responsibilities, although they do not have the equivalent of senior enlisted advisors to provide input to commands above the brigade level.[25] In practice, their value primarily lies in the experience gained through their decades of service, during which they master complex technical skills and processes, and provide continuity as the conscript force frequently turns over. However, there remains a difference from Western NCO corps, in which senior enlisted members are considered part of a unit's leadership. In the PLA, by contrast, NCOs usually do not serve on party committees, although some are party members. Moreover, while pay for both NCOs and officers has increased, there remains a vast disparity in the benefits and social status.[26]

There are several ways for individuals to become a PLA officer. Some are enlisted members handpicked, based on their leadership potential, to undergo officer training. A select handful of PLA officers join from civilian colleges. In the 1990s, the PLA established officer training programs on college campuses, similar to the Reserve Officers' Training Corps in the United States, but this program was eliminated in 2017. Explaining the demise of the program, some graduates of PLA academies complained that their civilian-educated colleagues lacked military discipline, and there was also a culture clash between the two communities. This was replaced by a system in which some officers are directly recruited from graduates of civilian colleges based on their majors (especially in-demand fields such as computer science or engineering).

Nevertheless, most PLA officers arrive as cadets in one of the PLA's academies, where they complete three or four years of study prior to commissioning.[27] PLA cadet academies are organized by branch, so a new PLA officer recruit might attend the PLA Navy Submarine Academy or the PLA Army Air Defense Academy, which means that they immediately specialize but have little contact with cadets from other branches. The system is thus quite unlike Western academies, where cadets receive similar training and only later divide into branches. The admission requirements not only include merit qualifications, but also strict quotas that limit the number of entrants by province as well as gender. Indeed, only about five percent of China's new academy students are female.[28] Applicants also need to pass a rigid political screening, which probes not only political beliefs, but also issues such as foreign connections and criminal records – of both the applicants and their family members. As a condition for service, all officers must remain a party member in good standing.

Officers advance in their careers along predictable trajectories. Soon after they enter service, they are assigned to a specific career track and rarely transfer between different fields: a logistics officer will likely remain one until retirement. Other fields include operational commanders, political commissars, equipment officers, and technical specialists. Officers typically stay within a particular unit and do not rotate geographically until reaching a senior level. This produces officers with deep expertise in their functional and regional roles but who lack the career-broadening experience prized in the U.S. military, where officers are often transferred between very different kinds of assignments. Promotions are handled by local party committees, which evaluate an officer's performance and their political bona fides. Officers who are not promoted typically retire from the PLA at ages determined by their grade, though some leave early to pursue opportunities in the civilian sphere.[29]

Despite efforts to attract high performers, the PLA has consistently critiqued itself for lacking competent officers. Many factors have informed these self-assessments. One problem is that very few officers have experienced combat, a result of China having not fought a war since 1979 and the intermittent border clashes with Vietnam that ended in 1991. Moreover, even in those conflicts, only the army was involved. This produces what Chinese leaders call a "peace disease," under which its officers are too accustomed to peacetime conditions and cannot imagine what combat would entail. A second problem is weaknesses in military skills, such as leading troops across unfamiliar terrain, or in exercising good judgment. These shortcomings are captured in frequent propaganda phrases such as the "two incompatibles" and the "five incapables," underscoring the need to achieve a higher degree of professional aptitude.[30] PLA analysts have also suggested the need for a more coherent way of providing officers with joint experience, often referencing the joint duty assignment system that was created to reduce institutional myopia and promote cross-service collaboration under the U.S. Goldwater-Nichols Act in 1986, but PLA assignments and promotions remain service-centric. This is arguably out of step with a military strategy focused on joint operations.[31]

Nevertheless, PLA self-critiques are designed to spur improvements, and the military has taken many steps to cultivate a more capable officer corps in recent years. Officers return to military academic institutions such as service command colleges at different points in their career to learn about the strategic environment, the principles of modern warfare, and other skills necessary for leadership. PLA academies have refreshed their curricula and are incorporating modern methods such as wargames and simulations to encourage agile thinking. In 2017, a Joint Operations College was established within China's National Defense University to promote joint education for mid-career officers – previously, officers only began to study joint operations when they neared flag rank. Xi Jinping has paid several visits to the National Defense University to highlight that institutions' role in producing joint commanders. Each theater command has also adopted on-the-job training programs for staff officers in functions such as planning, operations, and intelligence, building a cohort of skilled personnel from scratch.

Educational reforms have paralleled ongoing improvements in training. While field exercises enhance general readiness, they are of special value in sharpening commanders' and staff officers' skills. In recent decades, training innovations have involved maneuvers across theater boundaries, more joint and combined arms training, and fewer scripted exercises. In 2007, the PLA opened a combined arms training range in Inner Mongolia. This center features a dedicated opposition force based loosely on the U.S. military (the "Blue Force"), which conducts mock battles with visiting units. Almost on a *de rigeur* basis, visiting commanders lose to the Blue Force, instilling a need for self-reflection and improvement. Opposition force training is now routine in the navy, air force, and in the theater commands. Sitting atop the system is a new CMC Training and Management Department, which sets training guidelines and dispatches inspectors to assess performance.

As the PLA ventures out beyond China's borders, officers also increasingly have real-world opportunities to develop their skills. Opportunities to participate in UN peacekeeping missions regularly rotate between the PLA's group armies. This gives unit commanders and staff a chance to demonstrate their leadership skills in remote and sometimes hostile situations. The navy similarly dispatches ships from its three fleets to the Horn of Africa, offering experience in expeditionary operations for their crews. Closer to home, as discussed in Chapter 6, naval and air force units regularly operate along China's maritime periphery, where they are responsible for enforcing territorial claims and may encounter rivals. The officers in charge of those units must be able to protect China's interests but not create unintended escalation. Similar decisions need to be made by ground force officers leading patrols along the contested Sino–Indian border. While these efforts do not substitute for wartime experience, they do provide ways for the PLA to evaluate their own personnel and promote the most promising officers.

The final resource necessary to execute China's military strategy is technology. China's acquisition approaches have significantly evolved over the years. In the 1950s, China procured Soviet hardware and relied on Soviet advisors to establish massive state weapons factories. Only slow progress was made during the 1960s and 1970s when China was isolated and internally distracted by the Cultural Revolution (although advances continued to be made in core strategic deterrent areas, such as nuclear and ballistic missile technology, where Beijing needed to be more self-reliant). Deng's imperative for modernization combined with the collapse of the Soviet Union created new opportunities as arms were once again acquired from abroad. Some were supplied from ex-Soviet states including Ukraine, which sold the aircraft carrier *Varyag* to China in 1998, though most came directly from Russia. These included *Sovremenny*-class destroyers, *Kilo*-class submarines, Su-27 fighters, and S-300 air defense missiles. Technology was also acquired from foreign states in other ways: China hired scientists and technicians from former Soviet states, entered joint production ventures with Israel, and Chinese spies and hackers stole information on Western platforms such as the F-35.

China's post-Cold War acquisition strategy was not simply to rely on imports but to use those inputs to strengthen its own defense industrial base. University of California-San Diego professor Tai Ming Cheung notes that China relied on a standard process of "introducing, digesting, assimilating, and re-innovating" foreign technology.[32] This implied large-scale undertakings pursued over many years between the military, state corporations, and others, to disassemble foreign weapons systems, understand how they worked, and reverse engineer them into systems built to PLA specifications. The most notorious cases were those involving Chinese variants of licensed products, such as the J-11B fighter, which was based on the Su-27. Most key platforms are now produced domestically, and some are being sold on international arms markets. Only in a few areas does the PLA still rely on foreign imports, including jet engines and S-400 air defense missiles, both from Russia.

The problem with a foreign absorption strategy is that the PLA would always remain a generation behind the technology frontier. Since Deng, there has thus been a parallel push on domestic innovation. At the heart of this was the idea to better integrate civilian science and technology advances with military planning. In the twenty-first century, China's leaders began to speak of a deeper "military–civil fusion," a term that in the 2020s evolved into "national strategic systems integration."[33] Xi has taken a personal interest in this pursuit by chairing meetings, unveiling a formal strategy, and rolling out new policies that encourage civilian researchers to work with the military and civilian firms to design products and sell directly to the PLA. The focus has been on integrating disruptive technologies such as artificial intelligence, quantum computing, nanotechnology, and new materials into military systems, which could put China at an advantage in future conflicts. PLA theorists refer to this as "intelligentization," which would be a step beyond the "informationization" of the military pursued since the 1990s.[34]

However, several factors complicate the potential for China's defense innovation. Internal problems include lack of an effective intellectual property regime, which dampens incentives for innovation, limited enthusiasm by private enterprises to sell to the military (which is a minor player compared to the vast consumer market), and resistance by state defense corporations, who have long enjoyed protection from competition. Externally, China faces strategic competition from the United States and its allies. Washington is finding new ways to partner with other countries to stay ahead of the technology curve – one example being the Australia–U.K.–U.S. (AUKUS) partnership, which includes cooperation in nuclear-powered attack submarines and other high-tech areas such as artificial intelligence and quantum computing. The United States has also worked with allies to restrict China's access to sensitive dual-use technologies such as advanced semiconductors. Gaining a decisive advantage in this contest will be difficult for either side.

Conclusion

Since the early 1990s, China's military strategy has focused on short duration, high-intensity conflicts. These would not be the massive "general wars" envisioned against the superpowers during the Cold War but "local wars" against regional opponents, albeit with likely U.S. support. Taking a page from U.S. strategy in the Gulf War, the PLA developed operational concepts involving close collaboration between the services and integrating technologies such as satellite-based targeting and long-range precision weapons that would enable it to operate with greater lethality across an extended front. It would not only need the capacity to prevail in the main theater but also be able to address challenges across China's long coastal and land borders. Forces were thus carefully distributed in different theaters. Xi Jinping took a step forward through a momentous structural reform, whose centerpiece was a modern joint command structure. Complementing the strategy was steady increases in military budgets, cultivation of combat-focused talent, and acquisition of "world-class" hardware. Rather than giving the PLA a new mission, Xi instructed his forces to be better at their current assignments.

Several factors will influence how the strategy evolves in the future. One variable is Taiwan's status. The situation across the Taiwan Strait remains a focus for military planning but, if it is resolved on China's terms, the PLA would be able to reallocate capabilities to other contingencies. This could encourage China's leaders to escalate tensions with other neighbors to resolve its remaining territorial disputes. On the other hand, an unsuccessful campaign – or a successful but costly one – could leave the PLA in a weakened state, from which it would need to recover. An inconclusive campaign could produce continued hostilities in the strait, such as a long-term blockade, or evolve into a protracted struggle with the United States; the result would rest on which side is better able to exhaust the other. One lesson that Chinese observers have noticed from Russia's war with Ukraine is that plans for a short conflict might fail. This means that military planners will have to think through requirements for a protracted conflict, implying stockpiles of critical resources, such as munitions and oil, far beyond their current levels.

Another variable is the direction of the strategic rivalry between China and the United States. China's military strategy has long demanded that the PLA counter U.S. intervention in a regional conflict, and respond to incursions of U.S. forces near China's periphery in peacetime. An intensification of U.S.–China competition could also have other results, such as spurring Beijing to deepen its security partnerships in Africa, the Middle East, and Latin America, further indigenize production of key military and dual-use technologies, expand military cooperation with Russia and Iran, and increase military budgets to support a larger buildup. In a worst-case scenario, the PLA might actively work with foreign proxies to create trouble for U.S. forces abroad or seek a stronger capability for conducting strikes on U.S. interests beyond Asia. However, those steps would require major adjustments to China's diplomatic strategy as well as its military systems, as discussed in Chapter 8.

Domestic resources will also shape the prospects for China's military strategy. Funding for the PLA has increased under Xi but remains at a relatively low share of GDP and government spending. Official documents depict economic development and military modernization as mutually reinforcing, a rhetorical gambit that denies the need to set clear priorities. Nevertheless, Xi or a future Chinese leader could decide to reprioritize spending toward defense, even if it came at the expense of other government priorities. Significantly higher budgets would fuel more ambitious acquisition programs, allow the PLA to maintain ever larger conventional forces, and shore up its ability to attract the high-end expertise it will need to plan and operate on the future battlefield. Moreover, the PLA's ability to integrate artificial intelligence and other cutting-edge technologies being developed in the civilian sector will influence its ability to prevail in an "intelligentized" war. Yet its ability to do this will depend on the outcome of the technology contest now escalating between China and the United States.

A final consideration is China's internal politics. Xi Jinping used his political capital to require the PLA to make necessary changes that had eluded his predecessors. Key elements of his reforms, including rebalancing the services, inculcating "jointness" in a military not accustomed to it, and achieving greater cooperation between the PLA and civilians, could stagnate if his own power is diminished or if his successor has less influence. Other developments, such as severe economic setbacks, domestic discontent, or even an increase in large-scale natural disasters brought on by climate change, could dampen the Chinese leadership's enthusiasm for external military campaigns and mean that the PLA's attention would shift inwards. In short, China's post-Cold War military strategy is not etched in stone. But a shift to something else would depend on developments that point to different answers to the questions of where, against whom, and how the military needs to be prepared to fight.

Further Reading

Cheung, Tai Ming, *Innovate to Dominate: The Rise of the Chinese Techno-Security State* (Ithaca, NY: Cornell University Press, 2022).

Cozad, Mark et al., *Gaining Victory in Systems Warfare: China's Perspective on the U.S.–China Military Balance* (Santa Monica, CA: RAND, 2023).

Finkelstein, David M., *The PLA's New Joint Doctrine: The Capstone of the New Era Operations Regulations System* (Arlington, VA, Center for Naval Analyses, 2021).

Fravel, M. Taylor, *Active Defense: China's Military Strategy Since 1949* (Princeton, NJ: Princeton University Press, 2019).

Johnston, Alastair Iain, *Cultural Realism: Strategic Culture and Grand Strategy in Chinese History* (Princeton, NJ: Princeton University Press, 1998).

Saunders, Phillip C. et al., eds., *Chairman Xi Remakes the PLA: Assessing Chinese Military Reforms* (Washington, DC: NDU Press, 2019).

Xiao, Tianliang, ed., *Science of Military Strategy* (Beijing: National Defense University Press, 2020). English translation at https://www.airuniversity.af.edu/CASI/Display/Article/2913216/in-their-own-words-2020-science-of-military-strategy/.

Yasuyuki, Sugiura, *China Security Report 2022: The PLA's Pursuit of Enhanced Joint Operations Capabilities* (Tokyo: National Institute of Defense Studies, 2022).

4

Conventional Forces

China's high command – the Central Military Commission (CMC) – has outlined a military strategy focused on joint warfare and has instituted organizational changes to enhance cooperation between units from the different services. It has also allocated the equivalent of hundreds of billions of dollars annually to fund the people, training, and equipment necessary for the PLA to become a combat-ready force that can translate strategy into action. The services are responsible for ensuring successful modernization. Under the reforms, their mandate is force building, or what in the U.S. system is known as the responsibility to "man, train, and equip" forces. While there has also been significant progress in strategic capabilities, including land-based nuclear and conventional missiles, as discussed in Chapter 5, most PLA assets belong to the army, the air force, and the navy. The development of land, air, and maritime power forms the core of the PLA's ability to field effective joint forces.

This chapter reviews the history and recent modernization of the PLA across the three conventional domains. It begins with the ground forces, which are the oldest and largest of the services. They absorbed the bulk of a major personnel reduction under Xi Jinping but have sharpened their ability to project power across the region and globally. This section also discusses the People's Armed Police, which has assumed much of the responsibility for China's internal security. The chapter then turns to the air force, which has modernized its capabilities as it pivots from an earlier focus on territorial air defense to a newer mandate to conduct offensive operations. The air force shares responsibilities for delivering air power beyond China's borders with the navy's aviation branch, though the latter has begun to focus primarily on carrier-based aviation. This is followed by a discussion of China's maritime services. The navy retains important missions for coastal defense but has also built a blue water force that contributes to joint operations in the region and conducts missions beyond the first island chain. The navy, including its marine corps, also helps enforce China's contested claims in the South and East China Seas, increasingly supported by the Coast Guard and the maritime militias.

All major militaries have wrestled with contestation between the services for influence, resources, and missions. As suggested in the final section, this reality is no less true in the PLA where continuing army influence, service interests in retaining control of some operational forces, and the push for expensive "prestige" systems to justify large budgets are factors hindering the PLA's transition into a capable, and cooperative, joint force. Yet the services have also fostered collaboration in joint training and operations, and some of the conflict between them for missions has been reduced over the years through streamlined divisions of labor. The conclusion suggests that the services are already well on their way to fielding "world-class forces" by mid-century – and, in some cases, they have already achieved modernization progress that places them near or at the world's forefront today.

Ground Forces

The history of the PLA is a history of land warfare. From the onset of the Chinese Civil War in 1927 until the founding of the People's Republic of China in 1949, the PLA was almost constantly at war. Mao employed his zealous but poorly equipped troops as a guerilla movement against the ruling Nationalist (Kuomintang, or KMT) army, until he retreated during the 1934 Long March to remote bases in central China. The two sides joined forces against Japan during the anti-Japanese war from 1937 to 1945, following which the Civil War resumed.[1] With greater combat experience, morale, and modern equipment left behind by the retreating Japanese, Mao was able to pivot from guerilla to conventional warfare and gradually weakened the Nationalists, ultimately forcing them to retreat to Taiwan in 1949.[2]

During the Cold War, the PLA saw combat against several neighbors. In November 1950, after a series of internal debates and at the behest of the Soviet Union, Mao deployed forces across the Yalu River into Korea to oppose U.S. and South Korean troops under UN command, troops that had advanced close to China.[3] Mao's roughly 270,000 troops launched a major offensive, relying on numerical superiority and flanking maneuvers to push UN forces nearly to the southern tip of the peninsula. This was supplemented by a role for the fledgling air force, though Chinese bombers generally did not venture south of the 38th parallel to reduce the risk of U.S. retaliation against mainland bases; PLA fighters were limited in range and avoided operating from vulnerable Korean bases. Without close air support, however, Chinese forces were vulnerable and overextended. This allowed UN forces to counter-attack in May 1951, and the PLA retreated to the 38th parallel. Following months of heavy fighting, a stalemate ensued, and Chinese troops left after an armistice was signed in July 1953.

Chinese forces also crossed international borders in 1962 and 1979. In October 1962, Beijing precipitated a border war with India to dislodge Indian troops from forward positions along the disputed border. 80,000 PLA troops advanced in two border regions and pushed Indian forces back to the Line of

Actual Control. The result was that New Delhi abandoned its controversial "forward policy" of erecting outposts behind Chinese lines. The PLA retreated to its prewar positions but established some new outposts along the border.[4] In February 1979, about 200,000 Chinese troops and 200 tanks entered Vietnam in retaliation for Hanoi's military intervention that had toppled the China-backed Khmer Rouge regime in Cambodia in 1978. This was styled as a "self-defensive counter-attack" without an intent to occupy territory. The PLA withdrew after a few weeks, claiming it had taught Vietnam a lesson.[5] Both wars focused on the ground forces, with almost no participation from the other services.

Chinese military strategy also focused on preparations for even larger conflicts against the superpowers, though these wars never materialized. The "military strategic guidelines" promulgated by the CMC during the Cold War required the PLA to respond to an envisioned U.S. attack in the 1950s and 1960s, and to counter Soviet aggression, following the Soviet occupation of Czechoslovakia in 1968, Sino–Soviet clashes along the Ussuri river in 1969, and the Brezhnev buildup in the 1960s and 1970s.[6] The main approach, like the PLA's combat operations against the KMT and Japanese, would have been to allow U.S. or Soviet forces to invade far into Chinese territory and then weaken them through brutal guerilla raids on their supply lines – a concept that Mao called "luring the enemy in deep." This approach took advantage of the country's strategic depth and reflected the lagging state of the air force and navy, which in the absence of modern capabilities could not mount a credible forward defense.

The PLA's early history and Cold War-era strategic imperatives promoted a land-centric organizational culture that persisted into the new century. Most of the PLA's top brass hailed from the ground forces, though in a show of symbolic "jointness," the air force, naval, and strategic missile force chiefs were added to the CMC from 2004 to 2017. Moreover, the commanders of the former military regions and general departments were always army officers. The army remained by far the largest service, holding approximately 69 percent of total manpower as late as 2015. Indeed, the army was so dominant that it did not even have its own headquarters: the PLA writ large was synonymous with the ground forces, and its affairs were managed by the military regions and general departments. The stiffest resistance to structural reform came from the army, which did not wish to lose its status or resource advantages, even as China's formal military strategy shifted in 1993 to emphasize joint campaigns and offshore operations.

Army dominance did not begin to wane until the Xi-era reforms commenced at the end of 2015. As noted in Chapter 3, the army suffered the bulk of a 300,000-person downsizing, bringing its manpower share down to 49 percent. More than half of the cuts were to the officer corps, especially staff officers and other non-combat personnel. It also lost five group armies, reducing the total from eighteen to thirteen. A few non-army officers were selected for roles such as defense minister, CMC department directors, and theater commanders, although army officers continued to hold the large majority of these positions. The reforms also created a separate army headquarters on the same bureaucratic level as the other services. This meant that the army chief, as head of a distinct service – awkwardly styled the People's Liberation Army Army (PLAA) – would have to lobby the CMC for resources, alongside his air force, naval, and strategic missile force counterparts.[7]

While the reforms humbled the ground forces, they remain by far the largest service and are tasked with diverse roles and missions. Domestically, the army ceded most of its role in internal security to the People's Armed Police in the 1980s, but would continue to provide the ultimate backstop to party control if mass protests were to sweep the country. It also maintains a sizeable presence across western China, which increased after riots broke out in Tibet and Xinjiang in 2008 and 2009, respectively. Army forces are also prepared to respond to natural and humanitarian disasters at home; for instance, the ground forces supplied many of the capabilities used to respond to the 2008 Sichuan earthquake, including helicopters and heavy construction equipment, and mobilized to support the response to the Covid pandemic in 2020. Army troops are also responsible for safeguarding China's extensive land borders, which stretch for more than 20,000 kilometers across varied terrain, and encompass fourteen neighbors.

Regionally, the army's major role is supporting a Taiwan contingency. Its six amphibious brigades would form the first echelon in an invasion (as discussed below, the marine corps trains for a broader range of regional and global expeditionary missions). Other army units would act as the follow-on forces necessary to occupy the island. The army also operates long-range artillery systems such as the PCH-191, with a range of 500 kilometers, that would be instrumental to a joint firepower strike against the island.[8] In addition, the ground forces train for other regional contingencies. In the Northeast, they prepare for various Korean Peninsula scenarios, such as handling a refugee crisis, securing weapons of mass destruction, and safeguarding Chinese territorial interests, if another war were to break out. In the southwest, they have reinforced the border defense regiments permanently stationed along the Line of Actual Control with India, with troops rotating in from Xinjiang and the Western Theater. These troops patrol the disputed border and have occasionally been involved in minor skirmishes with Indian troops.

Outside Asia, the army is the PLA service with the greatest number of boots on the ground in foreign countries. Most of the roughly 2,000 Chinese participants in UN peacekeeping operations, which take place primarily in Africa and the Middle East, are from the army. Historically, these troops were mostly combat support personnel, such as logisticians, engineers, and military medics. In the 2010s, the PLA also began dispatching infantry units to South

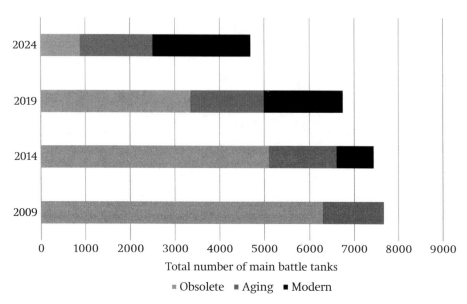

Figure 4.1 PLAA Main Battle Tank Modernization, 2009–2024
Source: Authors' figure based on data from IISS *Military Balance*, 2009–2024.

Sudan, at the battalion level, and Mali, at the company level, providing real-world experience for small combat units.[9] Most of China's military diplomats, who staff defense attaché offices in more than 110 locations worldwide, are career army officers. In addition, the army is second behind the navy in participation in foreign military exercises. As discussed in Chapter 6, this has involved sending large contingents to exercises in Russia and other countries.

These multifaceted missions have translated into upgraded hardware and organization. Historically, China's focus on land warfare meant that the PLA developed a strong industrial base for army equipment; most of this is still produced by the state-owned enterprise Norinco. China's Cold War vintage main battle tanks have gradually been replaced by newer Type-99s, which entered service in 2001, and the Type-99A, which appeared a decade later (see Figure 4.1 above). These systems have firepower, armaments, and mobility characteristics generally on par with their U.S. and Russian counterparts.[10] In 2018, the army fielded the Type-15 light tank, which is designed to maneuver quickly around difficult terrain in areas such as the Sino–Indian border.[11] Underscoring its range of missions, the army has also updated its inventories in uncrewed aerial vehicles, armored personnel carriers, attack and utility helicopters, multiple rocket launders, self-propelled artillery, mortars, grenades, and rifles. China's defense industry has also designed some of this equipment for export to foreign partners.

Improvements in equipment accompanied an increase in combat realistic exercises since the 1990s. PLAA training focuses on combined arms maneuvers, with more complex exercises often taking place in the spring and summer, after conscripts have received basic training. Exercises themselves have become less scripted and more demanding, including nighttime, poor weather, and live-fire drills. Troops have also endured long-distance mobility exercises, in which commanders need to handle the logistics requirements of moving and sustaining forces far from their home garrisons and across unfamiliar terrain for extended periods. Moreover, the army has created a dedicated opposition force brigade at the national training range in Zhurihe, Inner Mongolia, modeled after the U.S. national training center at Fort Irwin, California. The resident "blue" unit tries to emulate U.S. tactics and has routinely defeated the visiting "red" units. The PLA regards this experience as necessary to overcome its commanders' weak ability to exercise ingenuity and boldness on the battlefield.[12]

In terms of organization (see Figure 4.2 below), there is a division of authority in which PLAA headquarters in Beijing is responsible for manning, training, and equipping forces, while operational command for domestic and regional contingencies is exercised by the theater commands. This is a result of the shift to a joint command structure in the mid-2010s, as discussed in Chapter 3. Army headquarters also supervises the Xinjiang and Tibet military districts, as well as the Beijing Garrison, which have a range of operational forces.[13] Each of the five theaters contains an army theater component command; the Eastern Theater Command, for instance, has an Eastern Theater Command Army. These echelons report administratively to army headquarters in Beijing and operationally to the theater headquarters. Each theater army supervises two or three group armies, ensuring that major army formations are dispersed around the country and available for a wide set of potential contingencies.

At lower levels, the PLAA has sought a more standardized composition since the 1990s. The structure of the nearly one-million-strong service has mostly shifted from four tiers (group army-division-regiment-battalion) to three (group army-brigade-battalion). Most brigades are combined arms brigades; these are based on a common composition of units and equipment across the PLA's thirteen group armies and are usually categorized as heavy (with tracked armored vehicles), medium (with wheeled armored vehicles), or light.[14] Below this level, the combined arms battalion is considered the smallest unit capable of independent combined arms maneuver on the battlefield. Following the earlier moves of the U.S. and Russian armies to a brigade model, the shift to a flatter structure was intended to promote mobility, interoperability, and modularity as units could be reconfigured based on mission needs. Strikingly, the PLA embraced this model even as the U.S. and Russian armies converted some brigades back to divisions, based on experience that units with greater organic support might be necessary to defend against more precise and lethal firepower in modern warfare, as witnessed most recently in Ukraine.[15]

Aside from combined arms brigades, the PLAA also features other brigades designed for combat and combat support purposes. These include more than

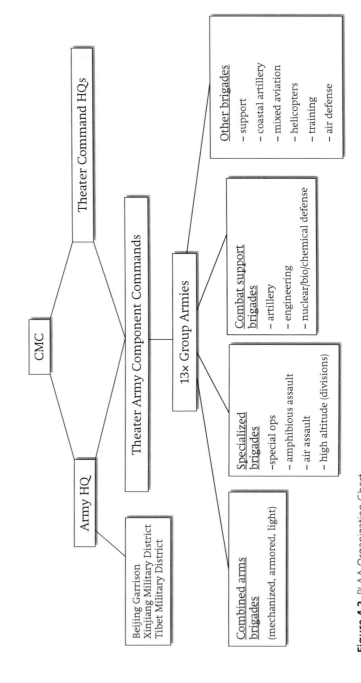

Figure 4.2 PLAA Organization Chart

Source: Authors' figure based on data from IISS *Military Balance, 2024*.

one hundred brigades distributed across the group armies and the theater service components, such as those focused on reconnaissance, combat engineering, special operations, army aviation, and air assault. Standardization needed to be balanced against the need to preserve specialized units purpose-built for specific missions. For instance, some of the army's few remaining divisions are mountain warfare units deployed as large-scale formations in the Xinjiang military district. The army also has engineering and chemical defense brigades that operate in all the group armies; the relevant units in the Northern theater, for instance, prepare for Korean Peninsula contingencies involving nuclear, biological, or chemical weapons. The army's six amphibious brigades, based in the Eastern Theater, train for a large-scale island landing scenario.

Though technically not part of the PLA, the People's Armed Police (PAP) provides additional land power. The Chinese Communist Party has organized armed paramilitary forces since the 1930s, and the PAP was given its current name in 1982 under Deng Xiaoping. Prior to the Xi era, it was jointly supervised by the Ministry of Public Security and the CMC. This dual command system reflected the organization's twin responsibilities. On one hand, it augmented local law enforcement and was periodically mobilized by local authorities to deal with social unrest and natural disasters. On the other hand, it was a member of the broader Chinese armed forces – an umbrella term that encompasses the active duty and reserve PLA, the PAP, and local militia units – and trained with the military for joint operations. During wartime, its responsibility would be to provide security at home so that combat forces can focus on their external missions.[16]

In the 1980s, the PAP was composed of poorly equipped units at low levels of readiness. During the 1989 Tiananmen crisis, the PAP was initially called in but was quickly overwhelmed by the scale of the demonstrations, leading party leaders to summon the PLA. The PAP's failure prompted a decades-long process of modernization. In 1996, fourteen mobile divisions were transferred from the army to the PAP, providing the latter with modern rapid reaction capabilities (while allowing the party to claim that it had "downsized" the PLA). More recently, the PAP has modernized along similar lines as the ground forces, focusing on procuring "new-type capabilities," such as helicopters, special operations troops, and un-crewed aerial vehicles to support land operations. There also continue to be strong ties between the ground forces and the PAP and, on occasion, officers will rotate through senior positions in both services.

Under Xi, the PAP underwent a major reorganization. Politically, the pivotal change was eliminating the dual command system and placing the PAP under the full control of the CMC. This was necessary to consolidate Xi's authority over the armed forces, especially since Xi's former political rivals, including Zhou Yongkang and Bo Xilai, had strong connections with the PAP. It was also necessary to reduce temptations by local officials to lean too heavily on the armed police to maintain order. This came against the backdrop of several incidents in the 1990s and 2000s when local officials had deployed heavily armed police to deal with civilian protesters, including some that ended with deadly violence. This conflicted with the party center's preference to handle those incidents peacefully, thus avoiding domestic and international embarrassment. Today, localities can still use local PAP units to deal with major emergencies, but they must request them through the CMC.

The current PAP consists of approximately 660,000 troops divided into three main components. First is the China Coast Guard, which, under Xi-era reforms, was transferred from the State Oceanic Administration (more on this below). Second are provincial contingents. Every province has a provincial-level PAP headquarters, which oversees various internal security forces. There are higher concentrations of PAP troops in major cities such as Beijing and Shanghai, as well as in western China, where they form part of the party's approach to stability maintenance in Xinjiang and Tibet. Third are two large "mobile contingents," one based in northern China near Beijing, the other based in the south in Fuzhou. These group army-sized formations, composed of rapid response, special operations, helicopter, engineer, and transportation troops, can be deployed at long distances to deal with major emergencies. During the 2019 protests in Hong Kong, for instance, the southern mobile contingent deployed to Guangzhou, where they staged to be called into the city (but were ultimately not needed to restore order).[17]

Air Forces

Originally a few planes at a Beijing airport, the PLA Air Force (PLAAF) has emerged as one of the world's most capable air forces. Seeking to convert his guerilla movement into a modern military, Mao relied on Soviet advice and equipment after the People's Republic was established in 1949, including MiG-15s delivered on the eve of the Korean War. Lacking qualified pilots, Soviet aviators flew about two-thirds of China's fighters during that conflict, scoring some victories over U.S. F-86s in "MiG Alley" near the Yalu River.[18] However, technical limitations meant that Chinese planes did not operate farther to the south where much of the fighting took place later in the war, leaving ground forces exposed. The PLAAF also participated in two Taiwan Strait crises in the 1950s. In January 1955, fighters and bombers provided air cover for a successful landing on Yijiangshan, a Taiwan-held island twelve kilometers off the Chinese coast.[19] Three years later, MiG-17s engaged in roughly two dozen aerial battles with Taiwan fighters near another offshore island, Kinmen, but suffered heavy losses due to their vulnerability to the air-to-air missiles supplied to Taiwan by the Eisenhower administration.

The PLAAF remained hobbled through the 1970s, for several reasons. First, the Sino–Soviet split meant that China could no longer receive critical technological assistance needed to maintain and upgrade its fledging air force. Second, the decision to build ballistic missiles and nuclear weapons required scarce resources to be shifted away from the other services and toward the new Second Artillery Force. Third, the Cultural Revolution (1966–1976) debilitated training and readiness across the air force. Fourth, the apparent attempted coup by Lin Biao against Mao in 1971 resulted in suspicions of a conspiracy inside the air force, which was Lin's power base; Mao removed its leadership and replaced them with ground-force officers for several years. Due in part to its technical limitations, a lagging PLAAF was of little help in the later Cold War. It could not provide air support to Chinese troops during the Sino–Indian conflict in 1962, and only conducted "deterrence patrols" inside China during the 1979 Sino–Vietnamese war. Its only major combat role was during the U.S. war with Vietnam, when PLAAF anti-aircraft artillery units were deployed to support Ho Chi Minh. However, Beijing's desire to control escalation risks meant that air force fighters were largely absent from that conflict.[20]

The PLAAF emerged from its Cold War slumber during the Deng era. In the 1980s, the United States assisted China in upgrading the avionics on the J-8 fighter through the "Peace Pearl" program (part of a strategic alignment against the Soviet Union). The urgency of air force modernization increased with PLA observations of the role of long-range precision bombing during the 1991 Gulf War and the CMC's adoption of a new military strategy that focused on the Taiwan Strait, which implied air superiority against Taiwan; the PLA would also need advanced air and missile defenses against the United States as well as an ability to project air power farther into the Pacific to hold U.S. forces at risk. With U.S. aid suspended after the collapse of the Soviet Union and the 1989 Tiananmen massacre, China turned to Russia, from which it purchased Su-27 and Su-30 fighters and for decades relied on for jet engines. It also entered into agreements with Moscow to co-produce the Su-27 fighter as the J-11 and developed the J-10 with technical assistance from Israel.[21] Eventually, China's aerospace industry was able to reverse engineer these systems, facilitating a push toward indigenous modernization. As with army equipment, some Chinese-produced fighters have also been marketed for export, including a batch of J-10s that entered service in Pakistan in 2022.

A focus on modern equipment and higher quality personnel after the Cold War supported a transition in the PLAAF's missions. The air force's traditional primary mission was territorial air defense, which remains one of its key assignments. The current integrated air and missile defense system includes S-300 and S-400 air defenses purchased from Russia, indigenously built surface-to-air missiles, anti-aircraft artillery, ground-based radars, fighter interceptors, and airborne early warning and control aircraft, connected by a highly redundant command and communications network. While the ground forces also continue to operate some air defense brigades, the PLAAF plays the key role in this system, which is underscored by its leadership of joint air defense exercises. The PLAAF also developed the concept for and enforces an air defense identification zone over the East China Sea, declared in November 2013 after tensions erupted with Japan over the Senkaku/Diaoyu islands. An air force general was appointed as one of the first commanders of the Central Theater, which provides air defense for the capital Beijing.

Nevertheless, territorial air defense is only one of several major missions for the PLAAF. In 2004, the CMC promulgated a new strategy that required the air force to conduct "both offensive and defensive missions." Other PLA discussions began to refer to the PLAAF as a "strategic air force."[22] Its primary combat tasks are projecting power across the Taiwan Strait. In peacetime, the PLAAF has increasingly carried out coercive air campaigns in Taiwan's air defense identification zone and across the midline of the Taiwan Strait. It has also simulated long-range bombing runs past the first island chain toward Guam, which is intended to signal a capability to strike intervening U.S. forces in their rear bases. In wartime, the PLAAF would pursue what it calls "command of the air" in the skies above Taiwan,[23] conduct strikes on military and government targets on the island (including from H-6 bombers operating at standoff distances inside the mainland's air and missile defense network), execute airborne operations,[24] deliver reinforcements and supplies, and prepare to execute bombing missions against U.S. bases.

Regionally, the PLAAF has also become more active in patrolling and intercepting beyond China's borders. After the 2016 UN arbitral tribunal ruling that invalidated China's claims in the South China Sea, Beijing announced that it would conduct "combat air patrols" in the South China Sea.[25] This involved flights across the region, some operating from three new air bases constructed on reclaimed land in the Spratlys.[26] There have also been joint air and naval patrols in the South China Sea, as well as joint patrols involving both the air force and naval aviation. In a different mode, air force fighters also routinely track and follow U.S. and allied aircraft operating in international airspace near China, which have sometimes resulted in dangerous or unsafe intercepts. More generally, air force units across the five theaters need to be ready for conflicts beyond the Taiwan Strait, including in the East China Sea with Japan, on the Korean Peninsula, and across the Sino–Indian border.

Like the other services, the air force's focus is domestic and regional, though it has also been expanding its global expeditionary role. The PLAAF does not operate any overseas air bases or maintain a permanent presence in foreign countries, making it reliant on host countries to provide facilities. Nevertheless, this arrangement suits the service's relatively modest global tasks, including delivering Chinese peacekeeping troops to Africa and the Middle East, transporting medical supplies and aid in crises such as the 2020

Covid pandemic, and participating in international air force competitions, such as Aviadarts with Russia. To accomplish these missions, the PLAAF has relied on a growing fleet of domestically produced Y-20 transport aircraft (seventy in 2024), which have a range of about 4,500 kilometers.

As a "strategic" air force, the PLAAF has upgraded its hardware across the board. It continues to operate hundreds of older fighters such as the J-10 and J-11 but is best known for its fifth-generation fighter, the J-20 (see Figure 4.3 below).[27] The J-20's major innovations include stealthy design, greater maneuverability, and more advanced avionics. Reflecting China's growing ability to produce advanced aviation equipment, it was developed by a subsidiary of the state-owned Aviation Industry Corporation of China (AVIC), although some of its avionics and stealth technology have been traced to stolen designs of U.S. aircraft such as the F-22 and F-35.[28] Initially tested in 2011, it entered service in 2017 and first deployed to the Eastern Theater. It then entered serial production and has been deployed to all five theaters, giving pilots everywhere a chance to train with the latest equipment; in 2024, roughly 200 were in active service. Early versions relied on Russian engines, although in 2019 a new variant was equipped with a domestically produced WS-10C engine; in 2022, a new WS15 engine, reportedly with greater thrust and reliability, came

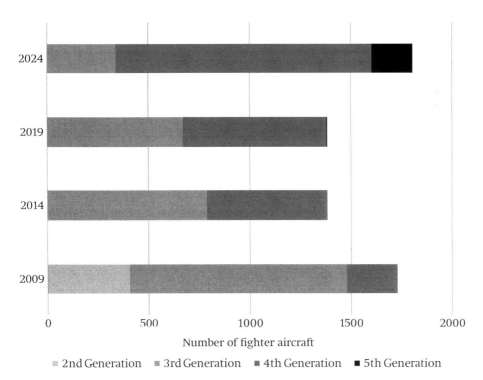

Figure 4.3 PLAAF Fighter Modernization, 2009–2024
Source: Authors' figure based on data from IISS *Military Balance*, 2009–2024.

online.[29] The PLAAF was thus making progress even in an area – jet engine technology – where it was historically weak.[30]

The PLAAF has also integrated advanced uncrewed aerial vehicles (UAVs) into its operations. All the services have worked to incorporate UAV technology, in roles such as logistics, intelligence, surveillance, and reconnaissance, communications, electronic warfare, and strike. The air force has built systems such as the GJ-1, equivalent in function and payload to a U.S. Predator drone, for surveillance and strike missions. Designed and produced by AVIC, the GJ-1 was introduced in 2011 and later marketed for export. The latest variant, the Wing Loong-3, made its appearance at the 2022 Zhuhai air show, where potential buyers learned that its range exceeds 10,000 kilometers with a 2,000-kilogram payload. China has focused heavily on marketing these products because, unlike the U.S. or European firms, it does not abide by arms control regimes for military drones. These systems have proliferated to countries such as Saudi Arabia, Morocco, Egypt, and Nigeria, sometimes appearing on foreign battlefields, although there have also been reported quality-control problems, including frequent crashes.[31]

The workhorse of China's bomber fleet has long been the H-6. The aircraft was originally developed by the Soviets as the Tu-16 and transferred to China in 1959. Like the U.S. B-52 bomber, the airframe design dates from the early Cold War, but there have been a series of advances over the years in avionics and engine technology. The key innovation of the current H-6K variant, which entered service in 2009 and now consists of about 100 units, is turbofan engines, which increase fuel efficiency and thus range and payload (see Figure 4.4 below). Built by another AVIC subsidiary, the H-6K has a range of about 3,500 kilometers and carries six YJ-12 or six CJ-20 air launched cruise missiles, with ranges of roughly 400 and 2,000 kilometers, respectively. An upgraded H-6N entered service in 2018 and features a refueling capability that extends its range by about 2,500 kilometers. This bomber is also capable of launching ballistic missiles, which could be tipped with a nuclear warhead, offering China an air-leg in its nuclear deterrent force.[32] A follow-on bomber, the H-20, resembles the U.S. B-2; its contributions come from its stealthy design and a range that could far surpass the H-6 variants.

Aside from hardware upgrades, the PLAAF has also improved its personnel quality. As in other countries, China has invested in recruitment of pilot candidates; to fill its quotas, the PLAAF needs about 1,000 new pilots annually, compared to about 1,500 for the United States. Historically, a constraint on pilot development was a low monthly quota of flight hours, which reflected the poor reliability of PLAAF aircraft (which often needed to be taken out of service for maintenance). However, higher performance jets and more sophisticated maintenance practices have probably reduced those limitations. Like the other services, air force training has also become more combat-realistic, featuring opposition forces, flying at nighttime, in poor weather conditions,

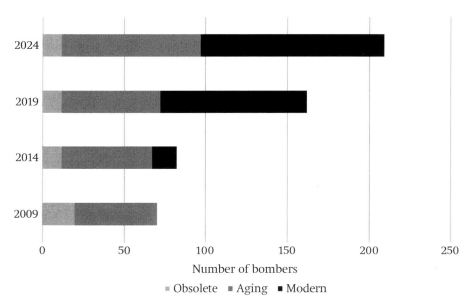

Figure 4.4 PLAAF H-6 Bomber Modernization, 2009–2024
Source: Authors' figure based on data from IISS *Military Balance*, 2009–2024.

and overwater, and combined arms drills. To cultivate elite pilots, the PLAAF has also instituted several high-profile competitions, such as Golden Helmet, Golden Dart, Blue Shield, and Red Sword.[33] China has also tried to improve its pilot proficiency by hiring foreign trainers, including a South African company that contracted elite Western pilots to conduct training sessions for the PLAAF.[34] Nevertheless, continuing human capital weakness for the PLAAF, as in the rest of the PLA, include the retention of highly skilled personnel given higher wages in the private sector, and lack of combat experience.

As with the army, advanced PLAAF capabilities are integrated into a modern structure and organization. By number of personnel and aircraft, it already fields the region's largest air force, and its inventory of fourth and fifth generation fighters has come close to surpassing the U.S. Air Force (roughly 1,300 vs. 1,500 in 2024). The PLAAF's five branches include aviation (its largest and most important), the airborne corps, ground-to-air missiles, radars, and electromagnetic countermeasures. As depicted in Figure 4.5, air force headquarters controls the airborne corps, bombers, strategic transport, and bombers, but most tactical aircraft are allocated to the five theater commands. There is a roughly even distribution of capabilities among the five theaters, which helps to ensure readiness across China's periphery. Each theater has an air force component headquarters, which in turn oversees two to three air bases, which control operational units. Tactical aviation units have transitioned from a division to a brigade model, mirroring similar reforms in the ground forces meant to promote agility and mobility. Air force brigades

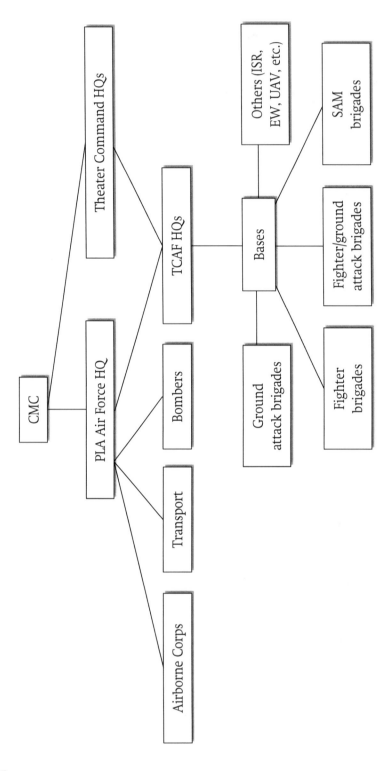

Figure 4.5 PLAAF Organization Chart
Source: Authors' figure based on data from IISS *Military Balance*, 2024.

are usually organized by aircraft type, which in turn comprise battalion-level flight groups (8–10 aircraft) and company-level flight squadrons (4–5 aircraft).[35]

Distinct from the PLAAF, the navy has had an aviation branch for most of its existence. It was created in 1952 to provide air defense for China's coastal defense forces and continued in this role for decades. During the 1979 war with Vietnam, naval aviators conducted strikes on Vietnamese atolls in the Spratlys. In April 2001, a naval J-8 fighter pilot, Wang Wei, infamously collided with a U.S. EP-3 reconnaissance plane over the South China Sea, triggering an international crisis. Yet naval aviation was always a much smaller force than the PLAAF: in 2023, it consisted of 26,000 personnel, compared to 395,000 for the PLAAF, fielding five fighter and ground attack brigades, compared to about fifty for the PLAAF. Nevertheless, the PLAAF's transition into a "strategic" service with a mandate to project power over water resulted in a challenge to the navy's monopoly on this mission. A new division of labor came into the picture in 2023. Under the new arrangement, most remaining land-based naval aviation units were transferred to the PLAAF; the naval aviation branch would focus on carrier-based aviation.[36]

Maritime Forces

The PLA Navy (PLAN), like the PLAAF, was antiquated in its early days but has since become a modern and capable force. Established in April 1949, the navy's initial missions focused on coastal defense, and to support the army in campaigns against Taiwan.[37] One early success was establishing sea control for the PLA's invasion of Hainan Island in April 1950, which was still held by Taiwan forces after their withdrawal from the mainland. With China cut off from Soviet military aid after the Sino–Soviet split in 1960, however, the PLAN lacked modern equipment or the industrial base to build large surface combatants and submarines. A fleet of mostly light-tonnage coastal patrol craft stood in contrast to the U.S. and Soviet navies – and to China's own proud seafaring tradition, which reached its peak with the voyages of Admiral Zheng He to Africa in the early fifteenth century (Zheng's 400-ton ships easily outclassed the 50-ton Portuguese galleons of the era). China's Cold War fleet might not have been a serious threat to major rivals but did prevail in minor skirmishes against even less well-equipped South Vietnamese forces in 1974, resulting in China's consolidation of control over the Paracel Islands in the South China Sea and, in 1988, when it evicted Vietnamese commandos from Johnson South Reef in the Spratlys.

The expansion of Soviet naval power in the Pacific in the 1970s prompted the drive for a more capable blue water navy. Mao reportedly instructed the PLAN to counter Soviet naval expansionism in 1975, a task that Deng continued after 1979. In 1985, the CMC endorsed a new naval strategy titled "near seas defense." Michael McDevitt argues that China tried to replicate the Soviet naval strategy of a "layered defense," in which the navy would be instrumental in pushing the country's security perimeter outwards.[38] This mission took on added importance in the 1990s: China became a net importer of oil in 1993, and thus needed to secure shipping lanes across the South China Sea; economic growth required access to fisheries and hydrocarbons in the contested waters of the South and East China Seas; and a 1993 shift in China's military strategy meant that the PLAN would need to support joint operations against Taiwan and counter U.S. intervention in wartime. In McDevitt's analysis, fulfilling these "near seas" missions required an ability to achieve local dominance – what Mahan called "sea control" – inside the first island chain, as well as a more modest "sea denial" ability to challenge foreign adversaries operating in the Philippine Sea, between the first and second island chains.

In the 2000s, the PLAN extended its operational reach beyond the Asian littoral. In December 2008, Beijing deployed a flotilla to the Horn of Africa to protect Chinese shipping against Somali piracy and has continued those deployments ever since. This was necessary to safeguard maritime traffic in the "far seas" past the first island chain but was also a symbol of China's contributions to global governance – responding to the George W. Bush administration's call for Beijing to become a "responsible stakeholder" and not a free rider.[39] In 2011, the PLAN played a minor role in the evacuation of Chinese citizens from Libya following the outbreak of conflict there.[40] By 2015, the CMC updated the navy's strategy to call for a balancing of "near seas defense and far seas protection."[41] The latter term meant that the navy would have to expand China's security perimeter outwards, protect critical sea lanes across the Indian Ocean, and be prepared to safeguard Chinese citizens abroad, even if its major combat preparations remained fixed on China's near periphery. Supporting these missions was the opening of an overseas naval base in Djibouti, close to key sea lanes and China's anti-piracy patrols, in 2017. Based on its own set of missions, the PLAN was certainly no less "strategic" than the PLAAF.

The navy's structure and organization reflect its expanding responsibilities. The total number of ships in the PLAN inventory increased from 216 in 2005 to 328 in 2023. This makes the PLAN the region's largest; it also has more ships than the U.S. Navy (289 in 2023). Among the surface fleet, the navy has replaced older coastal patrol vessels with new *Houbei*-class (Type-022) fast-attack catamarans beginning in 2004. More than eighty Type-022s have been produced, each equipped with eight YJ-83 anti-ship cruise missiles. Their armaments and ability to quickly swarm adversary vessels in large numbers makes them ideal for a "near seas defense" mission, although indications from Chinese interlocutors suggest concerns about readiness and manning.

The bulk of the increase in PLAN inventory, however, can be traced to production of larger surface combatants that can operate in both the "near seas" and the "far seas."[42] Beijing started its surface force modernization path

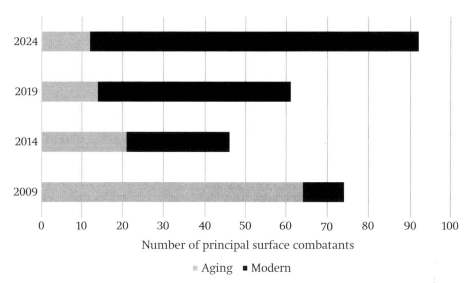

Figure 4.6 PLAN Principal Surface Combatant Modernization, 2009–2024
Source: Authors' figure based on data from IISS *Military Balance*, 2009–2024.

in the 1980s with development of the *Luda*-class (Type-051) destroyers, and picked up speed in the 1990s with the purchase of four *Sovremenny* destroyers from Russia. China has since developed a stronger industrial base to support domestic innovation and production, including the world's largest shipbuilding industry by output.[43] The number of destroyers doubled from 21 to 42 between 2005 and 2023. The most advanced destroyer, developed and built in China by the Dalian Shipbuilding Industry Company, is the 7500-ton *Luyang III* (Type-052D), which entered service in 2012 and features air defenses comparable to the U.S. *Aegis* system (a critical feature for operating beyond the range of China's shore-based air defenses) and 64 vertical-launch system (VLS) tubes designed for long-range strike. In 2020, the navy commissioned its first 11,000-ton *Renhai* (Type-055) cruiser, with 112 VLS tubes. Underscoring its ability to manufacture at a large scale, the navy commissioned seven more *Renhai* cruisers in the following three years. Figure 4.6 above depicts the modernization of the PLAN's major surface combatants.

Most symbolic of China's blue-water ambitions are aircraft carriers and large-deck amphibious assault ships. Acquisition of carriers began in the 1980s with then-naval chief Liu Huaqing, who envisioned them playing a wartime role against Taiwan as well as a peacetime role in strengthening China's overseas influence.[44] In 1998, Liu's vision became a reality, when Beijing purchased a former Soviet carrier, the *Varyag*, and eventually incorporated it into the PLAN in 2012 as the *Liaoning*. A second carrier, the *Shandong*, was modeled on the *Liaoning* and entered service in 2019. These are both small compared to U.S. *Nimitz* and *Ford* class ships and can only launch smaller aircraft such as the J-15 and not heavier ones such as airborne early warning aircraft. However, in 2022, the navy launched an indigenously designed third carrier, the *Fujian*; it is larger than its predecessors and has an electromagnetic catapult launch system that can support larger planes. Work also commenced on a fourth carrier, which, unlike its diesel-powered predecessors, could be nuclear powered.[45]

The PLAN has also quickly developed the world's second largest expeditionary amphibious projection capability. The first *Yushen*-class (Type-075) ship was commissioned in 2018, and was capable of transporting 800 troops and 28 helicopters. Two more Type-075s came online in 2022, with several more planned. The PLAN also has at its disposal eight 25,000-ton *Yuzhao*-class (Type-071) amphibious transport dock ships. Altogether, these large blue-water capable "amphibs" can deploy several thousand marines to any littoral area on the planet.[46]

The PLAN has also modernized and expanded its submarine force. Older diesel-electric attack submarines were noisy, but the latest *Yuan*-class (Type-039) features an air independent propulsion system that makes them more difficult to track. They can stay submerged for up to a few weeks before needing to return to port to recharge their batteries, which makes them ideal for "near seas" missions but not for long-duration global deployments.[47] Complementing traditional submarines are new uncrewed underwater vehicles, some more than 50-feet long, which assist in intelligence, surveillance, and reconnaissance and some combat missions such as minelaying and anti-submarine warfare. Given its focus on the "near seas," the navy has invested less in nuclear attack submarines, which are more expensive to build and operate than their diesel counterparts. The current fleet consists of six *Shang*-class (Type-093A) boats, although the navy has been developing a follow-on Type-093B slated to enter the fleet in the 2020s. There are also six *Jin*-class (Type-094) ballistic-missile submarines (SSBNs) based on Hainan Island. These have begun to carry out deterrence patrols under a Soviet-style bastion strategy in the South China Sea. Some *Jin* SSBNs carry the JL-3 ballistic missile, which can reach parts of the continental United States from their patrol areas, making the SSBNs a key part of China's emerging nuclear triad.[48] Figure 4.7 shows the modernization of the PLAN's submarine fleet.

While naval aviation has had its missions narrowed, the marine corps has expanded. The marines were established as a naval branch in 1953, with an original mission to prepare for assaults against Taiwan and its offshore islands. When Mao abandoned plans to seize the island in the mid-1950s, the marines were disbanded, only to be revived in a much smaller form by Deng in 1979. As late as 2016, the marines consisted of roughly 12,000 troops in southern China. But, during the Xi era, they grew to around 40,000 personnel based along the eastern seaboard from north to south; new units were drawn from former army divisions and regiments.[49] The current marine corps is designed

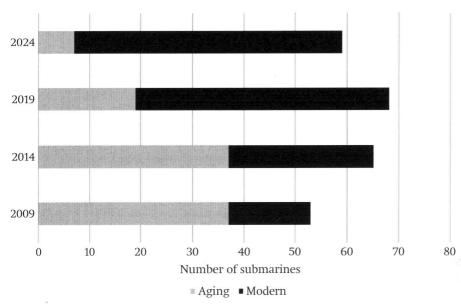

Figure 4.7 PLAN Submarine Modernization, 2009–2024
Source: Authors' figure based on data from IISS *Military Balance*, 2009–2024.

for a diverse range of regional and global expeditionary operations, including small island seizure in the South and East China seas, special operations, and jungle warfare. They also operate China's base in Djibouti and will likely be responsible for staffing future overseas bases. As noted above, however, they would *not* be the main landing force in an invasion of Taiwan; that responsibility is under the purview of the army.[50]

Naval modernization not only encompasses equipment, but also the people required to conduct a demanding set of assignments. As with the other services, naval training has become more combat-realistic, gradually expanding from a focus on surface warfare to include other disciplines, such as fleet air defense and anti-submarine warfare. There are also periodic multi-fleet maneuvers, as well as joint exercises involving the other services. The navy has also tried to improve its capabilities through exercises with Russia, although a questionable level of interoperability and limited mutual trust between Moscow and Beijing raise doubts about how much the PLAN has been able to learn from these interactions. Some assessments suggest that these exercises are more symbolic than substantive.[51] The PLAN has also begun to conduct occasional joint patrols with its Russian counterpart.

In terms of talent management, the navy has strengthened its non-commissioned officer corps, which may account for up to 80 percent of personnel aboard ships and embodies the technical expertise required for maintenance and operations. The steady drumbeat of naval patrols in the "near seas" provides practical on-the-job training for naval officers, who must possess

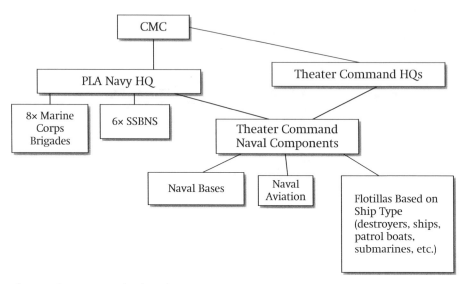

Figure 4.8 PLAN Organization Chart
Source: Authors' figure based on data from IISS *Military Balance*, 2024.

the professional competence to perform their missions without embarrassing failures, such as unintended collisions with foreign warships. Opportunities for participation in the Gulf of Aden anti-piracy patrols have been parceled out between the three fleets to develop their junior and mid-level commanders. A few naval officers have even risen into top joint positions, including theater commanders and defense ministers.

The navy's organization follows its mixed regional and global missions. Because of its diverse and extra-regional responsibilities, the marine corps is a national asset that reports to PLAN headquarters. The SSBN force also reports to PLAN headquarters, but the CMC has ultimate control over SSBNs as part of its centralized control over PLA nuclear forces.[52] Most ships and submarines, however, are assigned to one of three fleets under the coastal theater commands (northern, eastern, and southern). The fleets are responsible for training and operating in adjacent waters: the Northern Theater Navy in the Yellow Sea, the Eastern Theater Navy in the Taiwan Strait and East China Sea, and the Southern Theater Navy in the South China Sea. Promoting general readiness, the three fleets have a similar composition, although there are some variations; for instance, the Eastern Theater, responsible for Taiwan, has the bulk of the PLAN's landing craft. As with theater land and air force components, the fleets report to the theater commander. Nevertheless, when ships transit into the "far seas," control often reverts to PLAN headquarters. This system supports the goals of "far seas protection," which does not require a similar level of jointness as in the "near seas." Figure 4.8 above depicts the PLAN's organization.

Two other maritime forces – the Coast Guard and the maritime militias – support the PLAN in carrying out its "near seas" missions. China's maritime law enforcement functions were originally performed by several small forces, each with a distinct set of responsibilities.[53] The system was civilian in nature because oversight was exercised by civilian agencies such as the State Oceanic Administration rather than the military, and because their duties were equivalent to those carried out by many other coast guards, such as search and rescue and counter-narcotics. In 2013, Xi initiated a reform that consolidated four agencies into a unified Coast Guard. At the same time, Beijing acquired a larger Coast Guard fleet, sometimes by converting retired naval vessels into Coast Guard ships. Large (more than 1,000 tons) vessels nearly quadrupled from forty in 2012 to more than 150 a decade later. Introduced in 2015, the largest were a pair of 12,000-ton *Zhatou*-class cutters. These ships are heavier than typical U.S. and Chinese destroyers by tonnage but less well equipped; their primary weapon is a single 76-mm naval gun. The main advantage of these ships, however, is not their weaponry but their size – a key asset in intimidating foreign rivals while limiting the risks of unintended escalation.

In 2018, the Coast Guard underwent a reform to its lines of authority. Instead of reporting to civilian authorities, the Coast Guard was placed under the PAP, which itself fell within the military chain of command. With a new command structure and larger fleet, the Coast Guard became a more useful tool in regional maritime disputes. China's adversaries would need to face the sheer tonnage of the region's largest coast guard. This was an advantageous form of harassment because these "white hull" ships supported the narrative that Beijing was patrolling its own territory, rather than aggressively using "gray hull" naval ships in foreign conflicts. Attempts to challenge China's Coast Guard vessels were also difficult, given coordination between the Coast Guard and the navy, whose assets often loitered just over the horizon. Indeed, it was more frequently the case that Coast Guard ships would coordinate with the theater commands and conduct joint training with the navy, even if they retained their original mandate to conduct law enforcement missions, wore different uniforms, and operated somewhat different equipment. Hence, the Coast Guard's paramilitary identity began to eclipse its status as a regular law enforcement service.[54]

Aside from the Coast Guard, the navy is also supported by the maritime militias. These are not a single entity under unified command but rather a collection of militia units based in local townships, villages, and state-owned enterprises throughout southern China, with an operational focus on the South China Sea.[55] The maritime militias operate roughly 300 ships from ten ports. Most militia units are composed of regular fishing fleets, which Beijing occasionally mobilizes for intelligence-gathering or coercive purposes.[56] However, in 2015, a new full-time militia outfit was established at Sansha City in the Paracels, which offers a convenient base from which to conduct more regular patrols in the South China Sea. This professional unit operates larger ships with features such as reinforced hulls and water cannon designed for intimidation tactics. Like the Coast Guard, the maritime militias have improved their coordination with the theater commands and other maritime forces. Put differently, while the navy handles regional warfighting and global expeditionary missions, the three maritime services work alongside each other in the "near seas" to enforce China's territorial claims from a position of strength.

Service Politics

The main trajectory of China's conventional modernization has been pursuit of "world-class" capabilities by each service within their respective domain. This is consistent with a strategy that focuses on joint operations where each service contributes in its unique and distinctive way without excessive duplication of effort. As noted in Chapter 3, the main form of operations the PLA has needed to prepare for since 1993 has been "integrated joint operations." This is relevant to Taiwan as well as major campaigns in other theaters, such as with India or on the Korean Peninsula. More recent PLA analyses have tried to absorb U.S. concepts of "joint all-domain operations," suggesting an interest in achieving a higher degree of interoperability between forces from the different services and branches.[57] The aspirational PLA goal is to be able to conduct multi-domain integrated joint operations, as discussed in Chapter 5. The army, air force, and navy are now better integrated at the theater level, where commanders oversee a stronger regimen of joint planning, training, and peacetime operations than existed prior to the Xi-era restructuring.

From a hardware perspective, each service is building platforms and weapons useful for achieving dominance in their respective domain relevant for high-end joint campaigns. In a Joint Island Landing Campaign against Taiwan, for instance, the air force would take responsibility for control of the skies with its fleet of J-20s and conduct strike missions with its H-6Ks, the navy would gain control of the seas through its *Luyang III* destroyers, *Renhai*-class cruisers, and quiet *Yuan*-class submarines, and the army would gain a foothold through amphibious brigades equipped with the latest amphibious fighting vehicles. The Rocket Force, as discussed in Chapter 7, would also play a key role through its land-based ballistic and cruise missile forces. Many of the systems being fielded by the services are also fungible across a range of contingencies, including multi-mission destroyers and cruisers, modern fighters and bombers that can quickly pivot between theaters, and standardized air force and army brigades that can be plugged into units in different theaters in a large contingency.

Even when the services share similar capabilities, they have increasingly streamlined their roles to prevent overlapping missions. Since the 1980s, the PAP has taken the lead on internal security from the PLAA, freeing up the army to focus on its professional warfighting functions (although it has still been called in to handle domestic emergencies, including in the 1989 Tiananmen crisis). The navy, Coast Guard, and maritime militias have reached a *modus vivendi*, in which each plays their own role in enforcing China's maritime territorial claims. The air force and the navy once competed for the overwater aviation mission,[58] but the 2023 reforms decided that the PLAAF would handle all land-based aviation, including flights bound for the "near seas." This outcome was the reverse of the service's loss of its aspiration for a space mission, which some air force leaders had discussed in the 2000s under the banner of "integrated air and space operations," to the newly created Aerospace Force in 2016 (originally part of the Strategic Support Force).[59] There has also been a division of labor between the army amphibious brigades and the marine corps, with the former focused on the cross-Strait mission and the latter a more diversified set of assignments.

Service equities, however, have impeded progress toward building a joint force in other ways. Chapter 3 noted that army dominance in key positions and force composition remains a concern. Another problem is that, despite the ambition to fully empower joint commanders, each service headquarters has retained some vestigial operational functions. All the services continue to supervise forces: army headquarters supervises the Xinjiang and Tibet military districts, the air force retains the bombers, transport aircraft, and the airborne corps, and the navy is responsible for the marine corps and the SSBNs. This reflects both operational reasons – the desire to centralize control over scarce assets – as well as the political reality that services in any system are loathe to give up too much control over their own forces. For similar reasons, service chiefs have held onto control of some overseas operations, which fall outside the scope of the theater command system.

There is also competition for resources between the services that might have contributed to the procurement of systems not well suited for joint operations. The creation of a separate army headquarters in 2016 and the subsequent removal of the service chiefs from the CMC in 2017 meant that the chiefs are on the same bureaucratic level and must make an argument for resources. Advocacy for the most expensive acquisition programs may rest on an appeal to national pride or jobs rather than an operational rationale connected with the PLA's focus on "integrated joint operations." Liu Huaqing's justification for aircraft carriers as vital for the projection of airpower across the Taiwan Strait was superseded by advances in long-range precision munitions. Nevertheless, the program continued under the populist guise of "naval nationalism" and international respect.[60] The Army procured 1,200 Type-99 main battle tanks after 2011, an expensive system that cannot necessarily operate in difficult terrain such as the Himalayas compared to lighter tanks but which is a source of pride. Being "world-class," for the services, does not necessarily translate into fielding the forces necessary for joint campaigns.

Conclusion

Acquisition of modern land, air, and maritime forces is integral to the Chinese leadership's ability to manage the domestic, regional, and global challenges they face today. At home, the PAP takes the lead in internal security, supported by the PLAA. Both play a critical role in responding to humanitarian and natural disasters. The army and the air force work together to protect territorial airspace, managing a maturing integrated air and missile defense system intended to keep the country safe from foreign attack in wartime. The navy's historical mission has been safeguarding the littoral waters near China's vulnerable east coast, which continues today even as attention has turned to building a more capable blue water navy.

Regionally, the ground forces have shifted their attention to external missions, including patrolling along the Sino–Indian border, preparing for a Korean Peninsula contingency, and defending China's borders with other neighbors. The PLAAF enforces an air defense identification zone above the East China Sea, conducts "combat air patrols" in the South China Sea, and has operated beyond the first island chain to place U.S. bases in the western Pacific in their sights. The PLAN operates in concert with the other maritime services to enforce China's maritime territorial claims and has established a "layered defense" with surface and submarine forces that patrol the key sea lanes toward the Strait of Malacca and beyond. All three services train for Taiwan contingencies, contributing in their distinctive ways to joint firepower strikes, blockades, and a full-scale island landing.

All three services also play a global role, albeit in different ways. The army supplies most of the more than 2,000 Chinese personnel regularly deployed to UN peacekeeping missions and handles China's defense relations with foreign countries. The navy utilizes its large surface ships to conduct anti-piracy patrols in the Horn of Africa region and operates the first of what will likely be multiple overseas naval bases. The air force delivers troops and assistance through its burgeoning strategic transport fleet and has supported the navy in preparing to execute non-combatant evacuations when major crises occur.[61] As discussed in Chapter 8, the PLA's global role to date has been modest but could travel along new trajectories in the future.

To accomplish these missions, the services have all modernized their hardware, updated their organizational structures, and cultivated more capable personnel. The army already had the industry to develop modern tanks and fighting vehicles. The air force and navy needed to catch up after the Cold

War by purchasing combat systems from abroad or co-producing them with foreign partners. This contributed to the growth of a stronger industrial base in these domains, exhibited by the domestic production of systems at or near the world's leading edge, such as the indigenous (Type-003) aircraft carrier *Fujian*, the *Renhai*-class cruisers, and the J-20 fighter. Future generations of equipment, some of them undeniably "world-class" in their effectiveness, are also likely to be the product of an industrial base whose core feature is technological self-sufficiency. Personnel quality remains a self-acknowledged weakness, though the services have paid attention to recruiting the high-end talent needed to operate advanced hardware and improving the quality of training to be more "combat-realistic," even if they continue to lack real combat experience.

As in any military, there is undoubtedly competition and even rivalry between the PLA's three major services. Army dominance in senior positions, bids by the services to retain control over some forces and operations, and the pursuit of prestige systems not well suited to the demands of the modern battlefield could all slow the PLA's progress toward fielding a modern joint force. Yet it is also striking that the CMC has been able to avoid overlapping roles and missions between services, which has sometimes required sacrifices by services or branches. Ultimately, the PLA appears to be well ahead of its self-declared goal of fielding "world-class forces" by mid-century; this is true not only in the conventional domains, but also, as discussed in Chapter 5, in the strategic domains of space, cyber, and nuclear weapons.

Further Reading

Allen, Kenneth W. and Cristina Garafola, *70 Years of the People's Liberation Army Air Force* (Washington, DC: China Aerospace Studies Institute, 2021).

Blasko, Dennis J., *The Chinese Army Today: Tradition and Transformation for the 21st Century* (London: Routledge, 2012).

Cole, Bernard D., *The Great Wall at Sea: China's Navy in the Twenty-First Century*, second edition (Annapolis: U.S. Naval Institute Press, 2010).

McCaslin, Ian Burns and Andrew S. Erickson, "The Impacts of Xi-Era Reforms on the Chinese Navy," in Phillip C. Saunders et al. (eds.) *Chairman Xi Remakes the PLA* (Washington, DC: NDU Press, 2019), 125–170.

McDevitt, Michael A., *China as a Twenty-First Century Naval Power* (Annapolis: U.S. Naval Institute Press, 2020).

Wuthnow, Joel, *China's Other Army: The People's Armed Police in An Era of Reform*, China Strategic Perspectives 14 (2019).

5

Nuclear, Space, and Cyber Forces

Chapter 4 detailed the efforts the PLA has made to improve the ability of its army, air force, and navy to wage joint warfare in the land, air, and maritime domains. However, modern warfare increasingly revolves around acquiring, exploiting, and transmitting information about friendly and enemy forces via the electromagnetic spectrum and in the space and cyber domains. Chinese strategists view information dominance as the key to military success. Satellites, computer networks, and electromagnetic communications are critical force multipliers for modern militaries, allowing commanders to employ troops, ships, and aircraft in a networked manner that dramatically increases their effectiveness. This chapter explores Chinese thinking about information warfare and discusses the creation and eventual dissolution of the Strategic Support Force (SSF) to support PLA conventional warfighting efforts. It also explores PLA capabilities in the space and cyber domains, both as force enablers for PLA conventional operations and as critical vulnerabilities for PLA adversaries that can be exploited. It briefly considers other technologies useful for information warfare, such as precision-guided munitions and artificial intelligence.

The chapter then turns to the PLA Rocket Force (PLARF), which operates most of the PLA's land-based nuclear and conventional missiles, and examines Chinese thinking about nuclear weapons and the relationship between conventional and nuclear warfare. Chinese leaders historically have viewed nuclear escalation as impossible to control once nuclear weapons have been used in a conflict. Accordingly, they have viewed the primary purpose of nuclear weapons as deterring nuclear attack and nuclear intimidation and responding to nuclear strikes, and been satisfied with a relatively small nuclear arsenal. However, China has recently embarked on an unprecedented buildup of its nuclear forces and appears to be rethinking the utility of nuclear weapons for China's security. The chapter concludes with a discussion of the drivers of China's nuclear force expansion and the consequences of China's shift to a larger nuclear arsenal and a nuclear triad.

Information Warfare and the Strategic Support Force

The PLA views the information domain as critical for modern warfare. This focus derives from the study of U.S. and Russian military doctrinal writings and operations, with the 1991 Gulf War being especially influential on PLA thinking. PLA leaders endorsed a focus on "informationized warfare" by the early 2000s, and the concept subsequently has been studied, debated, and incorporated into PLA doctrinal materials, textbooks, operations regulations, and training guidance. Information dominance is the essential enabler of "integrated joint operations," which envision close cooperation among all the PLA services at the strategic, operational, and tactical levels to produce battlefield success. The 2013 edition of the *Science of Military Strategy*, an important PLA textbook, states that "information dominance is the foundation for seizing battlefield initiative; without information dominance it will be difficult to effectively organize friendly forces to seize command of the air and command of the sea."[1] The PLA envisions using a wide range of information operations – including cyberspace, electronic, space, and psychological warfare operations – to achieve information dominance. PLA experts believe that the struggle for information dominance requires an emphasis on offensive operations, especially for a military in an inferior position.[2]

The PLA has made extensive investments to improve its command, control, communications, computers, and intelligence, surveillance, and reconnaissance (C4ISR) capabilities. These investments include land-line communications links (with an extensive fiber-optic cable network), multiple mobile radio voice and data communications systems, and a growing network of military and civil communications satellites. These hardware investments, coupled with the reorganization launched in 2015, are intended to enable rapid information collection, processing, sharing, and decision-making. The goal is to collect and distribute real-time data – including intelligence, battlefield information, logistics information, and weather reports – to commanders at all levels via redundant, resilient C4ISR networks. By networking sensors, command posts, and combat platforms into an integrated system, the PLA seeks to help commanders make faster and better decisions.

The Chinese concept of "system destruction warfare" views modern warfare as a confrontation between the intelligence, information, logistics, and command systems of the contending militaries.[3] If the PLA can keep its critical systems operating at high efficiency, it can fight as an informationized and networked force, multiplying the effectiveness of individual combat platforms, seizing the initiative, and forcing the adversary to react to its moves. At the same time, the PLA plans to employ physical, cyber, and electromagnetic attacks against adversary sensors, communications links, computer networks, and command and support nodes to blind enemy sensors, degrade links between forces, slow decision-making, and force the enemy to fight as individual units rather than as a coordinated force. PLA strategists believe the military that can most effectively protect its critical systems and keep them functioning while attacking and degrading its adversary's systems will have a decisive advantage.

The PLA views the electromagnetic spectrum and the space and cyber domains as crucial arenas in the struggle for information dominance and critical for its ability to conduct "integrated joint operations." One clear marker is the Xi-era reorganization to bring the PLA's various space, cyber, electronic warfare, and psychological warfare forces together into one organization – the SSF. The decision to establish a new organization focused on information warfare reflected the PLA's belief that electronic warfare and space and cyber operations play a decisive role in modern warfare and that important synergies could be realized by bringing these capabilities together in one organization.

SSF operational forces were originally organized into two departments: the Network Systems Department (also known as the Cyberspace Force) and the Space Systems Department (also known as the Aerospace Force), both supervised by the SSF Staff Department. These two forces directly supported national and theater level commanders in developing plans and conducting operations.[4] In April 2024, the SSF was dissolved, with the Cyberspace Force and the Aerospace Force becoming independent entities and a new Information Support Force established to oversee PLA network information systems.[5]

The Cyberspace Force's missions include cyberspace warfare, technical reconnaissance, electronic warfare, psychological warfare, and information operations. By bringing these functions together in one organization, the PLA hopes to promote information sharing and achieve operational synergies in cross-domain operations, including the ability to practice "integrated network and electronic warfare" operations that combine cyberspace and electromagnetic attacks against key adversary targets. The force operates five technical reconnaissance bases aligned with the theater commands and a range of ground-based intelligence collection assets to support national, theater, and operational level intelligence needs.

The Aerospace Force controls PLA space and space-support assets. Its missions include military space launch and support; space surveillance; space information support; space telemetry, tracking, and control; and space warfare. The department is responsible for nearly all PLA space operations and operates at least eight bases to launch, track, and operate Chinese satellites and to support satellite and ICBM launches. These satellite constellations provide critical space information support in the form of intelligence, communications, and precision navigation and timing data to support PLA ground, maritime, aerospace, and missile operations.

As part of the PLA's overall intelligence system, the Cyberspace Force and the Aerospace Force play key roles in intelligence collection. Other key components of the PLA intelligence system reside in the Central Military

Commission (CMC) Joint Staff Department as well as the theaters, and include tactical intelligence gathered from conventional and uncrewed reconnaissance platforms, human intelligence functions carried out by China's defense attachés, and analytic capabilities at the national and theater levels. This information is fused together in Joint Operations Command Centers at the theater and national level to provide commanders with a common operational picture.

In the pre-reform PLA, cyber and space operations were conducted independently. Placing the Cyberspace Force and the Aerospace Force together within the SSF was intended to facilitate cooperation in shared missions, such as counter-space operations and strategic intelligence collection. However, the SSF appears to have been unable to achieve the desired operational synergies, perhaps due to its awkward organizational structure, which created ambiguity about command relationships by giving the SSF Staff Department, Cyberspace Force, and Aerospace Force commanders the same grade. The PLA leadership was not satisfied with the SSF's performance, and broke the organization up in April 2024.

At the ceremony establishing the new Information Support Force, Xi Jinping described it as "a newly created strategic force and a key support for coordinating the construction and application of network information systems" with "great responsibilities in promoting the high-quality development of our army and winning modern wars."[6] Xi listed its tasks as effectively supporting operations, adhering to information-led and joint victory, smoothing information links, integrating information resources, strengthening information protection, deeply integrating into the military's joint operations system, accurately and efficiently implementing information support, and serving to support military struggles in all directions and fields. The Information Support Force will develop and operate PLA command, control, communications, and computer systems, including responsibility for cyber defense. Its functions appear roughly analogous to those of the U.S. Defense Information Systems Agency.

The SSF was established to improve the PLA's ability to conduct "integrated joint operations," which, as noted in Chapter 3, are enshrined in China's current military strategy as the "main form of operations" troops need to be prepared to conduct. SSF support to theater commanders was provided primarily through support bases in each of the five theater commands. In principle, this provided a means of integrating PLA information support capabilities with the theater commander's direct control over land, air, and maritime forces (including Rocket Force conventional missile capabilities) to achieve operational synergies. These support bases are likely to continue, probably under the auspices of the Cyberspace Force. PLA units have also begun to conduct joint exercises at the theater level that integrate SSF capabilities, such as an army battalion air defense exercise that included support from air force radar units and the SSF.[7]

PLA thinking on the future of warfare increasingly focuses on what the 2020 *Science of Military Strategy* calls "multi-domain integrated joint operations."[8] Aerospace Force and Cyberspace Force operations to achieve dominance in the space and cyberspace domains and information support provided by the Information Support Force will play a key role in the PLA's ability to execute such operations. It remains to be seen whether dissolving the SSF into three component forces will improve the PLA's effectiveness in conducting informationized warfare across multiple domains. The PLA also envisions future "intelligentized warfare" that will incorporate artificial intelligence (AI) and autonomous systems to optimize the performance of individual weapon systems and to improve its ability to process and act on real-time information.

Cyberspace

China's 2019 defense white paper states that:

> Cyberspace is a key area for national security, economic growth, and social development. Cyber security remains a global challenge and poses a severe threat to China. China's armed forces accelerate the building of their cyberspace capabilities, develop cyber security and defense means, and build cyber defense capabilities consistent with China's international standing and its status as a major cyber country. They reinforce national cyber border defense, and promptly detect and counter network intrusions. They safeguard information and cyber security, and resolutely maintain national cyber sovereignty, information security and social stability.[9]

Although the PLA seeks to use networked C4ISR systems to improve the effectiveness of its own operations, its initial focus in cyberspace lay in exploiting U.S. civilian and military dependence on vulnerable computer networks. These networks were critical force multipliers that enabled U.S. military success, but they also created an asymmetrical vulnerability, where U.S. military forces were much more dependent on cyberspace than their less advanced PLA counterparts and thus much more vulnerable to cyber-attack. Accordingly, PLA theorists initially focused on how China could exploit this asymmetric vulnerability to collect information on U.S. civilian and military activities and to mount cyber-attacks against U.S. civilian and military targets in a conflict.[10] PLA writings view cyberspace as a domain that favors offensive operations and argue that cyber-attacks offer weaker militaries a number of advantages, including extended range, low cost, and the potential to degrade a sophisticated adversary's most advanced C4ISR capabilities.

China's key computer network operations concepts include computer network attack, computer network exploitation, and computer network defense.

Computer network attack involves offensive cyber operations to target adversary computer networks and to generate real-world effects by degrading the effectiveness of these networks and limiting use of the units, weapons, and systems they control. *Computer network exploitation* involves penetrating adversary networks to collect information of intelligence value, ideally without adversary awareness of the loss of the information. *Computer network defense* involves efforts to protect and secure friendly networks. Responsibility for computer network defense in the post-reform PLA originally lay with the CMC Joint Staff Department's Information and Communications Bureau, but this bureau has now moved to the Information Support Force, allowing for greater integration of offensive and defensive cyber capabilities.[11] The PLA is not responsible for defending civilian networks.

PLA and Ministry of State Security cyber units both conduct computer network attack and computer network exploitation attacks against foreign targets. Although PLA cyber units previously conducted operations against a range of civilian and military targets (and sometimes engaged in freelance operations on a commercial basis), since the 2015 reforms these units have been focused on foreign military and defense industry targets. The extensive anti-corruption campaign inside the PLA and centralized control over PLA cyber units appear to have introduced greater discipline into PLA cyber operations.

Computer network attack and computer network exploitation operations employ similar approaches to gain and maintain access to adversary computer networks. Initial Chinese offensive cyber operations employed relatively simple virus and phishing attacks to take advantage of poor adversary network security practices. An early assessment by a U.S. cyber expert noted that "interviews and [PLA] classified writings reveal interest in the full spectrum of computer network attack tools, including hacking, viruses, physical attack, insider sabotage, and electromagnetic attack."[12] Over time, PLA cyber units have raised their level of technological sophistication to mount much more complex attacks. More recent cyber operations involve more advanced tactics, techniques, and procedures, including "living off the land" by using built-in host network administration tools to perform operational objectives while evading detection. A Chinese state controlled cyber actor was detected in 2023 using these methods to gain access to U.S. networks controlling critical infrastructure.[13]

A 2023 U.S. Department of Defense report concludes, "the PRC poses a sophisticated, persistent cyber-enabled espionage and attack threat to military and critical infrastructure systems and presents a growing influence threat. The PRC seeks to create disruptive and destructive effects – from denial-of-service attacks to physical disruptions of critical infrastructure – to shape decision-making and disrupt military operations beginning in the initial stages and throughout a conflict." The report credits Beijing with the ability to launch cyber-attacks that can cause localized disruptions to U.S. critical infrastructure that could last days to weeks.[14]

Chinese computer network exploitation attacks have succeeded in exfiltrating large volumes of sensitive data from U.S. government and private industry targets, including technical data on the F-35 stealth fighter and an attack on the U.S. Office of Personnel Management that yielded fingerprints and sensitive background investigation data on millions of government personnel.[15] Chinese actors have also been detected conducting cyber reconnaissance of U.S. computer networks that control critical infrastructure, including power grids and transportation systems. Gaining access to these networks would position China to mount computer network attacks in wartime; China could also use this threat to try to deter U.S. attacks against its own vulnerable infrastructure. This highlights the inherent ambiguity in cyber deterrence – accesses to critical adversary networks are necessary to deter enemy cyber-attacks, but can also be used to mount first strikes against adversary networks. It is very difficult to distinguish between actions intended to create cyber deterrence and actions preparing for offensive cyber-attacks.

PLA writings suggest characteristics that might govern PLA employment of computer network attacks in a conflict involving the United States.[16] These include:

- using computer network attacks in the opening phases of a conflict, potentially even via a preemptive attack;
- targeting key nodes through which critical data passes, especially U.S. command-and-control and logistics networks;
- employing computer network and electronic warfare to temporarily paralyze enemy command-and-control systems, thus creating opportunities for attacks on command-and-control systems and on military forces via conventional precision strikes; and
- identifying military and contractor communications and logistics information that travels over civilian networks as particularly vulnerable to attack; these civilian networks may be vulnerable to relatively simple cyber-attacks, such as distributed denial-of-service attacks.

Chinese military writings characterize the cyber domain as offense-dominant, meaning that it is much easier to mount offensive cyber-attacks than to defend networks against attacks by sophisticated cyber actors. Some Chinese analysts see important gains from attacking first to obtain information dominance.[17] However, the cyber domain differs from the conventional and nuclear domains in that offensive capabilities do not necessarily provide defensive protection – that is, attacking adversary networks via preemptive strikes does not necessarily protect one's own networks. China's initial interest in exploiting asymmetrical U.S. dependence and vulnerability to achieve decisive strategic effects has morphed into a realization that cyberspace will be a contested domain that involves both offensive operations against an adversary's networks and defensive operations to protect one's own networks. Securing information dominance in cyberspace will require success in both offensive and defensive operations.

Space

The Gulf War highlighted the importance of space for military operations, with the United States using space-based intelligence, surveillance, and reconnaissance (ISR) assets to locate Iraqi forces and global positioning system satellites to target them with precision-guided munitions. PLA experts quickly recognized the critical role of the space domain in conducting informationized warfare – and that U.S. military dependence on space assets constituted a major vulnerability. China's 2015 defense white paper stated that "Outer space has become a commanding height in international strategic competition. Countries concerned are developing their space forces and instruments, and the first signs of weaponization of outer space have appeared."[18] PLA textbooks discuss space power as the glue of the modern integrated battlefield and space control as "the key to defeating the enemy in information warfare."[19]

China launched its first satellite in 1970 and has gradually built the technical capability to launch satellites to all orbits as well as crewed space vehicles and a lunar probe. China's formal arms control policies advocate the peaceful use and oppose the weaponization of outer space, but the PLA has developed an extensive array of satellites to support informationized warfare and a range of counterspace weapons to target foreign military space assets. These development efforts have proceeded in parallel, but building counter-space weapons to target vulnerable foreign satellites, ground-based space infrastructure, and electromagnetic communications traveling to and through outer space was a more urgent priority for the PLA. Over time, however, the PLA has deployed an increasing number of satellites to provide information support for its own military operations. What was once an asymmetric vulnerability due to greater U.S. military dependence on space is becoming more symmetric as the PLA integrates information derived from space into more of its operations. This is especially true because the vulnerability of satellites and ground-based space infrastructure to attack makes space an offense-dominant domain, where it is much easier to attack space assets than to defend them.

PLA analysts discuss five types of military space operations: space deterrence, space blockades, space strike operations, space defense operations, and space information support. *Space deterrence* is the use of space capabilities to deter or coerce an opponent to prevent the outbreak of conflict or limit its extent. *Space blockades* involve use of space and terrestrial forces to prevent an opponent from entering space or gathering or transmitting information through space. *Space strike operations* involve offensive operations against an adversary's assets on land, sea, air, and in space. *Space defense operations* counter an opponent's space strike operations by safeguarding space forces and defending key targets. *Space information support* involves supporting other PLA units by acquiring information on adversary forces from space or by transmitting information through space. Although space information support arguably is the most critical area for the PLA's ability to conduct its own operations, PLA military writings increasingly prioritize the other mission areas, which are viewed as critical for the PLA's ability to achieve space control and information dominance.[20]

Chinese military analysts think about space warfare in terms of the principles of "active defense" and "integrated joint operations." Although Beijing perceives itself to be on the strategic defense, active defense in the space domain envisions offensive operations as necessary to seize the initiative and secure space dominance. Chinese sources discuss space operations in an integrated manner that involves multiple domains. Ground-based satellite launch sites, tracking radars, and space operation centers provide critical support to space operations, as does China's fleet of space support vessels. Satellite control signals, voice and data communications, and information collected by intelligence satellites must be transmitted through the electromagnetic spectrum and processed and controlled by computer networks.

Satellites themselves are fragile systems vulnerable to a range of physical and electromagnetic attacks. The vulnerability of satellites to adversary attack depends partly on their orbits, with satellites in low-earth orbits more vulnerable to kinetic attack than satellites in higher medium-earth or geosynchronous orbits. However, kinetic attacks on a satellite that generate extensive debris can potentially damage other satellites in the same orbit, "trashing the beach" for friendly and enemy satellites alike. Vulnerability also depends on the ability of satellite communications systems to resist electromagnetic jamming and the type of sensors ISR satellites employ. For example, electro-optical intelligence satellites are potentially vulnerable to dazzling by directed-energy weapons that can blind or burn out their optical sensors. At a higher level, space resilience depends on the size of a satellite constellation and the ability to launch satellites quickly, to reconstitute lost capabilities.

China has developed a wide range of capabilities that can potentially be used to target space assets and support systems. A 2023 Pentagon report notes that:

> the PLA continues to acquire and develop a range of counterspace capabilities and related technologies, including kinetic-kill missiles, ground-based lasers, and orbiting space robots, as well as expanding space surveillance capabilities, which can monitor objects in space within their field of view and enable counterspace actions.[21]

The PLA successfully tested a direct-ascent anti-satellite (ASAT) weapon in 2007 against a satellite in low-earth orbit and is reportedly developing kinetic ASAT systems that can destroy satellites in geosynchronous orbits. The PLA is developing a range of counterspace capabilities such as satellite jammers, offensive cyberspace capabilities, and directed-energy weapons. The PLA could also use its conventional precision-strike capabilities to physically attack ground-based space launch sites, space radars, and satellite control systems. This range of capabilities gives the PLA the ability to mount both hard-kill attacks, which would physically destroy adversary satellites, and soft-kill attacks, which would seek to temporarily or permanently disable a satellite's ability to perform its functions.

The PLA is taking full advantage of the contribution space assets can make to military operations, emulating U.S. efforts to use space as an enabler for "integrated joint operations." Table 5.1 below shows the range of PLA military satellites that perform key information support functions. One function is ISR, which involves the use of remote sensing technologies on satellites to collect intelligence by regular surveillance of broad areas or reconnaissance of specific targets or locations. The PLA Aerospace Force operates various ISR satellites, including electro-optical (EO) satellites that use optical sensors to photograph adversary targets, synthetic aperture radar (SAR) satellites that can use radar to see through clouds or detect targets at night, electronic intelligence (ELINT) satellites that collect adversary communications or electronic signals, and early warning (EW) satellites that use infrared sensors to detect missile launches. These ISR systems play a critical role in locating adversary forces and providing near-real-time tracking information that can enable PLA units to target them.

Communications satellites also play a critical role in transmitting and relaying voice and data communications between PLA ground, sea, air, and space based systems and platforms. PLA units operating on the Chinese mainland can employ a variety of land-line and radio communications systems, but as PLA units operate further away from China, they become increasingly dependent on satellite communications. The Aerospace Force also operates Positioning, Navigation, and Timing (PNT) satellites that can precisely determine the position of an object at a specific time and allow course corrections to navigate to a desired location. This capability is important for mobile weapons and platforms, but is critical for precision-guided munitions, which use PNT data to allow maneuverable bombs and warheads to adjust course in mid-flight to hit their targets. The PLA's *Beidou* PNT satellites are roughly similar to the U.S. global positioning system (GPS), but also provide a limited capability for two-way text communications.

PLA writings on space in the 1990s and early 2000s emphasized U.S. military dependence on space systems and the potential for even the threat of counterspace attacks to deter U.S. intervention in a military conflict. If deterrence

Table 5.1 PLA Satellites

Satellite Type	PRC Capabilities	Orbit
Intelligence, Surveillance, and Reconnaissance (ISR) Use remote sensing technologies to collect intelligence by regular surveillance of broad areas or reconnaissance of specific targets or locations.	*Electro-Optical* (51) 4 Jianbing-6; 4 Jianbing-7; 3 Jianbing-11/12; 4 LKW; 4 Tianhui-2; 2 Yaogan-34; 15 Yaogan-35; 3 Yaogan-36; 12 Yaogan-39	Low Earth Orbit
	Synthetic Aperture Radar (5) 2 Jianbing 5; 3 Jianbing 10	Low Earth Orbit
	Electronic Intelligence (92) 5 Jianbing-9; 3 Jianbing-16; 15 Jianbing-10; 3 Yaogan-29; 30 Yaogan-30; 12 Yaogan-31; 4 Yaogan-32; 3 Qianshao-3; 10 Shijian-6; 7 Shijian-11	Low Earth Orbit
	Early Warning (5) 5 Huoyan-1 (EW)	Geosynchronous Orbit
Communications Use satellites to transmit and relay communications between ground, sea, air, and space based systems or platforms.	*Total* (11) 2 Shen Tong-1; 4 Shen Tong-2; 2 Feng Huo-1; 3 Feng Huo-2 The PLA can also use China's civilian communications satellites.	Geosynchronous Orbit
Positioning, Navigation, and Timing (PNT) Precisely determine the position of an object at a specific time and allow course corrections to navigate to a desired location. Useful for mobile weapons and platforms, especially precision-guided munitions (PGMs)	*Total* (27) 3 Beidou-2; 24 Beidou-3	Medium Earth Orbit
	Total (18) 12 Beidou-2; 6 Beidou-3	Geosynchronous Orbit
Meteorology/Oceanography Use satellites for weather forecasting and to assess water conditions	*Total* (8) 2 Yunhai-1; 6 Yunhai-2	Low Earth Orbit

Source: Authors' table based on data from IISS *Military Balance* 2024; Union of Concerned Scientists Satellite Database 2023. Note that some older satellites may no longer be operational.

failed, some Chinese military experts advocated preemptive attacks on U.S. space assets to take advantage of asymmetric U.S. vulnerability and seize the initiative in the fight for information dominance. Circumstances have changed since then. The PLA is still less dependent on space systems than the U.S. military, but its emphasis on fighting and winning informationized wars and specific operational requirements (such as the need to locate and target U.S. aircraft carriers) have increased PLA dependence on vulnerable space assets, especially when operating further away from China.

PLA space experts write that space dominance will be a critical and contested objective throughout any military conflict, with the PLA seeking both to maintain use of its space assets in the face of an adversary's attacks and to deny or degrade an adversary's ability to use its own space assets. Offensive counterspace capabilities will not necessarily protect Chinese space assets from U.S. attacks, and kinetic attacks that generate debris could also damage China's own satellites. As a result, the PLA has shifted to a space warfighting strategy that mixes offensive actions, defensive space operations, and efforts to use space deterrence to limit adversary attacks on Chinese space assets.

PLA authors discuss a range of defensive operations to protect Chinese space assets and defend against attacks from space. These include the use of camouflage and stealth measures to disguise a spacecraft's functions, the deployment of small and microsatellite constellations rather than single large satellites, maneuverability, the capability for autonomous operation, and the deployment of false targets and decoys to overload an adversary's tracking systems. They also envision offensive operations using both space-based and terrestrial assets to protect Chinese space assets.[22] The PLA is also exploring mobile launchers that could help surge additional space assets into low-earth orbit to either augment peacetime capabilities or replace damaged satellites.

Space deterrence rests on a foundation of counterspace capabilities but envisions exercising restraint in how those capabilities are used to avoid an all-out space war. Some PLA writings envision an escalation ladder that runs from testing space weapons to exercising space forces to reinforcing space capabilities (especially in a crisis) to limited attacks on adversary space assets. Chinese strategists argue that demonstrating the capability and willingness to attack an adversary's space assets is the most credible form of deterrence. Other PLA writings on space security highlight a preference for soft-kill measures over hard-kill attacks. Soft-kill attacks are seen as being more deniable and less diplomatically controversial than hard-kill attacks, which may generate debris or involve kinetic strikes on facilities in surrounding countries. Some PLA writings also stress the importance of centralized authorization and management of these attacks due to their diplomatic costs and potential for escalation.[23] China's challenge will be using the right mix of offensive space operations to degrade adversary space capabilities, while also conducting a mix of space deterrence and defensive space operations to preserve the Aerospace Force's ability to provide space information support for PLA operations.

Other Strategic Capabilities

The PLA is also developing other weapons with strategic effects that can be applied in modern warfare. These include precision strike capabilities that can attack adversary bases, ports, headquarters, and military assets and efforts to harness AI for a range of military applications. PLA advanced informationized warfare concepts envision leveraging PLA investments in C4ISR, space, cyber, electronic warfare capabilities with advances in big data and AI to rapidly assess and target adversary operational systems and then using precision-guided munitions from all the PLA services to strike key targets. Key precision strike assets would include the PLARF's large arsenal of conventional ballistic missiles and land-attack cruise missiles, navy land-attack cruise missiles launched from submarines and surface ships, air force long-range cruise missiles launched from H-6 bombers and precision-guided munitions launched from tactical aircraft, and army extended-range rockets and artillery.

The PLA has long envisioned conducting joint firestrike campaigns that combine strike assets across the various services in coordinated attacks on fixed targets that can overwhelm adversary defenses with strikes from multiple directions arriving simultaneously. Such attacks would initially target adversary radars, air defenses, and missile defenses with hard-to-intercept hypersonic weapons that travel more than five times the speed of sound. These include terminally guided ballistic missiles, hypersonic cruise missiles, and hypersonic glide vehicles mounted on the PLARF's DF-17 medium-range ballistic missile (MRBM). Once adversary defenses are degraded, the PLA could then mount sustained attacks using slower, less-maneuverable precision-guided missiles and bombs.

PLA advanced informationized warfare concepts have the even more ambitious goal of using near-real time intelligence and AI to identify critical mobile and fixed targets, and rapidly strike them with precision-guided munitions. The PLARF's anti-ship ballistic missile (ASBM) systems are consistent with this vision, using ballistic missiles equipped with terminal guidance systems to target moving aircraft carriers. The mobile DF-21D ASBM has a range exceeding 1,500 kilometers, is equipped with a maneuverable re-entry vehicle, and can reportedly reload rapidly in the field.[24] The DF-26 ASBM can potentially hit naval targets out to 3,000–4,000 kilometers and has been tested against a moving target in the South China Sea. The navy is also developing shorter-range ASBMs that could be launched from its *Renhai*-class cruisers.[25]

AI is "the ability of a computer system to solve problems and to perform tasks that would otherwise require human intelligence."[26] It is a general technology with a broad range of commercial and military applications. Current AI systems involve statistical machine learning that uses large-scale exemplar data sets or simulated interactions as inputs, employs algorithms to identify correlations for how particular inputs map to particular outputs, and then uses the resulting models to identify events, patterns, or anomalies in real-world data. "Deep learning" involves an interactive process of analyzing large data sets with a deep neural network and training the algorithm by adjusting parameters until the algorithm reaches a desired level of performance. This approach has proven effective for image classification, object detection, speech recognition, and natural-language processing.[27]

The large investments that China is making in AI have the potential to improve PLA information warfare capabilities. In 2017, the Chinese government announced an ambitious AI development plan that sought to catch up with leading countries by 2020 and make China "the world's premier artificial intelligence innovation center" by 2030.[28] The government backs this plan with commitments of public resources and incentives to mobilize commercial resources on behalf of national goals. China's "military–civil fusion strategy" seeks to facilitate the flow of technology between the military and civil sectors and to stimulate research cooperation between commercial, academic, and military entities. China's potential to make significant breakthroughs in commercial and military applications of AI could have significant implications for the U.S.–China strategic balance in particular areas and for bilateral strategic competition more generally.

The PLA is exploring a variety of AI applications that support its vision of information warfare. At the tactical level, AI applications include optimizing the performance and accuracy of missiles, improving the ability of weapons, platforms, and missiles to defeat defenses and countermeasures, and increasing the effectiveness of cyber-attacks and cyber-defenses. A second set of applications involves improvements in sensor and image-recognition technology that could reduce the ability of adversary platforms and systems such as nuclear submarines, mobile missiles, and stealth aircraft to avoid detection. This could erode strategic stability by making deterrent forces vulnerable to a first strike. A third set of applications involves the use of AI in autonomous or uncrewed systems, either acting independently in swarms or to augment crewed systems. At the strategic level, AI can be incorporated into command-and-control systems, either to develop and plan alternative courses of action for human commanders or to execute plans without human involvement. For the PLA, investments in military applications of AI are part of a planned shift from today's "informationized" warfare to tomorrow's "intelligentized" warfare.[29]

The Chinese AI infrastructure will have a significant influence on the PLA's ability to realize the potential of military AI. The Tortoise Media Global AI index and Stanford AI index use a range of metrics to assess relative national

AI capability. Their most recent reports both show the United States with a substantial lead over China.[30] Western export controls have begun to limit Chinese access to advanced processors optimized for AI applications, which will likely slow Chinese advances. China has the human research talent and is investing heavily to expand its pool of trained AI researchers but, so far, the United States retains an advantage in top talent and in the most cited AI research papers. Some assessments emphasize advantages of the Chinese system in mobilizing resources to support security and military applications of artificial intelligence,[31] while others highlight political and regulatory constraints that are likely to limit Chinese progress.[32] Relative performance will matter greatly for some applications where AI-empowered weapons and systems will compete head-to-head but, in other cases, "good enough" performance may be sufficient to produce significant military gains.

The PLA Rocket Force

The PLARF operates China's land-based nuclear and conventional missiles and associated support forces. PLARF missiles form the core of China's strategic nuclear forces, and nuclear deterrence is the PLARF's most important mission. However, the PLARF also operates one of the world's largest arsenals of conventional ballistic and land-attack cruise missiles, which are increasingly sophisticated in terms of range, accuracy, and responsiveness. These missiles provide the PLA with a long-range precision strike capability and would play an integral role in any major conventional conflict. Roughly half of Rocket Force personnel are believed to be assigned to conventional missile units.

The PLARF's origins date to 1966, when the Second Artillery Force was founded as an independent branch of the PLA to operate China's nascent nuclear forces. In the late 1980s and early 1990s, the Second Artillery Force began adding conventional ballistic missiles to complement its nuclear capabilities. Second Artillery DF-15 conventional missiles were fired into waters off Taiwan's major ports in July 1995 and March 1996 as part of a PLA campaign to deter Taiwan independence and influence Taiwan's first democratic presidential elections.

The 2015 PLA reforms changed the name of the Second Artillery Force to the PLARF and elevated it to a full service equivalent to the army, navy, and air force. Although the reforms relegated the other services to a force-building role, PLARF headquarters continues to have an operational command role as well as force-building responsibilities. One important change is that the reforms gave theater commanders operational control over PLARF conventional missile capabilities so they can integrate all PLA conventional strike assets into their operations. The CMC retains centralized operational control of PLA nuclear forces, operating through PLARF headquarters. Nevertheless, as

Table 5.2 Rocket Force Bases and Brigades

Base	Missile Brigade (Missile Type)			
61 (Huangshan)	611 (DF-26?)	612 (DF-31AG)	613 (*DF-15B*)	614 (*DF-17*)
	615 (*DF-11A*)	616 (*DF-17*)	617 (*DF-16A*)	618 (U/I)
62 (Kunming)	621 (DF-31AG)	622 (DF-31A)	623 (*CJ-10A*)	624 (*DF-21D*)
	625 (<u>DF-26</u>)	626 (<u>DF-26</u>)	627 (*DF-17*)	
63 (Huaihua)	631 (DF-5B)	632 (DF-31AG)	633 (DF-5A)	634 (DF-5*)
	635 (*CJ-10*)	636 (*DF-16A*)		
64 (Lanzhou)	641 (DF-31?)	642 (DF-31AG)	643 (DF-31AG)	644 (DF-41)
	645 (DF-41*)	646 (<u>DF-26</u>)	647 (<u>DF-26</u>)	
65 (Shenyang)	651 (DF-41)	652 (DF-31)	653 (*DF-21D*)	654 (<u>DF-26</u>)
	655 (*DF-17*)	656 (*CJ-100*)	657 (U/I)	
66 (Luoyang)	661 (DF-5B)	662 (DF-5*)	663 (DF-31A)	664 (DF-31AG)
	665 (DF-26?)	666 (<u>DF-26</u>)		

Sources: Authors' table based on data from *PLA Rocket Force Organization*, China Aerospace Studies Institute, October 24, 2022; *People's Liberation Army Rocket Force Order of Battle 2023*, James Martin Center for Nonproliferation Studies, July 2023.

Key
Italicized – brigades with conventional missiles
<u>Underline</u> – brigades with dual-capable missiles
? – uncertainty about missile type
U/I – unidentified "new missile type"
*Under construction

discussed in Chapter 1, corruption has been a concern. In June 2023, the Rocket Force commander and political commissar were both abruptly removed from their positions along with two deputy commanders, reportedly as part of an anti-corruption investigation, and replaced with navy and air force officers. The decision to reach outside the PLARF for new leaders may indicate that the current PLARF leadership was complicit in corruption or reflect deeper Chinese Communist Party (CCP) concerns about their political reliability.

PLARF missile forces are organized into brigades, which report to one of six operational bases (Base 61–66), as shown in Table 5.2 above. The location of the PLARF bases, coupled with the range of the missiles they operate, suggests their likely targets. For example, Base 61 (headquartered in Huangshan) operates numerous short-range missile brigades opposite Taiwan, while Base 65 operates theater-range ballistic and cruise missile brigades that could be used to strike Japan from operating locations in Shenyang. Each base commands six to eight nuclear and conventional missile brigades. Each brigade operates a single type of missile (either nuclear or conventional), but some brigades operate DF-26 missiles, which can rapidly swap between nuclear and conventional warheads. Three other bases play support roles: Base 67 manages the PLARF nuclear stockpile, including oversight of nuclear weapons handling regiments at the operational bases, Base 68 handles engineering and physical infrastructure, and Base 69 is responsible for personnel training and missile tests.[33]

As of 2024, PLARF conventional missiles include approximately 200 short-range ballistic missile (SRBM) launchers and about 1,000 missiles, including the DF-11A (600 km range), the DF-15B (725–800 km range), and the DF-16 (700 km range). It also operates about 300 conventional MRBM launchers and about 1,000 MRBMs, including the DF-21B/C (1,500 km range) and the DF-17 (1,500 km+ range), which is equipped with a hypersonic glide vehicle to penetrate missile defenses. The PLARF also has about 300 CJ-10 ground-launched cruise missiles and 150 launchers. In addition to these conventionally armed missiles, the PLARF operates about 500 DF-26 intermediate-range ballistic missiles (IRBMs) and 250 launchers. The DF-26 is a dual-capable missile that can rapidly swap between conventional and nuclear warheads; it is unclear how many DF-26 brigades are assigned to nuclear roles.[34]

China's initial ballistic missiles had poor accuracy, which limited their utility for conventional strike missions. However, by the mid-2000s the PLA had made significant advancements in targeting and guidance systems technology, such that its conventionally armed ballistic missiles may have circular error probables as small as ten to fifty meters. (This degree of accuracy depends partly on access to PNT data from PLA satellites.) The newer DF-16 SRBM reportedly features high accuracy, a short launch preparation time, and an improved maneuverable terminal stage. China's medium- and intermediate-range DF-21 and DF-26 systems also incorporate maneuverable re-entry vehicle technology, which allows for increased accuracy and gives the anti-ship variants the ability to strike moving targets such as U.S. surface ships.

The deployment patterns of the DF-11, DF-15, and DF-16 SRBMs suggest that the PLA envisions employing them in a conflict over Taiwan. Most of these conventionally armed short-range missiles are assigned to the Rocket Force's Base 61, headquartered in Anhui province, and the brigades operating them are arrayed across China's southeast coast, near the Taiwan Strait. China's DF-21 and DF-17s MRBMs and the DF-26 IRBM could be used to target U.S. military forces in the region, including bases on Guam and Okinawa. In a Taiwan conflict, the PLARF's conventional missile force would play an important role in a PLA joint firestrike campaign against targets on Taiwan and a critical role in striking U.S. bases, ports, and aircraft carriers throughout the region.

An Evolving Nuclear Deterrent

Chinese leaders decided to pursue nuclear weapons in 1955, justifying their decision in terms of defending peace, saving mankind from a nuclear holocaust, and facilitating agreement on nuclear disarmament and complete abolition of nuclear weapons. China's practical goal was to protect itself against nuclear coercion, which it had experienced several times from the United States. CCP leaders tasked their scientists to develop high-yield nuclear and thermonuclear weapons and long-range delivery systems for strategic deterrence, while eschewing tactical nuclear weapons and nuclear warfighting.[35]

China conducted its first nuclear test in 1964; Mao's statement after the test highlighted the limited political and military utility of nuclear weapons and committed China to the principle of "no first use" of nuclear weapons and to the ultimate goals of global nuclear disarmament and the abolition of nuclear weapons.[36] China's no-first-use pledge also reflected the belief of CCP leaders that it would be extremely difficult to control escalation once nuclear weapons were used; the value of nuclear weapons lay primarily in deterring adversary nuclear threats and use. This statement set the parameters of Chinese nuclear policy and continued to guide China's nuclear doctrine and PLARF operational practices for five decades.

China's first nuclear test occurred as the U.S.–Soviet nuclear arms race was accelerating, but Beijing declined to compete. Instead, China's leaders remained content with a modest force of nuclear ICBMs and theater-range missiles aimed at regional powers such as India (which tested its own nuclear device in 1974). This reflected their belief that even a few nuclear weapons capable of striking an adversary's homeland were sufficient to deter nuclear attacks or nuclear threats. A small arsenal was sufficient if retaliation was assured.[37] This nuclear posture was consistent with China's technological and financial limitations, and differentiated China from the two superpowers. As recently as 2005, China was assessed to have only the world's fifth-largest nuclear arsenal, behind those of the United States, Russia, France, and the United Kingdom.

For decades following its 1964 test, China maintained a relatively small, immature, and unalerted nuclear force. From the development of its first IRBMs and ICBMs in the 1970s until the early 1990s, China's nuclear forces consisted mostly of liquid-fueled, ground-based missiles operating in silo (DF-5) or rollout-to-launch (DF-4) basing modes.[38] These inaccurate missiles were equipped with single, large-yield warheads suitable only for use against cities. China did not have any meaningful air or sea based nuclear forces, and it lacked strategic early-warning capabilities.[39] China is believed to have kept its nuclear warheads, delivery vehicles, and launchers stored separately and at relatively low levels of readiness.[40] Although China's nuclear doctrine emphasized assured retaliation, its strategic deterrent was highly vulnerable to a first strike, especially if an adversary could use ballistic missile defenses to intercept any surviving Chinese missiles.

To improve survivability, the PLARF pursued a second generation of ground-based nuclear missiles with improved accuracy, solid fuel to reduce vulnerability during launch preparations, and mobile launchers to disperse missiles from garrison into concealed firing locations. The DF-21 MRBM was the first of these second-generation missiles, but it was eventually followed by the DF-31, DF-31A, and DF-41 ICBMs, the last of which are equipped with multiple independently-targetable re-entry vehicles. These missiles supplemented the PLARF's vulnerable silo-based ICBMs and were complemented by efforts to develop a naval nuclear capability via the Type-094 ballistic missile submarine (SSBN) and its JL-2 submarine-launched ballistic missile.[41] Although China has never provided official numbers for its nuclear forces, foreign analysts expected that this modernization effort would ultimately produce a larger, more diversified, and more sophisticated nuclear force of several hundred warheads.[42]

This understanding was overturned by the discovery in 2021 that China was constructing as many as 360 new ICBM silos.[43] If filled with missiles, this would constitute the largest expansion of China's nuclear forces in history.[44] The Chinese government has not acknowledged the existence of the new ICBM silos or provided any explanation for this unprecedented expansion of its nuclear forces. In addition to the new ICBM silos, China has also been developing and deploying hundreds of new nuclear-capable theater missile systems, including the dual-capable DF-26 IRBM.[45] China has also invested in more exotic and advanced nuclear delivery systems, probably including a strategic hypersonic boost-glide vehicle and a fractional orbital bombardment system.[46] It is also developing increasingly sophisticated supporting capabilities and infrastructure, such as early warning satellites that can detect missile launches, ground-based large phased array missile tracking radars, and more reliable command and control systems.[47] There are also hints that the PLARF may be changing its operational practices by mating warheads to some delivery vehicles in peacetime and by conducting training, exercises, and alerts to achieve a higher level of readiness.

China has also made progress in developing a full nuclear triad consisting of ground, air, and sea legs. As noted in Chapter 4, the navy has launched six *Jin*-class (Type-094) nuclear-powered SSBNs, which now regularly conduct at-sea deterrence patrols.[48] The navy's next-generation (Type-096) SSBN, which will be quieter and carry the longer-range JL-3 SLBM, is expected to enter service in the late 2020s or early 2030s.[49] Some late-production Type-094 submarines, sometimes identified as Type 094A vessels, are already equipped with JL-3 missiles.[50] The air force has also been reassigned a nuclear mission. H-6N bombers have begun training to launch a nuclear air launched ballistic missile based on the DF-21; the service is developing a next generation stealth bomber that will likely be nuclear-capable.[51]

These developments have caused the U.S. government to increase its estimates of current and future Chinese nuclear forces. The U.S. Department of Defense estimated that as of May 2023 China had a stockpile of more than 500 operational warheads and will have over 1,000 operational warheads by 2030, most on delivery systems capable of reaching the United States.[52] Table 5.3

Table 5.3 Estimated PLA Nuclear Forces, 2023 and 2030

	2023 Fielded Systems	Systems in Development	2023 Warheads Deployed	2030 Warhead Estimate
ICBMs			~254+	~660
Silo-based	DF-5A	DF-41 silo		
	DF-5B	DF-27	~66+	~400
	DF-5C			
	DF-31			
Mobile	DF-31	DF-31B		
	DF-31A/AG		~188+	~260
	DF-41			
IRBM			~120+	~200
	DF-26	DF-17 nuclear follow-on		
Naval			72	96
(SSBN/missile) (SLBM)	Type 94 + JL-2/JL-3	Type-96/JL-3		
Air			0	40
(bomber/missile)	H-6N/developmental ALBM	H-6N/ALBMs H-20 stealth bomber nuclear ALCM		
TOTAL			500+ (DOD)	~1000+ (DOD)

Sources: Authors' table based on data from U.S. Department of Defense, *China Military Power Report*, 2023; IISS, *The Military Balance*, 2024.

gives the Department of Defense's estimate of China's 2023 nuclear forces and adds the authors' projection of how 1,000 nuclear warheads in 2030 might be distributed across China's nuclear forces.[53] The estimates suggest a large increase in the number of silo-based DF-31 and DF-41 ICBMs and in dual-capable DF-26 theater-range IRBMs. The expectation of a much larger and more sophisticated Chinese nuclear arsenal is already affecting policy debates about U.S. nuclear modernization, regional security, and prospects for regional and global arms control.[54]

Foreign analysts are left to ponder whether this nuclear expansion represents an updated Chinese estimate of how many warheads are necessary for a survivable second strike, a new judgment by Chinese leaders that a larger nuclear arsenal will have significant political or military benefits, or a change in China's nuclear policy, strategy, or operational doctrine.[55] There have been periodic internal debates about adjusting nuclear policies in the past, but there is no clear-cut evidence that CCP leaders have shifted any of the core features of China's nuclear strategy.[56] Indeed, Chinese officials deny that there have been any changes in nuclear policy.

The growing discrepancy between China's declaratory policy and its advancing nuclear capabilities raises questions about both the current status and the future trajectory of China's nuclear forces and strategy. What political and military value do Chinese leaders place on additional nuclear forces? What are the goals of China's ongoing nuclear modernization and expansion? What might China's nuclear forces and strategy look like in the next decade? What are the drivers of China's nuclear strategy? What risks and implications do China's nuclear forces present for U.S. national security policy, and how can the United States most effectively reduce and manage those risks?[57]

One possibility is that China's goal is still to have a *secure second-strike capability* to deter nuclear attack, but that the technical requirements for a nuclear force that can survive a first strike have grown as adversary ISR, precision-strike, and ballistic missile defense capabilities have improved. Because successful deterrence depends on what adversaries believe, CCP leaders may now want a nuclear force that leaves no doubt that an adversary first strike could not succeed. Much of China's nuclear force modernization is consistent with this goal, including efforts to build the technical capability to shift to a "launch on warning" posture (which the PLA calls an "early warning counterstrike") where the PLARF would launch a retaliatory strike *before* inbound enemy missiles have landed.

The Aerospace Force and the PLARF have built many of the technical capabilities to support such a shift, including early warning satellites to detect adversary missile launches and long-range ballistic missile tracking radars to determine where inbound missiles will strike. This could also explain the PLARF shift to silo-based ICBMs. Silo-based missiles are more vulnerable to attack but are easier to place on alert and can launch faster than mobile ICBMs. Their vulnerability won't matter as much if the PLARF plans to launch them before an adversary first-strike hits. A shift to a launch on warning posture compresses the time available to decide whether to launch a retaliatory attack and requires ballistic missiles and their nuclear warheads to be physically mated, increasing the risk of an accidental or unauthorized launch. The key counter-argument against this explanation is that estimates of the future Chinese nuclear force are much larger than the requirements for a secure second-strike.

A second possibility is that China now seeks to construct a *"nuclear shield"* that can deter adversary limited nuclear strikes and conventional military intervention in order to gain freedom of action. This implies that Chinese leaders have broadened their view of the political and military value of nuclear weapons and now believe a more powerful nuclear force can help deter the United States from intervening in a conflict over Taiwan or at least confine the conflict to the conventional level, where the PLA might have a local advantage. By creating a stalemate at the nuclear level, China might gain the freedom to initiate a conventional conflict without fear of nuclear escalation, the so-called "stability–instability paradox." This explanation is broadly consistent with China's historical nuclear policies and its observed and predicted nuclear force development. It also fits readily within the PLA's broader strategy of active defense; the strategic goal is to deter outside intervention in what China regards as a domestic sovereignty issue. This explanation is also consistent with PLA interest in "integrated strategic deterrence," which envisions the use of a range of conventional, nuclear, and other strategic capabilities (including offensive cyber-attack and counterspace weapons) to deter strong adversaries.[58]

A third possibility is that a desire for *great power status* is driving China's nuclear expansion. This explanation views a large and sophisticated nuclear arsenal as a marker of superpower status, and suggests that CCP leaders are no longer satisfied with a limited nuclear force that is much smaller than the U.S. and Russian nuclear arsenals. Xi Jinping has called for building "world-class forces" commensurate with China's international standing, and has called for a more powerful nuclear capability in internal speeches to the PLA, calling China's nuclear capability a "pillar of our status as a great power."[59] In October 2022, Xi's 20th Party Congress work report spoke of the need to "build a strong system of strategic deterrence." Authoritative PLA textbooks also speak of the need to build a "a lean and effective strategic nuclear force commensurate with China's international status."[60] This explanation suggests that CCP leaders now view a large nuclear arsenal as having greater value in conveying China's political status and influence, and would explain why China appears to be building a large and technologically sophisticated force similar to the U.S. and Russian nuclear arsenals.

A fourth possibility is that CCP leaders have changed their views of the military value of nuclear weapons and now see value in *theater nuclear dominance*. China might seek theater or tactical nuclear weapons and delivery systems that would allow it to deter limited nuclear attacks or credibly threaten limited nuclear use against Japan or U.S. forces in the region. This explanation would predict future Chinese nuclear forces capable of conducting robust theater and tactical nuclear strikes, with a significant number of MRBMs, IRBMs, and cruise missiles equipped with lower- and variable-yield warheads. The ground, air, and naval forces operating these systems would be placed on higher levels of alert in a crisis. It would also predict development and deployment of the supporting capabilities necessary to support theater deterrence and nuclear warfighting, such as advanced ISR, theater BMD, and counterspace capabilities. It also implies a fundamental shift in Chinese leadership expectations about the ability to limit escalation in a limited nuclear conflict. China is reportedly developing a low-yield warhead that would be consistent with this explanation, and broader aspects of PLA modernization are developing some of the necessary supporting capabilities. However, thus far the PLA has not sought to develop and deploy tactical nuclear weapons or to change PLARF operational practices and training in ways that would support theater-nuclear deterrence and warfighting.

These four possible explanations are not mutually exclusive, though there is very limited evidence for theater nuclear dominance. China's observed and projected nuclear force modernization provides significant evidence to support the secure second strike, "nuclear shield," and great power status explanations.[61] All three predict larger, more sophisticated Chinese nuclear forces, but the nuclear shield and greater power status explanations imply progressively larger ultimate force structures.

The evidence suggests that China is likely to continue to increase the overall size of its nuclear forces to improve their survivability, deter U.S. military threats and intervention, and bolster its status by differentiating itself from second-tier nuclear states. The desire to demonstrate great power status might eventually encourage China to seek both quantitative and qualitative parity with U.S. and Russian nuclear capabilities. However, such a decision might be constrained by the increased costs and operational risks that accompany a larger nuclear force, tradeoffs with conventional force modernization, and political costs given China's desired image as a peaceful power different from the United States and Russia. A decision to deploy low-yield or tactical nuclear forces would signal a significant shift in Chinese thinking about the military and political utility of these weapons and about its nuclear policy and doctrine.

China's nuclear expansion has significant implications for the United States and other countries in the region. Since China appears determined to maintain a survivable second-strike capability, the United States should anticipate that China will respond to advances in U.S. offensive nuclear capabilities and ballistic missile defense systems and factor these responses into its investment decisions. A Chinese "nuclear shield" intended to deter U.S. intervention and consideration of nuclear escalation would place a greater premium on the local conventional military balance and force U.S. policymakers to make difficult choices about allocating scarce defense dollars across nuclear and conventional forces. U.S. nuclear force development will set the benchmark for what it means to be a nuclear great power; China is likely to seek to match or outpace perceived U.S. technological advances to showcase its status as an aspiring superpower. China will likely remain reluctant to enter arms control negotiations if it views such agreements as constraining its efforts to enhance force survivability or limiting its prestige by locking it into an inferior position vis-à-vis the United States and Russia.

Conclusion

The PLA's desire to fight and win "informationized" wars has driven it to seek information dominance in the space and cyber domains. This is captured in the PLA's emerging concept of "multi-domain integrated joint operations" and was an underlying rationale for the creation of the SSF to integrate PLA capabilities across the space, cyber, and electromagnetic domains. A focus on information dominance, especially in a high-end war against the United States, can explain the PLA's early interest in offensive cyber attack and counterspace capabilities as means of exploiting the vulnerabilities created by the U.S. military's dependence on computer networks and on space-based ISR, communications, and PNT capabilities.

Over time, however, PLA efforts to leverage space and cyber to support its own regional and global operations have created similar vulnerabilities. The result is that space and cyberspace will be contested domains in any conflict, with both sides seeking to degrade adversary access to space and cyber assets while preserving their own access. A vital but unanswered question is whether critical civilian infrastructure and nuclear-related assets such as launch detection satellites and nuclear command and control systems can be protected from counterspace and cyber-attacks, either by defenses, deterrence, or mutual agreement. The PLA's growing arsenal of conventional precision-strike weapons and interest in AI can also support its efforts to achieve information dominance.

The PLARF, which operates the PLA's ground-based nuclear and conventional missile forces, is an important contributor to joint campaigns and a strategic tool. Chinese leaders historically have viewed nuclear escalation as impossible to control, defined the primary purpose of nuclear weapons as deterring nuclear attack and nuclear intimidation, and been satisfied with a relatively small nuclear arsenal. China has now embarked on an unprecedented buildup of its nuclear forces and appears to be rethinking the political and military utility of nuclear weapons. One important goal may be to provide a "nuclear shield" that would give China the freedom of action to initiate a conventional use of force against Taiwan while reducing the risk of U.S. intervention or nuclear escalation. A larger Chinese strategic arsenal will also have important consequences for strategic stability and arms control. Chapter 6 will take up the question of how the PLA is using its new capabilities to shape its external security environment.

Further Reading

Cheng, Dean, "Space and Chinese National Security: China's Continuing Great Leap Upwards," in Joel Wuthnow, Arthur S. Ding, Phillip C. Saunders, Andrew Scobell, and Andrew N.D. Yang, eds., *The PLA Beyond Borders: Chinese*

Military Operations in Regional and Global Context (Washington, DC: NDU Press, 2021), 311–337.

Cunningham, Fiona S., *Under the Nuclear Shadow: China's Information-Age Weapons in International Strategy* (Princeton, NJ: Princeton University Press, 2024).

Cunningham, Fiona S. and M. Taylor Fravel, "Assuring Assured Retaliation: China's Nuclear Posture and U.S.–China Strategic Stability," *International Security* 40: 2 (2015): 7–50.

Costello, John and Joe McReynolds, *China's Strategic Support Force: A Force for a New Era*, China Strategic Perspectives 13 (2018).

Dahm, J. Michael, "China C4ISR and Counter-Intervention," Testimony before the U.S.–China Economic and Security Review Commission hearing on China's Evolving Counter Intervention Capabilities and Implications for the U.S. and Indo-Pacific Allies and Partners, March 21, 2024.

Fravel, M. Taylor and Evan S. Medeiros, "China's Search for Assured Retaliation: The Evolution of Chinese Nuclear Strategy and Force Structure," *International Security* 35: 2 (2010): 48–87.

Logan, David C. and Phillip C. Saunders, *Discerning the Drivers of China's Nuclear Force Development: Models, Indicators, and Data*, China Strategic Perspectives 18 (2023).

Smith, James M. and Paul J. Bolt, eds., *China's Strategic Arsenal: Worldview, Doctrine, and Systems* (Washington, DC: Georgetown University Press, 2021).

6

Shaping the New Security Environment

The PLA has historically been an insular institution with limited contact with foreign militaries, especially after the Sino–Soviet split in 1960 and during the Cultural Revolution. China's reform and opening created opportunities for contacts with other countries, and the PLA gradually expanded its interactions with its foreign military counterparts. However, the PLA's limited power projection capabilities restricted its ability to exercise with foreign militaries or to undertake overseas deployments or port calls. This situation was aggravated by an organizational culture that emphasized secrecy and the importance of avoiding embarrassment by revealing operational deficiencies in front of foreigners. Most of the PLA's interactions with other militaries prior to 2002 consisted of high-level visits, strategic dialogues, and educational exchanges.

Capability limitations also severely restricted the PLA's ability to project power within the region. The PLA's use of force to defend China's national interests mostly involved ground force operations against neighboring states (intervention in Korea in 1950 and China's invasion of Vietnam in 1979) or limited incursions as part of border disputes (border fighting with India in 1962 and with Vietnam in the 1980s). Its few air and maritime combat operations either took place immediately off China's coast (clashes with Taiwan and the United States over offshore islands in 1954 and 1958) or against weak and distracted opponents (China's seizure of the Paracel Islands in 1974 from South Vietnam).

The force modernization efforts discussed in Chapters 4 and 5 have given the PLA a greater ability to project power and to shape China's external security environment. The PLA supports China's overall foreign policy by engaging with foreign militaries to cultivate friendly relations and promote a positive image of China as a peaceful country that helps address international security challenges. Military diplomacy and cooperation on non-traditional security issues such as counterterrorism and humanitarian challenges are the friendly face of a more powerful Chinese military, but the PLA has also begun to play a more coercive role in the Indo-Pacific region. China's military and paramilitary forces are increasingly using coercive means to defend Chinese interests and to intimidate other countries. These measures include building infrastructure and conducting patrols in disputed areas to strengthen China's hand in territorial disputes with its neighbors. The PLA also regularly intercepts foreign military aircraft and vessels to enforce China's restrictive view of what activities are permitted in its exclusive economic zones, and conducts information operations to gather intelligence and shape foreign perceptions of China. These activities almost always remain below the threshold of lethal force to minimize international reactions and are examples of "gray zone coercion."

This chapter begins with an exploration of the objectives of Chinese military diplomacy, which include the strategic goals of supporting Chinese diplomacy and shaping the external security environment, and the tactical goals of collecting intelligence and improving PLA capabilities. It reviews the patterns of Chinese military diplomacy since 2002, with a focus on the types of activities the PLA conducts with foreign militaries and who its key partners are. It then focuses on Sino–Russian military relations, including a review of their combined exercises and their recent practice of conducting joint air and naval patrols in the region. The last section explores the PLA's coercive role, examining intimidation actions such as construction in disputed areas, sovereignty enforcement, dangerous intercepts of aircraft and ships in China's exclusive economic zones, and PLA information operations. The chapter concludes by noting the tension between PLA efforts to use military diplomacy to reassure foreign countries of its peaceful intentions and the negative impact of PLA efforts to coerce and intimidate its neighbors.

Military Diplomacy

PLA writings describe military diplomacy as a component of China's broader diplomatic efforts and stress that defense relations "must always take the overall diplomatic goals of the country as its goal and always grasp the right direction."[1] Most of the PLA's military diplomacy is focused on advancing Chinese strategic interests and managing key relationships. Chinese foreign policy emphasizes managing strategic relations with great powers such as the United States and Russia and engaging countries on China's periphery; these are the PLA's most frequent partners. China has become the world's largest importer of crude oil, with 56 percent of its 2022 imports coming from the Middle East and eleven percent coming from Africa.[2] PLA efforts to engage militaries in the Middle East and Africa, the PLA Navy's anti-piracy patrols in the Gulf of Aden, and the PLA ground force's participation in United Nations peacekeeping operations help develop China's strategic ties in these critical regions.[3] In addition, PLA interactions with militaries from Europe, Africa, Central Asia, and South Asia support Xi Jinping's signature foreign policy initiative – the Belt and Road Initiative (BRI).

Chinese military diplomacy reinforces broader PRC foreign policy initiatives such as the "community with a shared future for mankind" and the Global Security Initiative. These initiatives build upon previous foreign policy concepts such as the five principles of peaceful coexistence and the new security concept, all of which sought to advance China's preferred principles for international relations and project a positive image of China as a peaceful country. The Global Security Initiative repeats the PRC's longstanding emphasis on respect for sovereignty and territorial integrity for all countries and incorporates Xi Jinping's 2014 call for a new vision of "common, comprehensive, cooperative, and sustainable security."[4] A number of Western analysts view these initiatives as articulating a Chinese vision for a post-U.S. global order,[5] but these proposals are better understood as propaganda intended to shape foreign perceptions of China. As discussed later in this chapter, China's coercive behavior and lack of respect for the sovereignty and territorial integrity of other countries have been undermining the credibility and appeal of these foreign policy initiatives.

Chinese military diplomacy objectives can be divided into strategic and operational categories. Strategic objectives include *supporting overall PRC diplomacy* by engaging key countries and providing public goods and *shaping the security environment* by displaying or deploying PLA capabilities. Operational goals include *collecting intelligence* on foreign militaries and potential operating areas and *improving PLA capabilities* by learning from advanced militaries and militaries with more combat experience than the PLA.

The PLA conducts a range of military diplomacy activities to pursue these objectives. PLA leaders engage foreign militaries by conducting *senior-level visits* with their counterparts and by participating in *multilateral security dialogues* such as the Shangri-la Dialogue and the ASEAN Regional Forum Defense Ministers' Meeting Plus. The PLA also has regular *bilateral dialogues* with a number of European and regional militaries. These responsibilities fall primarily on the defense minister, the Deputy Chief of the Joint Staff Department with the intelligence and foreign affairs portfolio, and the director and deputy director of the Central Military Commission (CMC) Office of International Military Cooperation. CMC vice chairmen and service chiefs will sometimes meet with foreign counterparts and attend international meetings, but the PLA generally tries to limit foreign military interactions with its operational commanders.

Another type of military–military interaction involves combined exercises with foreign militaries. The PLA conducted its first *bilateral exercise* with a foreign military in 2002 and its first *multilateral exercise* in 2003.[6] In the years prior to the Covid pandemic, the PLA was conducting 40–50 exercises a year with foreign militaries, some sponsored by regional organizations such as the Shanghai Cooperation Organization (SCO), the Association of Southeast Asian Nations (ASEAN), and the African Union. Most PLA exercises focus on non-traditional security issues such as humanitarian assistance and disaster relief (HA/DR) with limited military content.[7]

The PLA Navy conducts and hosts *port calls* to demonstrate its presence overseas and to engage foreign navies. These typically include a welcome ceremony, a banquet with local officials and military officers, and sometimes a low-level naval exercise. Prior to the opening of the PLA naval base in Djibouti in August 2017, PLA Navy anti-piracy escort task forces would regularly conduct port calls to replenish their food and fuel stocks while conducting anti-piracy patrols. The escort task forces also usually conduct multiple friendly port calls on their way back to China after their deployment. This practice not only allows the task force to engage foreign militaries, but also lets China showcase the contributions its anti-piracy patrols make to regional security.

The PLA also conducts *functional and educational exchanges* with foreign counterparts. These exchanges sometimes have substantive military content, but are often focused on relatively innocuous non-traditional security issues. The PLA sends students to study at foreign military institutions; China's National Defense University and other PLA educational institutions also conduct classes for foreign military personnel, offering training in English, Spanish, French, and Russian.

PLA participation in *non-traditional security operations* such as HA/DR operations, United Nations peacekeeping missions, and counter-piracy patrols in the Gulf of Aden also falls under the PLA's expansive definition of military diplomacy. These activities showcase improving PLA capabilities and allow China to argue that a stronger military allows it to provide public goods and make greater contributions to maintaining regional security. Table 6.1 shows how these various activities support PLA military diplomacy objectives.

Figure 6.1 shows the number of PLA military diplomatic interactions from 2002 to 2023. The data suggest several conclusions. First, senior-level meetings make up most PLA diplomatic engagements. Beginning in 2009, naval port calls and international military exercises start to compose a growing share of total interactions, but senior-level meetings still represent the bulk of Chinese military-to-military interactions. Second, total interactions peak in 2015, and start to decline over the subsequent years. This can be attributed to the fact that Xi Jinping's military reforms started in late 2015, and the PLA dedicated more time and resources to internal matters than to outside engagements.

Finally, military interactions drop precipitously in 2020–2022 due to restricted travel associated with the Covid pandemic. The PLA conducted just 44 military engagements in 2020, about one quarter of the 2019 total. As China's focus shifted to pandemic containment, PLA operational capabilities were diverted to domestic medical response and construction projects and to providing medical supplies, personal protective equipment, and medical response missions to foreign partners. Strict quarantine regulations imposed as part of China's "zero-Covid" policy inhibited international travel. PLA senior leaders largely stopped traveling and hosting meetings but were able to participate in some multilateral and bilateral meetings virtually through

Table 6.1 Chinese Military Diplomatic Activities and Objectives

Activity	Strategic Goals		Operational Goals	
	Support PRC Diplomacy	Shape Security Environment	Collect Intelligence	Improve PLA Capabilities
Senior-Level Visits				
Hosted	✗	✗	✗	
Abroad	✗	✗	✗	
Dialogues				
Bilateral	✗	✗	✗	
Multilateral	✗	✗	✗	
Military Exercises				
Bilateral	✗	✗	✗	✗
Multilateral	✗	✗	✗	✗
Naval Port Calls	✗	✗	✗	✗
Functional Exchanges	✗		✗	✗
Non-Traditional Security Operations				
HA/DR	✗	✗	✗	✗
Peacekeeping	✗	✗	✗	✗
Counter-piracy	✗	✗	✗	✗

Source: Authors' table adapted from Kenneth Allen, Phillip C. Saunders, and John Chen, *Chinese Military Diplomacy, 2003–2016*, China Strategic Perspectives 11 (2017), 12.

video teleconference or phone conversations. Naval port calls ceased after March 2020 and did not resume until November 2022. PLA exercises with foreign partners declined dramatically, but the PLA continued some recurring exercises with close partners like Russia and Pakistan. PLA military diplomatic activity resumed in 2023 after China abandoned its zero-Covid policies, but still lags below pre-Covid levels.

Figure 6.2 breaks out PLA military diplomatic engagements by geographic region. The data show that Asia is the highest priority region for PLA military diplomacy, with Europe in second place and Africa a distant third.[8]

This pattern matches China's overall diplomatic priorities, which emphasize engagements with major powers, neighboring countries in Asia, and developing countries. The PLA interacts with different foreign militaries in different ways. Patterns in these interactions suggest differing levels of cooperation, trust, expediency, and effort between the PLA and specific foreign

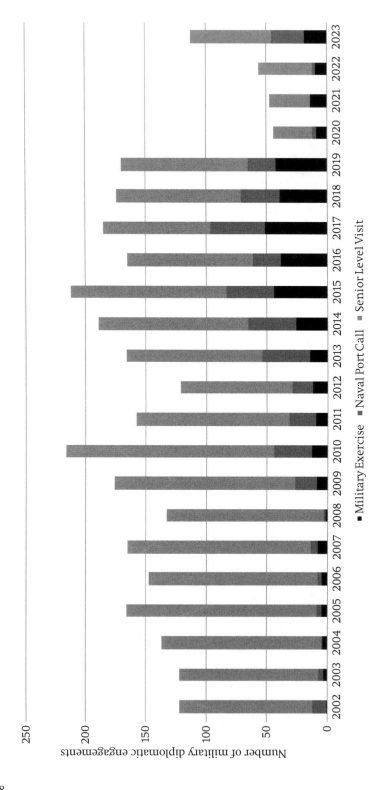

Figure 6.1 Total Military Diplomatic Interactions by Activity, 2002–2023

Source: Authors' figure based on data from National Defense University Chinese Military Diplomacy Database version 5.00.

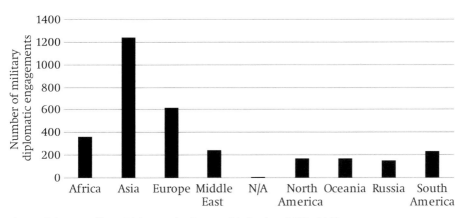

Figure 6.2 PLA Military Diplomacy by Geographic Region, 2002–2023
Source: Authors' figure based on data from National Defense University Chinese Military
Diplomacy Database version 5.00.

military diplomatic partners. The PLA appears to place a strong emphasis on senior-level contacts with countries in Asia and Europe. Within Asia, the PLA prioritizes the sub-regions of Southeast and South Asia. Russia, the United States, and Pakistan are the PLA's most frequent diplomatic partners, with the number of interactions with Russia increasing and interactions with the United States decreasing in recent years.

The data, coupled with PLA participation in an increasing array of multilateral meetings, highlight the growing importance of Southeast Asia as a battleground for U.S.–China strategic competition. Countries in Asia that are caught between the United States and China are increasingly using military diplomacy as a tool. U.S. treaty allies Thailand, South Korea, and Australia, and Southeast Asian countries such as Vietnam and Cambodia, all conduct senior-level military visits to China much more often than they host senior PLA officers, indicating that they are proactive in using military diplomacy to manage their relations with China. These countries have also conducted bilateral military exercises with the PLA.

Figure 6.3 focuses on senior-level visits. A pattern related to China's five-year political cycle can be observed as visits are lower for the party congress years in 2002, 2012 and 2017, with 2007 as an anomaly and 2022 as a Covid-related exception. Years when party congresses are held are characterized by political maneuvering as officials attempt to secure promotions for themselves or their protégés; this raises the opportunity costs of traveling to meet with foreign counterparts. In party congress years, the PLA is less willing to send senior leaders abroad, producing an imbalance between senior-level visits abroad and visits hosted. Unusual continuity in political and military leadership explains the anomaly in the 2007 data. CCP general-secretary Hu Jintao, Premier Wen Jiabao, and the two CMC vice chairmen all remained in their

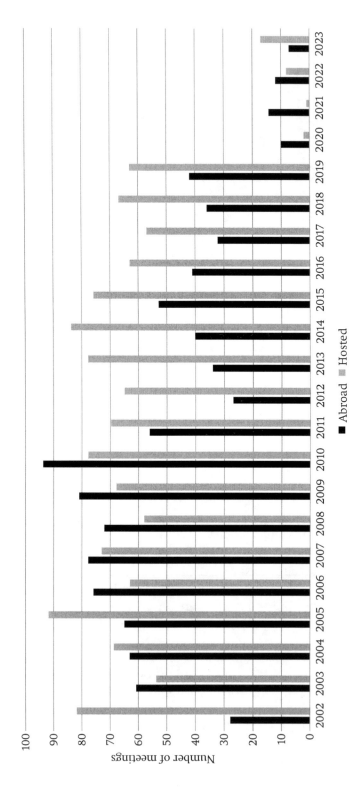

Figure 6.3 Total Number of Senior-Level Meetings, 2002–2023

Source: Authors' figure based on data from National Defense University Chinese Military Diplomacy Database version 5.00.

positions for second terms; PLA senior leaders may therefore have had more freedom to travel.

Figure 6.3 also shows a significant decline in senior visits by top PLA leaders overseas since 2010 due to Chinese austerity and anti-corruption campaigns. These campaigns, which continued and intensified under Xi Jinping, may have served as a disincentive for PLA leaders who did not want to take on the political risks of foreign travel. Prior to 2010, PLA senior-level visits abroad and hosting of foreign counterparts were roughly in balance, in accordance with diplomatic protocol that calls for alternating sending and receiving senior officials. However, as China's influence has grown, many foreign countries have become more willing to disregard protocol and send their senior officials to China without reciprocal visits. This highlights China's increasing strategic weight in the international sphere, and the willingness of other countries to engage on Chinese terms.

Another notable trend is increasing PLA senior-level representation in multilateral meetings (see Figure 6.4). This started with the Shanghai Five and SCO summits in 2000 and 2001, extended to the International Institute for Strategic Studies Shangri-la Dialogue in Singapore in 2007, and now includes regular attendance at multilateral meetings organized by ASEAN, the Western Pacific Naval Symposium, and other international organizations. SCO senior-level engagements include annual meetings of SCO Ministers of Defense and SCO Military Chiefs of Staff meetings. As of 2023, there have been twenty Ministers of Defense meetings and six military chiefs of staff meetings.

Once the PLA gained experience participating in multilateral settings, it began to host its own multilateral meetings, starting with the first China–Latin America Defense Forum in November 2012, extending to the Xiangshan Forum in 2014, and adding a China–Africa Defense and Security Forum in 2018. The regional defense fora allow senior PLA leaders to engage most of their counterparts at a single meeting in Beijing, rather than traveling to the region for individual bilateral meetings.

Naval port calls are another prominent type of PLA military diplomacy. Figure 6.5 shows the PLA's port calls in foreign countries, with the data separating PLAN escort task forces (ETF) conducting anti-piracy patrols in the Gulf of Aden from ports calls by other non-ETF ships (NETF). ETFs usually consist of two warships and a replenishment ship; they conduct replenishment port calls to support their deployment and friendly visits on the way home after a four-month operational deployment.[9] Non-ETF port calls can involve regular PLAN warships, hospital ships, and training vessels.

The 2002 data point is an anomaly, reflecting the Chinese Navy's first around-the-globe voyage, when the *Qingdao* DDG and a *Taicang* supply ship visited ten countries over a four-month deployment. In late 2008, the PLAN started anti-piracy deployments to the Gulf of Aden. These deployments generated new requirements for replenishment port calls and new opportunities

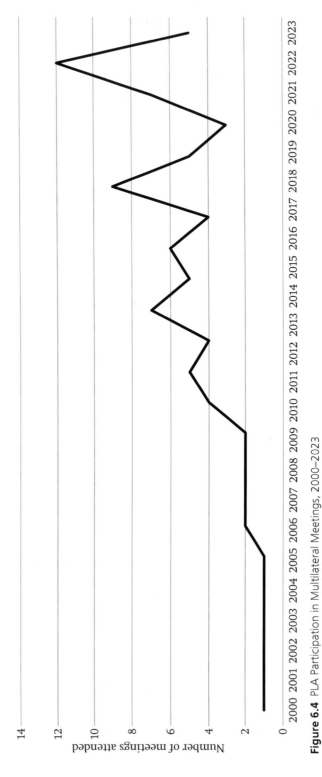

Figure 6.4 PLA Participation in Multilateral Meetings, 2000–2023

Source: Authors' figure based on data from National Defense University Chinese Military Diplomacy Database version 5.00.

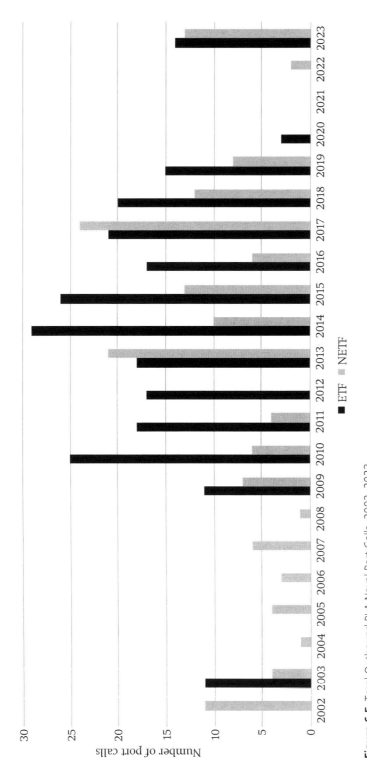

Figure 6.5 Total Outbound PLA Naval Port Calls, 2002–2023

Source: Authors' figure based on data from National Defense University Chinese Military Diplomacy Database version 5.00.

Legend: ETF=Escort Task Force; NETF=Non-Escort Task Force

for friendly port calls in the Indian Ocean region, which eclipsed non-ETF port calls from 2009 to 2012. In 2010, China's hospital ship *Peace Ark* made its first deployment, which started an increase in the number of non-ETF port calls.

The ports most frequently visited by PLAN ETFs are all along the Indian Ocean rim, including in Oman, Sri Lanka, Saudi Arabia, and Djibouti, where China's first overseas base is located. The opening of the Djibouti naval base in August 2017 greatly reduced the need for replenishment port calls elsewhere once the base was fully operational. Most ETF port calls since August 2017 have been friendly visits for diplomatic reasons once the PLA Navy anti-piracy task force has completed the operational portion of its deployment. (PLAN replenishment port calls to the Djibouti base are not shown because they do not involve engagement with foreign militaries and are not reported by the PLA.) The Covid pandemic prevented PLAN port calls other than replenishment port calls in Djibouti until the *Peace Ark* made a port call in Indonesia in November 2022.[10]

Aside from senior-level visits and port calls, a third major category of military diplomacy is combined exercises with foreign partners. The PLA uses these exercises to "learn from the advanced technology, operational methods, and management experience of foreign armies, focusing on the fundamental goal of seeking victory for war."[11] This objective is best achieved by combat and combat support exercises with advanced militaries and with militaries with extensive combat experience. However, the PLA is willing to use a strategy of "pragmatic cooperation" that begins with high-level visits, dialogues, and non-traditional security exercises with the goal of eventually developing military relations to include cooperation on military technology and joint exercises and training more directly related to combat skills.[12]

Figure 6.6 shows total PLA combined exercises by type. Starting in 2009, the PLA increased bilateral exercises with foreign militaries and subsequently increased participation in multilateral exercises beginning in 2014. Several factors explain the change. First, the PLA has grown more confident in the ability of its equipment and personnel to engage in increasingly complex exercises and military competitions with foreign militaries without risk of failure or embarrassment. Second, military exercises provide an opportunity for the PLA to show off its capabilities to the rest of the world and shape the regional security environment. This is particularly true of multilateral exercises, which have larger audiences and are therefore better vehicles for demonstrating PLA capabilities.

The number of PLA bilateral exercises peaked at 42 in 2017, but the increased numbers mask a shift toward smaller-scale exercises as PLA ground-force units were preoccupied by the requirements of the PLA reorganization and the transition into a group army-brigade-battalion structure, as discussed in Chapter 4. PLA exercises with foreign militaries declined significantly in 2020–2022 due to the impact of Covid. The PLA made some effort to develop virtual exercises

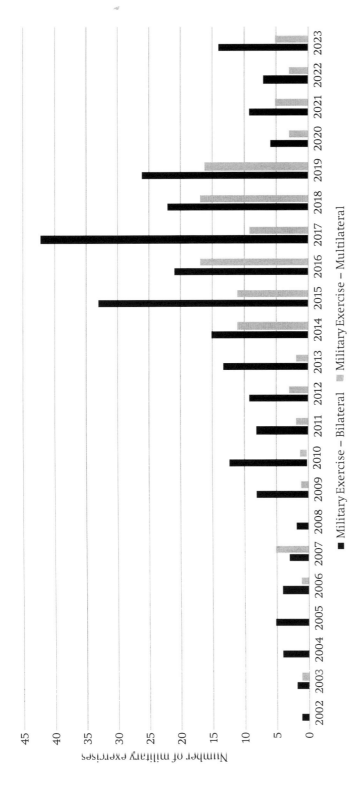

Figure 6.6 Total PLA International Military Exercises by Type, 2002–2023

Source: Authors' figure based on data from National Defense University Chinese Military Diplomacy Database version 5.00.

145

as a substitute, but these are not shown because they do not involve interactions between fielded forces.

Most PLA exercises with foreign militaries focus on "military operations other than war (MOOTW)." MOOTW exercises focus on non-traditional security issues such as anti-terrorism, anti-piracy, HA/DR, non-combatant evacuation operations, and peacekeeping missions, all of which help project an image of the PLA as a reliable partner and a military with global responsibilities.[13] This also reflects the fact that many countries have political concerns about conducting combat-related exercises with the PLA and are more comfortable if the exercises involve less politically sensitive content. More than three quarters of PLA exercises with foreign militaries focus on non-traditional security issues rather than skills directly relevant to combat.

The focus on non-traditional security highlights the role of military exercises in signaling positive political relations between the participants. Countries have become more willing to exercise with the PLA, even if they have territorial disputes or suspicions about China's intentions. Chinese exercises with South China Sea claimants like Vietnam, Malaysia, and Brunei and U.S. allies like the Philippines and South Korea indicate that even countries that have security tensions with China have become willing to exercise with the PLA. About two thirds of the PLA's exercises with other militaries are in Asia or with Russia. The PLA's most frequent partners for combat and combat support exercises are Russia and Pakistan. Both countries have close strategic relations with China and are willing to use combat exercises to demonstrate their military cooperation to third parties.

Another new phenomenon is PLA participation in multilateral exercises sponsored by regional organizations or by individual countries. The PLA began participating in multilateral exercises in 2003, but Figure 6.7 shows that the volume increased significantly beginning in 2014. This included participation in the U.S.-sponsored Rim of the Pacific (RIMPAC) exercises in 2014 and 2016. The military content of PLA participation in RIMPAC was carefully limited, but the invitation served as a signal of the U.S. desire to build trust between China and other countries. Conversely, the U.S. decision to disinvite China from RIMPAC in 2018 due to its "continued militarization" of the South China Sea was a political rebuke.

Another important multilateral exercise series is the SCO's Peace Mission. Beijing views the SCO, founded by China and Russia in 2001, as an important means of projecting Chinese influence into Central Asia without alienating Russia. The SCO organizes a range of multilateral military exercises involving its member states. The biggest is Peace Mission, which has been held almost annually since 2007 and has become geared toward anti-terrorism efforts in recent years. Peace Mission 2021 was a combined military exercise that involved over 4,000 military participants from China, Russia, Kazakhstan, Tajikistan, Kyrgyzstan, India, Pakistan, and Uzbekistan. Although branded as

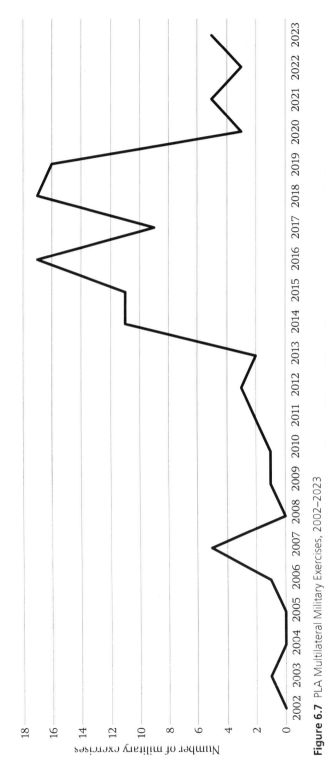

Figure 6.7 PLA Multilateral Military Exercises, 2002–2023

Source: Authors' figure based on data from National Defense University Chinese Military Diplomacy Database version 5.00.

an anti-terrorism drill, it is classified here as a combat exercise due to elements such as forces conducting live-fire drills and using infantry fighting vehicles and assault vehicles against targets. Since 2015, China and Russia have increasingly relied on bilateral military exercises rather than SCO exercises to signal the significance of their military cooperation.

The PLA has also participated in multilateral exercises sponsored by ASEAN, the European Union, the Western Pacific Naval Symposium, and the Indian Ocean Naval Symposium, as well as multilateral exercises sponsored by individual countries including Australia, Indonesia, Thailand, Malaysia, Mongolia, Russia, and the United States. Most focused on MOOTW issues that are relatively innocuous from a military point of view but allow the PLA to posture itself as contributing to global security cooperation. The PLA's increased engagement with Southeast Asian countries in general and with ASEAN in particular starting around 2014 can be seen as an effort to repair bilateral tensions, especially with countries that have territorial and maritime disputes with China. As the PLA gains more experience and becomes more confident in its capabilities, it is likely to seek to participate in more combat-oriented exercises in the future.

Sino–Russian Military Relations[14]

Since the collapse of the Soviet Union, China and Russia have sought individually and together to expand their global influence and challenge U.S. dominance. Figure 6.8 shows that Sino–Russian military cooperation has increased significantly since 2013. Arms sales have always been an important factor in the relationship; in the early 2000s, the PLA was one of the main purchasers of Russian military equipment, and Russian air defense systems, fighters, and air-to-air missiles revolutionized China's capabilities. As China has become more capable of building domestic weapons platforms and less dependent on Russian equipment, Sino–Russian military engagement has turned toward other forms of cooperation.

Since 2015, Sino–Russian military exercises have increased in quantity and complexity, including more combat and combat support elements. 34 percent of the PLA's combat and combat-support exercises have been with the Russian military, the most of any partner. Almost half of China–Russia military interactions have occurred since 2015, showing an intensification of military interactions. This reflects Russia's increasing isolation from the West since its seizure of the Crimean Peninsula in 2014, which makes China a relatively more important partner. The PLA sees Russia as a military with both combat experience and advanced technology and seeks to learn from Russia's experience in conducting joint operations.

The PLA and the Russian military have engaged in a variety of bilateral

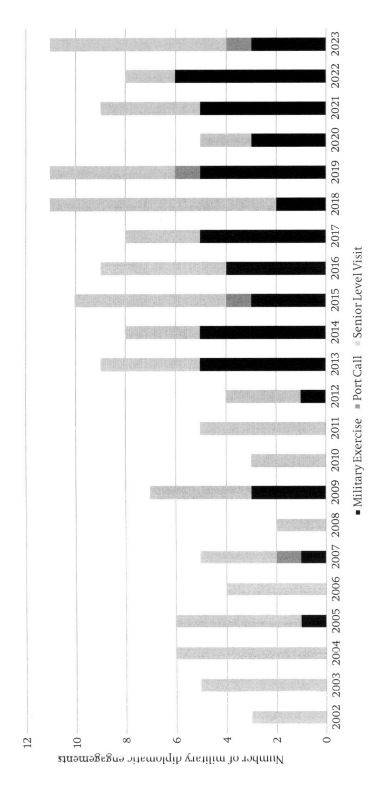

Figure 6.8 PLA Military Diplomacy with Russia, 2002–2023

Source: Authors' figure based on data from National Defense University Chinese Military Diplomacy Database version 5.00.

military exercises since 2003, including the Joint Sea naval exercise series and trilateral exercises with Iran and South Africa. The military significance of these exercises can be analyzed in terms of training, learning, and strengthening interoperability (the ability of the militaries to work together). They also have political significance in signaling to third countries that the militaries can work together in strategically significant ways. Sino–Russian exercises have increased in military sophistication since 2015 and are often conducted in ways that send stronger political signals, including by exercise location, the involvement of advanced weapons systems, and press coverage in English.

The exercises with the most military significance have been the major field exercises that have taken place in Russia. These include Vostok 2018, Center 2019, Interaction 2021, and Vostok 2022. In the Vostok 2018 theater-wide exercise, the PLA deployed a brigade-sized force of 3,000 troops and senior leaders to Russia, including some of the PLA's most advanced weapon systems. The exercise included live-fire elements, an opposition force, and PLA and Russian troops working together in mixed groups. It also featured four levels of combined command and control from the theater level down to the battalion level. Vostok 2018 is arguably the most militarily significant China–Russia exercise to date, but it lacks elements of interoperability and integrated command and control found in major U.S.–South Korea and NATO exercises such as Foal Eagle 2016 and Trident Juncture 2018.

China and Russia have become more willing to hold military exercises in sensitive areas to signal their strategic cooperation to third countries. For example, the Joint Sea naval exercises, which began in 2012, have been held in increasingly sensitive waters in recent years, including the Mediterranean Sea, the Baltic Sea, the East China Sea, and the Yellow Sea. China and Russia began conducting joint bomber patrols in Northeast Asia in 2019 and joint naval patrols beginning in 2020. Although the military training value of these patrols is limited, they send an important political signal to the United States and its allies in Northeast Asia.

Sino–Russian military exercises and patrols have continued after Russia's invasion of Ukraine in February 2022, although the demands of the conflict have limited Russia's ability to organize and participate in large-scale ground exercises. China has been reluctant to sell arms to Moscow due to fear of sanctions from the United States and the European Union, but exercises and patrols were a means by which Beijing could show solidarity with Russia at an acceptable political cost. (According to an unclassified U.S. intelligence report, Chinese companies have also supplied Russia with military spare parts and dual-use equipment that can be used to produce weapons.)[15]

Increasing Sino–Russian military cooperation does not mean the two countries are allies or are building mutual trust, but rather that they have a common adversary in the United States and are cooperating in areas of common interest. In the end, China and Russia recognize each other as neighbors and important strategic partners and choose to engage each other militarily to expand their individual and collective geopolitical influence. Trends in Sino–Russian military engagements indicate a deepening relationship and suggest increased cooperation in the future, especially on efforts to limit U.S. freedom of action and influence. At the same time, mutual suspicions exist, and the military content of their exercises falls well short of U.S. exercises with its allies.

Coercive Tactics

In the PLA's dual-track approach to shaping the regional security environment, military diplomacy sits uncomfortably alongside intimidation tactics. Foreign observers often discuss the latter under the heading of "gray zone coercion," though some also reference "hybrid warfare." Frank Hoffman provides a useful definition of "hybrid warfare": "those covert or illegal activities of non-traditional statecraft that are below the threshold of armed organized violence; including disruption of order, political subversion of government or non-governmental organizations, psychological operations, abuse of legal processes, and financial corruption as part of an integrated design to achieve strategic advantage."[16] For China, military intimidation is only one feature of this approach; others include disinformation campaigns, bribing foreign officials, retaliating against foreign firms or individuals when their governments engage in political disputes with Beijing, or carrying out "lawfare," such as rejecting a 2016 UN arbitral court ruling that invalidated China's claims in the South China Sea.

Military intimidation reflects the Chinese Communist Party leadership's attempts to reconcile competing objectives. On one hand, the party hopes to expand China's effective control over disputed territories, such as in the South China Sea, and achieve other strategic goals, such as exerting pressure on Taiwan to accept Beijing's preferences on cross-Strait relations. The party's confidence in its ability to use the PLA, Coast Guard, and maritime militia to pursue these goals reflects stronger capabilities, a more effective organization, and stronger resourcing, as discussed in Chapters 3 and 4. Chinese leaders are thus more confident that the risks of escalation can be managed. On the other hand, the party needs stable relations with neighboring states to advance China's own economic goals; strategically, the party also hopes to drive wedges between the United States and its Indo-Pacific allies and partners, which supports diplomatic outreach in the region. Chinese strategists sometimes frame this delicate balancing act as one between *weiwen* (stability maintenance) and *weiquan* (rights enforcement).

Within these boundaries, China has used military and paramilitary force in several ways consistent with Hoffman's definition (see Table 6.2). The first

Table 6.2 Types of PLA and Paramilitary Intimidation Tactics

	Construction in Disputed Areas	Sovereignty Enforcement	Dangerous Intercepts	Information Operations
Purpose	Establish new facts on the ground, extend the range of PLA operations	Bolster narrative of China's rights to disputed territory; intimidate foreign leaders	Raise costs for U.S, allied operations along China's periphery, deter intervention	Intimidate foreign decision-makers and military personnel
Activities	Land reclamation, infrastructure construction in disputed areas	Routine patrols, assistance to PRC commercial actors, aggressive tactics in disputed areas	Shadowing, warning, harassment of naval and air force assets	Exercises, tests, parades, misinformation
Actors	Army, air force, navy, civilian construction firms	Army, air force, navy, Coast Guard, militia	Air force, navy, Coast Guard, maritime militia	Cyberspace force, political work department
Examples	Doklam (2017), South China Sea land reclamation	East and South China Sea patrols, HY-981 (2014), Taiwan operations (2022–)	EP-3 (2001), *Decatur* (2018), B-52 (2023)	2019 military parade, social media manipulation

category is military infrastructure construction in disputed areas. The purpose is to establish new "facts on the ground," thereby strengthening China's practical ability to control territory and increasing its bargaining leverage. The most prominent example concerns China's land reclamation efforts in the South China Sea, which were initiated following Beijing's declaration of vast but ambiguous claims in a 2009 submission to the United Nations and the Philippines' 2014 lodging of a complaint against China's claims.[17] China subsequently dredged about 3,200 acres of land in the Spratly archipelago, erecting military bases on three reclaimed features: Mischief Reef, Fiery Cross Reef, and Subi Reef. These facilities allow for the more consistent projection of naval and air power into the sea and could facilitate military operations against rival claimants and even the United States if tensions were to boil over.

China has pursued similar tactics in the Himalayas. The PLA has long been increasing its construction of roads, storage facilities, airstrips, and other infrastructure throughout the region to support a larger scale military presence, ultimately giving it stronger leverage in its discussions with India. Tensions have periodically spiked, including in 2017 when Chinese engineers were found to be building a new road through Doklam – a disputed region in the tri-junction region between China, India, and Bhutan. The specific location alarmed New Delhi because of its proximity near the Siliguri corridor, a strategic valley that connects the main part of India with its northeast.[18] Indian troops intervened to block China's road construction, resulting in a military standoff that lasted two months until China agreed to leave the area. The withdrawal, however, did not prevent China from constructing other roads through the Doklam plateau, thereby serving its goal of creating new "facts on the ground."[19]

A second category of military intimidation is conducting air, maritime, and ground patrols in contested or sensitive regions. Such patrols underscore China's legal claims by framing its presence as enforcement of domestic laws while dissuading foreigners from operating in these areas. They also leverage China's status as possessing the region's largest air force, navy, and Coast Guard. One example is the increase in Chinese patrols in the East China Sea near the Senkaku islands, which Beijing refers to as the Diaoyus. The trigger was an escalating dispute between Beijing and Tokyo when the latter sought to purchase three of the islands from a private owner in 2012. This prompted an uptick in Chinese maritime patrols near the islands, which rose and abated in subsequent years depending on the state of Sino–Japanese relations.[20] In 2013, China also declared an air defense identification zone above the East China Sea, justifying a larger presence of air force fighters and underscoring its controversial territorial assertions.

China has also increased its Coast Guard and naval patrols in the South China Sea. The construction of new bases has permitted Chinese forces to stay on patrol for long durations and in locations much farther from mainland China, including the southern reaches of the sea near Indonesia. Those bases have also facilitated a greater presence of PLA fighter aircraft and bombers in the theater, since their runways and hangars are designed to accommodate larger planes. Improvements in China's ability to jointly command and control forces has also led to innovations in its ability to conduct patrols in the South China Sea. On many occasions, for instance, the Southern Theater Command has organized joint patrols involving air force and naval assets, and has also been responsible for leading patrols of naval, Coast Guard, and maritime militia ships.

China's patrols in the South China Sea have also involved support for commercial activities in contested areas or harassment of forces belonging to rival claimants. In 2012, Chinese government vessels arrived to assist fishermen locked in a tense standoff with a Philippine Navy frigate at Scarborough Shoal, a site of fish-abundant waters about 125 miles from Luzon. Despite a U.S.-brokered deal to resolve the crisis through a mutual withdrawal, Chinese ships soon returned and ultimately gained control over the shoal. Some incidents have involved aggressive tactics such as ramming or firing water cannons, with foreign boats occasionally damaged or lost. In 2014, China's navy and maritime law enforcement ships assisted a Chinese oil exploration rig, HY-981, operating in a stretch of the Paracels within Vietnam's exclusive economic zone. Vietnam responded by dispatching patrol vessels, and China sent more ships to protect the rig. During the standoff, a Vietnamese fishing boat was rammed and sunk. Beijing backed off only when deadly anti-China protests erupted in Hanoi and other Vietnamese cities. China has used similar tactics to block Filipino attempts to resupply the BRP *Sierra Madre*, a naval vessel that Manila intentionally grounded in 1999 at Second Thomas Shoal in the Spratlys. Beijing has sought to dissuade the Philippines from maintaining a presence at this outpost, but as in other disputes has not escalated to the level of lethal violence.[21]

Taiwan has been another frequent subject of Chinese air and maritime coercion. As discussed in Chapter 7, China's "gray zone" tactics against Taiwan have been ongoing for three decades (or longer, if one considers the shelling of Taiwan's offshore islands in the 1950s as an early intimidation tactic). Paired with economic and diplomatic coercion, military operations and exercises pressure Taiwan's leaders to avoid declaring independence and signal disapproval of specific policies, including Taipei's warming ties with the United States. Following then-Speaker of the House Nancy Pelosi's visit to Taiwan in August 2022, the PLA significantly increased air force incursions into Taiwan's southwestern air defense identification zone and across the midline of the Taiwan Strait – long considered an informal boundary between the two sides – while naval vessels encroached on Taiwan's twelve nautical mile territorial sea. These tactics increased Taiwan's sense of vulnerability and countered the notion that Taipei could exercise de facto sovereignty in the air and maritime spaces near its main island.

Patrols to undercut the sovereignty of China's rivals can also be found on land. The buildup of PLA forces on the Tibetan plateau has allowed for larger and more persistent patrols near the Line of Actual Control. The low level of strategic trust between Beijing and New Delhi, proximity and intermingling of forces, and concerns that both sides are seeking to change the status quo through infrastructure development have increased the prospects for conflict.[22] There have been several brawls and standoffs in recent years, and in June 2020 a deadly clash broke out in the Galwan Valley, located in the disputed Aksai Chin region controlled by China, with Chinese and Indian troops beating each other with rocks and clubs. The incident marks a rare exception to China's avoidance of lethal violence, leading some analysts to conclude that the escalation was not centrally directed.[23] It was notable that in the aftermath both sides tried to cool tensions and talks between military commanders resumed.

Third is the harassment of U.S. and allied forces in international airspace and waters close to China. Beijing has long contended that the United States is using military operations near China's borders to further its containment strategy. Legally, it also claims a right to regulate foreign military transits, exercises, and other operations in its exclusive economic zone, although the United States and most other countries reject this claim as inconsistent with international law.[24] Nevertheless, growing PLA power projection capabilities and a more advanced intelligence, surveillance, and reconnaissance network have allowed Beijing to track, shadow, and intercept foreign air and naval operations. Chinese crews are trained to deliver stern warnings, and some have conducted dangerous maneuvers. The most famous example came in April 2001, when a Chinese naval aviator collided with a U.S. EP-3 reconnaissance aircraft above the South China Sea. The Chinese pilot died, and the U.S. crew crash landed on Hainan Island, where they were held for ten days and released only when the George W. Bush administration issued a letter of "regret and sorrow."

Similar incidents took place in the following years, though none has involved loss of life. In 2018, for instance, a Chinese destroyer approached within 45 yards of the bow of the U.S. destroyer *Decatur* in the South China Sea, forcing the U.S. ship to conduct an emergency maneuver to avoid a collision. In 2023, a Chinese J-11 pilot came within ten feet of a U.S. B-52 bomber flying above the South China Sea at nighttime. Other incidents involved U.S. allies, such as Australia, Canada, and the United Kingdom. Based on rising concerns, in 2023 the U.S. Defense Department declassified images and videos of fifteen cases of what it called "coercive and risky operational behavior" by the PLA over the previous two years. These included "reckless maneuvers, close approaches at high speeds in the air, releasing objects and projectiles like flares, and other dangerous behavior."[25] Many observers worried that it was just a matter of time until a repeat of the deadly April 2001 collision occurred.

In both sovereignty enforcement and intercepts, Beijing has managed the risks that incidents could escalate into "armed organized violence," per Hoffman's definition, and thus threaten its interests in stability. At times, as in the Doklam and Vietnam oil rig cases, China backed off before tensions could boil over and create more severe political consequences. China has also often relied on assets that lack heavy weapons, such as Coast Guard and maritime militia ships, and in the Himalayas, Chinese and Indian troops have resorted to primitive weapons such as knives and clubs due to an agreement that patrols not carry firearms. Chinese air and naval crews appear to be increasingly well trained, reducing the chances of an accident, although some incidents, such as the 2023 B-52 case, suggest poor skills or daring risk-taking from some individual operators. Beijing has also pursued confidence building and crisis communications mechanisms with the United States, Japan, South Korea, Singapore, and other states to prevent or manage accidents, and holds dialogues to better understand its opponents' bottom lines.

A final category of coercive activity concerns information operations. Shaping foreign perceptions is an objective of all areas of "gray zone" coercion: military construction, patrols, and intercepts all influence foreign decision-making by signaling the costs and risks of continuing down a certain path. What makes information operations unique is the intentional manipulation of information to alter the ways in which foreign audiences perceive China's intentions and capabilities. The selective release or publication of facts about the PLA, the blending of real and false information, or outright disinformation all fall in this category. While other types of intimidation are mainly conducted by the services and paramilitary forces, information operations are the remit of certain institutions designed for this purpose, including the Cyberspace Force (which conducts cyber and psychological warfare) and the Political Work Department, which handles foreign propaganda.

Military parades are a classic example. Typically, the PLA stages a major parade in Beijing on key anniversaries of the founding of the country (every ten years since 1959). The parades involve thousands of troops, hundreds of pieces of equipment, and the participation of foreign dignitaries, as well as the country's top leader. One purpose is to burnish the party's image among a nationalist domestic audience. However, the parades can also be described as an information campaign orchestrated to shape foreign views about PLA capabilities. In the 2019 parade, the PLA intentionally revealed several new systems, including the DF-41 intercontinental ballistic missile, JL-2 submarine-launched ballistic missile, DF-17 medium-range ballistic missile fitted with a hypersonic glide vehicle (designed to evade enemy missile defenses), and new uncrewed aerial and underwater vehicles. State television commentaries noted that these systems offered powerful new ways to resist enemy intervention.

Other information operations involve a mix of truth and fiction or total fabrications. In the aftermath of then-Speaker of the House Nancy Pelosi's August 2022 visit to Taiwan, images of PLAN vessels operating in close range of Taiwan appeared on social media. While the navy was indeed conducting exercises, the images (known as deepfakes) were created to suggest that the units were far closer to Taiwan than they actually were.[26] This was likely intended to accentuate fears in Taiwan about the PLA's ability to operate with impunity near their territory. Similarly, images of PLA air force jets flying in visual range of Taiwan's highest point, Jade Mountain, have circulated on social media, which Taiwan authorities have dismissed as disinformation.[27] During the 2020 Covid pandemic, Chinese officials claimed that not a single PLA soldier had been affected, a dubious assertion that foreign analysts dismissed as an attempt to dissuade foreign leaders that the time was right to press their own agendas in disputes with China.[28]

Conclusion

China's efforts to maintain stability (*weiwen*) by cultivating good relations with major powers and neighboring countries are in tension with Beijing's desire to protect national interests (*weiquan*) and strengthen its claims to disputed land borders and maritime territory. PLA military diplomacy attempts to use positive interactions to support China's foreign policy goal of maintaining a stable regional environment for economic development, and to drive wedges between the United States and its supporters in the region by increasing China's own attractiveness as a security partner. PLA efforts to provide public goods by participating in United Nations peacekeeping operations, conducting anti-piracy patrols, and participating in HA/DR operations are intended to support China's desired image as a powerful but peaceful country and the CCP narrative that China's "peaceful development" is an opportunity and not a threat for other countries.

Nevertheless, this benign message is undercut by PLA coercive activities that attempt to intimidate neighbors and coerce them into making concessions in their territorial disputes with China. Xi Jinping himself ordered an increased emphasis on sovereignty protection in a 2013 speech that was widely studied within the party and the military.[29] China has attempted to balance the two goals by restricting military coercion to "gray zone" activities that fall below the threshold of lethal force to minimize international reactions. China has also generally pursued a divide and conquer strategy, singling out only one target at a time for coercive pressure to avoid collective responses.

This approach has faltered as China has widened and stepped up the intensity of its coercive activities after Xi's arrival in 2012 as the party's paramount leader. Since then, China has intensified its territorial disputes with Japan (over the Senkaku Islands), India and Bhutan (over disputed land borders), and several Southeast Asian countries (over territorial disputes in the South China Sea). These disputes fit within a larger pattern of belligerence in China's foreign policy under Xi, as reflected in contentious disputes with Australia over the origins of the Covid pandemic and its interference in Australian elections, as well as in increased pressure on Taiwan after Democratic Progressive Party leader Tsai Ing-wen was elected president in 2016 and 2020, and after her vice president, William Lai, was elected in 2024. China's support for Russia's 2014 invasion of Crimea and increasing use of economic and military coercion has also damaged relations with the United States and the European Union; Beijing's refusal to condemn the 2022 Russian invasion of Ukraine further aggravated already strained relations.

These coercive actions have strengthened China's effective control in contested regions, especially in the South China Sea, but have not successfully resolved any of the underlying issues. They have also undermined some of the political gains from military diplomacy and efforts to promote a positive image of China as a peaceful country whose rise is more of an opportunity than a threat.[30] Public opinion toward China, especially in countries involved in territorial disputes with Beijing, has grown more negative due to China's aggressive tactics. To hedge against uncertainty and better defend their own sovereignty, many countries in the Indo-Pacific have sought to improve their diplomatic and security ties with the United States, the European Union, and major Asian powers such as Japan, India, and Australia.[31]

The unintended outcome of these coercive campaigns has been a strengthening of U.S. regional alliances and security partnerships and the invigoration of regional security cooperation mechanisms that do not include China.[32] This is occurring partly through enhanced bilateral diplomacy across the region – in July 2021, for instance, Filipino president Rodrigo Duterte reversed a decision to cancel an agreement for increased U.S. military presence in the Philippines, and his successor, Ferdinand Marcos, Jr., further expanded access for U.S. forces – and partly through multilateral arrangements such as the Quadrilateral Security Dialogue (with the United States, Japan, India, and Australia), the Australia–U.K.–U.S. (AUKUS) security partnership, and U.S.–Japan–South Korea trilateral security cooperation. These mechanisms are not aimed explicitly against China and do not constitute an anti-China military alliance. However, they are a political reaction to increased Chinese coercion and stand as a potential balancing coalition if Chinese pressure increases in the future. Beijing has arguably succeeded in shaping the regional security environment, but not in the manner party leaders intended.

While much of the PLA's day-to-day operations focuses on navigating the balance between military exchanges and coercive diplomacy, it is also preparing itself for the chance that conflicts could escalate beyond the "gray zone." The next chapter evaluates the PLA's preparations for its single most important set of contingencies – major combat operations with Taiwan and the United States.

Further Reading

Allen, Kenneth, Phillip C. Saunders, and John Chen, *Chinese Military Diplomacy, 2003–2016*, China Strategic Perspectives 11 (2017).

Diamond, Larry and Orville Schell, eds., *Chinese Influence and American Interests: Promoting Constructive Vigilance* (Stanford, CA: Hoover Institution, 2018).

Gorenburg, Dmitry, Paul Schwartz, Brian Waidelich, and Elizabeth Wishnick, *Russian-Chinese Military Cooperation: An Increasingly Unequal Partnership* (Arlington, VA: CNA, 2023).

Green, Michael, Kathleen Hicks, Zack Cooper, John Schaus, and Jake Douglas, *Countering Coercion in Maritime Asia* (Washington, DC: CSIS, 2017).

Siebens, James A., ed., *China's Use of Armed Coercion: To Win Without Fighting* (London: Routledge, 2024).

Sutter, Robert, *China–Russia Relations: Strategic Implications and U.S. Policy Options* (Washington, DC: National Bureau of Asian Research, 2018).

Zhang, Ketian, "Cautious Bully: Reputation, Resolve, and Beijing's Use of Coercion in the South China Sea," *International Security* 44: 1 (2019): 117–159.

7

Preparing for War with Taiwan

Russia's 2022 invasion of Ukraine generated countless international headlines asking the same question: could Taiwan be next? The sensationalism surrounding the threat faced by Taiwan in some quarters clouded an undeniable reality – for thirty years, China's military has built up capabilities it would need to deter Taiwan independence and, if ever summoned by the party, to compel unification by using force. Under Xi Jinping, military coercion of Taiwan has reached new levels of intensity, partly in response to perceived negative developments on Taiwan and in U.S. policy toward the island, and partly as a result of stronger military capabilities that make those tactics possible. Xi has also overseen a major reform of the PLA, an increase in its conventional forces, and a nuclear expansion that could be relevant to Beijing's attempts to deter foreign intervention in a conflict.

There is little question that Taiwan confronts a "new normal" in which it will face greater coercive threats from China. This could involve close-range air and maritime maneuvers, Chinese attempts to interfere with shipping, or even more dramatic displays of force, such as a PLA campaign to blockade or seize one of Taiwan's offshore islands. It is less clear that Beijing will initiate a full-scale war. One path to such a decision would be political necessity. This is likeliest if Taiwan declares formal independence but is also possible if Beijing concludes that Taiwan, inspired by more active support from Washington, has moved irrevocably toward permanent separation from the mainland. Another path involves the calculated decision that the rewards of unification outweigh the costs and risks of conflict. This is less likely because of the high military, diplomatic, and economic price that Beijing would pay. Xi or a future leader would be putting their legacy and even their political survival on the line for a prize that does not need to be won today. Nevertheless, a war of choice could become more likely as the PLA develops more capable forces, as China takes steps to reduce its exposure to sanctions (based on lessons it is deriving from recent Russian experience), and if Taiwan's defense fails to keep pace.

This chapter begins with a discussion of how China has applied military pressure short of war against Taiwan, and how those "gray zone" tactics could evolve in the coming years. It then outlines the alternative paths to a war, highlighting the major challenges Beijing faces in a deliberate decision to use force. The following three sections focus on the military dimensions of a future conflict. The first introduces the three major campaigns the PLA has been developing since the 1990s – a Joint Firestrike Campaign, Joint Blockade Campaign, and Joint Island Landing Campaign. This section focuses on the impediments to mounting an invasion and how the PLA is working to overcome them. The next section explains that countering foreign intervention is a key task in any combat scenario and describes several ways China could attempt to achieve this goal. This is followed by an exploration of the lessons that China has been considering from Russia's invasion of Ukraine. Those include insights into the character of modern conflict and broader lessons on the potential strategic consequences of going to war and how to reduce those risks.

The final section evaluates Taiwan's defense. There has been movement in recent years to reorient the island's defense posture toward the same asymmetric methods that have allowed Ukraine to oppose Russia's invasion. This involves procurement of large volumes of anti-ship and anti-air weapons while reorganizing the military to be able to fight a successful defensive campaign. Yet Taiwan has had to balance this approach with the need to respond to Chinese coercion in peacetime, which requires conventional naval and air forces. Limited resources and bureaucratic challenges also complicate Taiwan's ability to accelerate its war preparations. Meanwhile, the United States has put more attention on deterring aggression, considering how to impose penalties so that, as one U.S. official put it, "the Chinese leadership wakes up every single day and says 'today is not the day' to launch an invasion across the Taiwan Strait."[1] Nevertheless, the Pentagon has also refined its operational concepts to fight and win if deterrence fails, just as other countries are beginning to think more about their own roles in such a conflict.

Gray Zone Campaigns

China's military activity around Taiwan has sought to deter formal independence, while registering dissatisfaction with undesired elements of Taiwan and U.S. policy, as noted in Chapter 6. These "gray zone" intimidation tactics have had some success in reducing the appetite of Democratic Progressive Party (DPP) leaders for pursuing formal independence. As new patterns of more intense air and maritime activity take shape, however, the stage has been set for further escalation. No longer content with periodic demonstrations, Beijing could conduct more provocative actions that might pass the threshold into lethal violence. Those steps could include close in military operations, a quasi-blockade, or even the seizure of one of Taiwan's offshore islands. As China ascends the escalatory ladder, it will have to consider whether the benefits of more forcefully registering its concerns outweigh risks that could begin to approximate what it would face in a war.

Use of military power to influence Taipei and Washington has long been part of China's coercive repertoire. During a 1995–1996 Taiwan Strait crisis, the PLA conducted amphibious drills, live fire exercises, and missile tests near major Taiwan ports to signal opposition to the Clinton administration's decision to allow then-Taiwan leader Lee Teng-hui to travel to the United States to deliver an address at Cornell University and to influence Taiwan's first presidential election in March 1996.[2] China also conducted major exercises in the early 2000s to pressure the first DPP president, Chen Shui-bian, who advocated a "two states theory" of cross-strait relations and pushed for UN membership under the controversial name "Taiwan."[3] Throughout this period, the PLA expanded its inventory of short-range ballistic missiles opposite Taiwan, serving as a reminder that steps toward independence could prompt a violent response. These tools augmented other coercive activities such as persuading other countries to sever diplomatic relations with Taiwan and imposing economic restrictions on the import of fruits and other goods from independence leaning parts of Taiwan.

Following a relatively peaceful period under Kuomintang (KMT) president Ma Ying-jeou (2008–2016), tensions increased when another DPP president, Tsai Ing-wen, was elected in 2016. Tsai's offenses, from Beijing's perspective, included failing to support a "one China" vision of cross-strait relations and referring to Taiwan as a "country." China also opposed what it saw as tacit support for Taiwan independence from the Trump and Biden administrations through arms sales and high-level contacts. A full-blown crisis erupted in August 2022, when Tsai met with U.S. Speaker of the House Nancy Pelosi in Taipei. Underscoring a broader range of capabilities and a new command structure able to plan and coordinate operations, Beijing's response was larger and more dramatic in some ways than the 1995–1996 crisis (see Table 7.1 below). Military activities included firing ballistic missiles over the island, conducting live-fire drills in seven zones around Taiwan, and sending an unprecedented number of fighters across the mid-line of the Taiwan Strait (long considered an informal boundary between the two sides) and into Taiwan's southwestern air defense identification zone. Another uptick of tensions occurred in April 2023 when Tsai met with new U.S. Speaker Kevin McCarthy during a transit visit through the United States. As Tsai's administration concluded, and the new era of DPP president William Lai began, the PLA had settled into a new normal of elevated coercion around the island. In a move designed to send a message to Lai prior to his May 2024 inauguration, Chinese Coast Guard ships conducted patrols and boarded a Taiwan-flagged civilian vessel near Kinmen – a Taiwan-held island near the Chinese coast.[4]

Military coercion has had some success in shaping political decisions in Taipei and Washington. Wary about threats of punishment from the mainland, recent DPP leaders have carefully avoided overt steps toward *de jure* independence, such as calling for a public referendum to amend the constitution or

Table 7.1 Comparison of 1995–1996 and 2022 Taiwan Strait Crises

	1995–1996 Taiwan Strait Crisis	2022 Taiwan Strait Crisis
Exercise Zones	PLA exercises in three zones near the Chinese mainland.	PLA exercises in seven zones, which encircled Taiwan.
Exercise Duration	First stage included DF-15 MRBM launches (July 21–24, 1995) and an 11-day naval live-fire exercise (August 1995); second stage included a week-long naval exercise (October 1995) and a three week amphibious exercise (November 1995); third stage include DF-15 launches (March 8–13, 1996) and a week-long joint amphibious exercise (March 18–25, 1996) curtailed by bad weather.	Two weeks in early August 2022.
Exercise Activities	Large-scale live-fire naval and air exercises; major amphibious landing exercise opposite Taiwan. An estimated 40 ships, 260 aircraft, and 150,000 troops participated.	Large-scale live-fire naval and air exercises, including the *Liaoning* aircraft carrier and at least one nuclear-powered attack submarine. PLA sent UAVs over Taiwan's Kinmen Island for the first time.
Missile Launches	Missile "tests" in July 1995 and March 1996, with DF-15 MRBMs launched from Fujian province to areas off the coast of Taiwan. One missile in March 1996 landed less than fifty miles from the southern port city of Keelung.	Live-fire missile and rocket launches into the various exercise zones, including DF-15B ballistic missiles. At least four missiles reportedly flew over Taiwan.
Airspace Incursions	PLA aircraft repeatedly flew close to the Taiwan Strait centerline but did not cross over.	PLA aircraft repeatedly crossed over the Taiwan strait centerline; 446 incursions into Taiwan's air defense identification zone (ADIZ) were reported in August 2022.
Command and Control	PLA established a "Headquarters for Operations Targeting Taiwan" and placed the exercises under the authority of the Nanjing War Zone.	Exercises supervised by the Eastern Theater Command. The PLA deployed military assets from other theater commands to participate.
U.S. Involvement	The U.S. military did not respond to the first two exercise phases, but sent two carrier battle groups, the *Independence* and the *Nimitz*, toward the Taiwan Strait in March 1996.	The U.S. military did not respond.

Sources: Authors' table based on data from Kristen Gunness and Phillip C. Saunders, *Averting Escalation and Avoiding War: Lessons from the 1995–1996 Taiwan Strait Crisis* (Washington, DC: NDU Press, 2022); Robert S. Ross, "The 1995–1996 Taiwan Strait Confrontation: Coercion, Credibility, and the Use of Force," *International Security* 25; 2 (2000): 87–123; "Tracking the Fourth Taiwan Strait Crisis," CSIS China Power Project.

changing the name from the Republic of China to Taiwan. Tsai's nuanced position was that there was no need to declare independence because Taiwan was already a de facto sovereign country (navigating a careful balance between political incentives to highlight Taiwan's separate status without provoking a conflict); Lai adopted a similar stance before and after his 2024 inauguration. Survey data indicate that most Taiwan residents support a continuation of the status quo, with any decisions on unification or independence avoided or shelved until later.[5] Successive U.S. administrations have reaffirmed opposition to Taiwan independence and explained that non-official relations with the island would be guided through the Taiwan Relations Act, which was passed in 1979 after diplomatic relations between the United States and China were established.

Despite Beijing's successes, foreign analysts anticipate an increase in Chinese "gray zone" tactics in the years ahead. There are several reasons. First is that past levels of military coercion were not completely successful in preventing DPP leaders from pursuing a separate Taiwan identity or in dissuading Washington from upgrading its unofficial miliary and political interactions with Taiwan. The second reason is that Beijing has been under increasing domestic pressure to respond forcefully to any undesired political developments on Taiwan. During the August 2022 crisis, for instance, netizens expressed disappointment in the amount of pressure exerted by the PLA.[6] Third, expanding military and paramilitary capabilities, as well as recent organizational reforms, have provided new options for China's leaders to exercise against the island. Of note is the creation of a joint theater command structure, as discussed in Chapter 3, which has increased the PLA's ability to coordinate offshore air, maritime, and missile activities.

There are many ways that the PLA could increase tensions without conducting a full-scale war. The most straightforward option would be to raise the frequency and scale of air and maritime incursions in airspace and waters near Taiwan. Fighters and ships could come closer to Taiwan to pressure its leaders, induce a sense of vulnerability among its people, test or wear down its defenses, and provide real-world experience for PLA crews. PLA units could also maneuver closer to or attempt to intercept U.S. naval ships or military aircraft operating around the Taiwan Strait. These tools would function as a knob that could be turned up or down in response to perceived external provocations. A downside, however, involves the risk of an accident or miscalculation, especially if Chinese assets are shot down, or if a collision occurs. Beijing could be forced into a larger conflict, unless it makes the politically difficult decision to de-escalate. Another risk is that even more aggressive incursions might lose their shock value if they become too routine or anticipated, forcing Beijing back to square one. At a certain point, repeated shows of force become a demonstration that one is not prepared to actually use force.

A different option would be a quasi-blockade of the island. Instead of declaring a formal blockade, which would constitute an act of war under international law, China could experiment with a more tailored campaign of interdicting shipping to and from Taiwan, possibly under a pretense such as a "health and safety inspection." This could weaken Taiwan's access to critical supplies such as oil or natural gas (most of which Taiwan imports via tankers). Such actions could also be combined with cyber operations against Taiwan's ports or other critical infrastructure. The goal would be to influence Taiwan's calculus while avoiding lethal violence, thus reducing the possibility that the international community would orchestrate an effective military response. Nevertheless, this campaign could also expose China to diplomatic pressure and international sanctions if it leads to social and economic upheaval – and it is possible that Taiwan or the U.S. Navy would ultimately act to counter it.

The most dramatic form of coercion short of war would be an assault on one of Taiwan's offshore islands. As a precedent, in 1955 the PLA conducted an amphibious landing on Yijiangshan, an island located twelve kilometers off the Chinese coast, defeating Nationalist forces after a short battle involving several hundred casualties on both sides. Beijing could similarly order troops to assault one of Taiwan's remaining islands such as Kinmen, Matsu, or Pratas. Such operations are feasible given relevant marine and air assault training, limited defenses on these islands, and their proximity to the mainland. This would send a bold signal of China's dissatisfaction, represent a political victory for the party, and offer the PLA some of the combat experience it currently lacks. The risks, however, would be significant. These islands are garrisoned by Taiwan troops, meaning that lethal force would likely be necessary. Some of them also have large civilian populations. Crossing this threshold could spark international condemnation and sanctions, prompt Taiwan to upgrade defenses on the main island, and even result in calls in Taiwan for formal independence. China could thus precipitate exactly the outcome it sought to prevent. The offshore islands also play a symbolic role in linking Taiwan to China; losing them could actually emphasize Taiwan's separation from China.

Strategic Decisions

Unification, rather than simply deterring independence, has always been China's goal for Taiwan. Since the 1980s, the preferred method has been a "one country, two systems" formula, through which Taiwan would retain some degree of political autonomy in exchange for acknowledging Beijing as the legitimate authority over a united China. There was some progress when Chinese Communist Party (CCP) and KMT representatives met in Hong Kong in October 1992 and agreed that there was only "one China," albeit with different interpretations. This became known as the "1992 Consensus."[7]

Beijing was optimistic that further progress could be made with Ma Ying-jeou, whose conciliatory mainland policy resulted in direct transportation, trade, and postal links. Nevertheless, China also faced DPP presidents Chen Shui-bian, Tsai Ing-wen, and William Lai, who did not endorse the "1992 Consensus." Moreover, support for unification, which has never been very strong in Taiwan, dropped to new lows after China curtailed civil liberties in Hong Kong following protests in 2019.

New questions emerged about China's intentions following Tsai's election. At the 20th Party Congress in October 2022, Xi told delegates that the party insisted: "We will continue to strive for peaceful reunification with the greatest sincerity and the utmost effort, but we will never promise to renounce the use of force, and we reserve the option of taking all measures necessary."[8] Such rhetoric was consistent with past admonitions, but was interpreted in a more threatening light, as Beijing railed against what it saw as an alarming DPP-led slide toward formal independence, aided by the United States. Not only did PLA-led intimidation tactics increase, but Xi also reportedly instructed the military to be ready to conduct major combat operations against Taiwan by the centennial anniversary of the PLA's founding in 2027.[9] There was intense international speculation that Xi had perhaps already made up his mind to use force later in the decade, although analysts generally agreed that the 2027 date was intended as a readiness milestone and not as an operational timeline.[10]

Whether the party's leadership chooses to use force to compel unification depends on the circumstances. A *war of necessity* is possible if Taiwan crosses what Beijing defines as its red lines. A formal declaration of independence would probably trigger a conflict, but China has not been explicit about what other actions would constitute unacceptable behavior. China's 2005 Anti-Secession Law states only that force would be used when "Taiwan independence forces ... accomplish the fact of Taiwan's separation from China," "if a major event occurs, which would lead to Taiwan's separation from China," or "if all possibility of peaceful reunification is lost."[11] The statements are purposefully vague, allowing Beijing flexibility but leaving others guessing about the limits of its tolerance. In the absence of clearer signals, observers worry that the accumulation of pro-independence DPP rhetoric, low public support for unification, efforts to reorient Taiwan's economy from the mainland, Taipei's pursuit of autonomy and a separate identity, and more high-profile U.S. military and political support for Taiwan will cross a threshold. The use of force would then be a political necessity, irrespective of the consequences.

By contrast, a *war of choice* would result from a deliberate appraisal that the benefits outweigh the anticipated costs and risks. The benefits of unification are relatively straightforward. A success would count as a legacy-defining achievement for Xi or any other Chinese leader: they would have achieved the final victory in the Chinese Civil War, which eluded Mao himself. There would also likely be a swelling of public support after a successful campaign against Taiwan and possibly the United States. This benefit would be most valuable in times of political crisis if a leader needs a "rally around the flag effect" to preserve the regime. There are also potential economic and military benefits to unification, though these are probably of secondary importance. These include gaining access to any advanced technology that survives the war – Taiwan has the world's largest semiconductor manufacturing industry – and removing a hostile regime on the first island chain, enabling greater access to the Pacific for the PLA.[12]

The downsides, however, have cautioned against a war. Militarily, there is no guarantee of success. Doubts are greatest in an island landing campaign, due to its complexity and scale, while a blockade could falter if Taiwan holds out or the United States intervenes. Even a campaign that achieves its goals could involve prohibitive military costs. Estimates of the PLA's prospects will flow not only from the military balance but also from leadership perceptions. The most reassuring scenario is that Xi or his successors harbor doubts about the PLA's likely performance – there is little direct evidence of how Xi assesses PLA capabilities, but his injunction for them to be ready by 2027 suggests that he was not confident in their ability in the early 2020s. It is also possible that those assessments could change. War would be more likely if Beijing becomes convinced or overconfident in its own military capabilities or, as discussed below, if it believes that the United States and U.S. allies can be deterred from intervening.

Use of force against Taiwan would also incur a heavy diplomatic price. There would be strong condemnation from the United States, its major allies, and Western-led institutions, such as NATO, the European Union, and the G7. Beijing would attempt to blunt the diplomatic costs by framing the dispute as an internal matter rather than as a violation of sovereignty, marshaling support from Russia and supporters in the developing world to echo that position, and preventing criticism from the UN Security Council or regional organizations such as ASEAN. Nevertheless, China would immediately over-turn decades of attempts to project a pacific and responsible image, returning to the pariah status it achieved after the 1989 student crackdown in the eyes of elites and the public in North America, Western Europe, and much of industrialized Asia.

The economic risks would be even more pronounced. Any use of force would entail financial, trade, and other sanctions levied by the United States and its European and Asian allies. U.S. consultancy firm Rhodium Group assessed that the most severe sanctions, targeting the Chinese financial sector, could result in the disruption of up to $3.7 trillion in assets and $3 trillion in cross-border trade, with hundreds of billions more in costs to specific industries and to the personal wealth of Chinese officials.[13] An escalating conflict with the United

States would also likely spark a global downturn, or even a depression, that would undermine China's long-term prospects. The CCP would face a tradeoff between achieving one element of "national rejuvenation" (unification), while jeopardizing the larger goal of building "a modern socialist country that is prosperous, strong, democratic, culturally advanced and harmonious."[14] Risks would remain, but lessen, if Beijing develops a credible counter-sanctions strategy, such as basing a larger share of international financial transactions in renminbi.

The military, diplomatic, and economic risks blend into a final, and most serious, problem – political risk for China's leadership. Victory would yield political benefits for the party and buttress the legacy of the top leader, but failure could open the leadership to challenges. Grievances that have accumulated during the first decade of Xi's leadership due to the anti-corruption campaign, for instance, could translate into a movement to oust him if an invasion fails.[15] At a minimum, his legacy would be tarnished, like Mao's reputation after the disasters of the Great Leap Forward and the Cultural Revolution. A more plausible option could be demonstrating progress toward unification through intimidation tactics, while grounding his legacy on other achievements, including social stability and better governance. Chances of a conflict are greatest if China's leadership faces severe pressures at home, which could result from an economic disaster or political unrest. If they believe they have nothing else to lose, they may gamble on a last-ditch effort to rally the public by escalating tensions with Taiwan.[16]

There has also been speculation in international commentary that Beijing could use force in the near term because the long-term anticipated costs and risks are even greater.[17] This argument assumes that China's leadership believes that slowing economic growth, demographic challenges such as an aging population, and relative advances in U.S. military technology, such as the advent of the next generation B-21 bomber and new hypersonic missiles, will make the use of force in the 2030s or 2040s even riskier than in the late 2020s. Skeptics point out that there is no direct evidence that Chinese leaders believe themselves to be in a closing window of opportunity on Taiwan; indeed, party rhetoric and documents tend to be optimistic about China's long-term prospects, driven by a sense that its market authoritarian model is superior to liberal democracy.[18] Moreover, even if some party officials came to believe that future options could be less attractive than current ones, it is far from certain that this would justify a decision that could involve existential risk for the regime.

Major Combat

While war might not be imminent, the role of the PLA is to provide options to the party that can be exercised either in a war of necessity, or if conditions change so that the benefits are perceived to outweigh the costs and risks. A shift in attention to the Taiwan Strait in the early 1990s preceded a new generation of operational doctrine, finalized in 1999, that conceptualized the missions the PLA would need to be ready to conduct against the island.[19] A theme of the doctrine is that any major combat across the strait would necessarily involve joint warfare. Three campaigns were developed to compel Taiwan to accept China's proposals or to seize and occupy the island.[20] Two of the campaigns – a Joint Firestrike Campaign and a Joint Blockade Campaign – can be carried out independently or as elements of the third and most extensive option, the Joint Island Landing Campaign. The first two options are likely feasible but would not guarantee control of Taiwan; the definitive third option would entail significant military risk.

Bombardments have long been part of China's toolkit. In 1954 and 1958, the PLA conducted artillery shelling on Kinmen and Matsu in response to Taiwan (Nationalist) military constructions on those islands. Periodic bombardments continued as late as 1979, but these evolved into symbolic acts, with shelling occurring only on alternate days to minimize casualties and allow for resupply. Ballistic missiles featured prominently in the 1995–1996 and 2022 crises. The Joint Firestrike Campaign envisions strikes against the main island to degrade its defenses to the point that its leaders would be forced to negotiate or to prepare for an invasion. Key targets would include radars, transportation networks, command and control nodes, airbases, shore and air defense batteries, and logistics sites. Strikes would be carried out by China's large inventory of short-range ballistic missiles, numbering more than 1,000 in 2023; cruise missiles launched from land, air, and sea, and long-range rockets, such as the army's PHL-16, which has a range exceeding 360 kilometers. These strikes may also be accompanied by electronic warfare and cyber-attacks.

A second option is the Joint Blockade Campaign. In PLA writings, this campaign is of greater intensity and scope than a lesser "gray zone" attempt to restrict maritime traffic to the island without triggering a war. It would instead attempt to seal Taiwan from the sea and air, while also cutting its access to information by severing Internet and cell phone connections – sometimes called an "information blockade." This would require missile strikes against port facilities and airports, mining, and cyber warfare. As U.S. analyst Lonnie Henley argues, a blockade could continue indefinitely after a failed invasion, to starve the island into submission.[21] This campaign is also likely within the technical capability of Chinese forces, which would include the air force, navy, and Coast Guard, but its escalatory nature means that China would pay some of the diplomatic and economic costs of a war, without the certainty that its target would concede.

The most ambitious option is a Joint Island Landing Campaign. This would begin with a mobilization phase that would involve calling personnel back from leave, increasing readiness levels, prepositioning critical materiel, posturing intelligence, surveillance, and reconnaissance assets, and moving ships and submarines to defend critical sea lanes. Hostilities would commence with a preparatory phase involving firestrike, and blockade activities carried out as special operations forces land on Taiwan, to clear obstacles and soften up defenses. Marines would land on major offshore islands such as Kinmen and Matsu to eliminate any remaining threats. These activities would hope to achieve what PLA doctrine refers to as the "three dominances" – superiority in the air, sea, and information domains, leveraging China's numerically superior forces across the Taiwan Strait (see Table 7.2 below). It is also likely that missile or special forces would target Taiwan's political leadership, hoping to

Table 7.2 Cross-Strait Military Balance, 2013–2023

Capability	PLA Eastern and Southern Theater 2023 (Total PLA)	PLA Net Increase or (Loss) from 2013	Taiwan 2023	Taiwan Net Increase or (Loss) from 2013
Ground Force Personnel	420,000 (1,050,000 total)	20,000	89,000	(41,000)
Tanks	1100 (4200 total)	(1900)	900	(200)
Artillery Pieces	2300 (7600 total)	(700)	1,300	(300)
Aircraft Carriers	1 (2 total)	1	0	0
Destroyers	30 (42 total)	14	4	0
Cruisers	4 (8 total)	4	0	0
Frigates	30 (47 total)	(14)	22	0
Landing Ships	50 (57 total)	26	14	2
Attack Submarines	31 (47 total)	4	(4)	0
Coastal Patrol Boats (Missile)	60 (60 total)	(7)	43	(2)
Fighter Aircraft	750 (1900 total)	420	300	(88)
Bomber Aircraft	300 (500 total)	140	0	(22)
Transport Aircraft	40 (500 total)	0	50	29

Source: Authors' table adapted from *Military and Security Developments Involving the People's Republic of China* (Washington, DC: Department of Defense, 2013, 2023). 2013 figures include PLA equipment in the "Taiwan Strait area" (land), East and South Sea Fleets (naval), and "within range of Taiwan" (air). The theaters were established in 2016.

reduce the prospects for an organized defense. The next phase would involve the delivery of tens of thousands of troops and their equipment (roughly six brigades) across the 185-kilometer strait to prearranged landing sites, complemented by airborne and air assault forces dropped in the interior that would attempt to seize an airfield to facilitate reinforcements. In the final phases, troops would secure a lodgment and move inland to mop up any resistance.

There are inherent tradeoffs in each of the three campaigns. The Joint Firestrike Campaign would be the most straightforward to execute, given China's large artillery and missile arsenals, but would cross the threshold of lethal violence and expose China to international sanctions and even military risks – Taiwan has its own missiles capable of striking the mainland. This might also trigger mobilization of foreign forces and thus reduce the chance of success for any follow-on operations. A Joint Blockade Campaign might spark economic and social upheaval on Taiwan, but would not necessarily result in Taipei agreeing to negotiations. The use of violence would similarly spark international sanctions, without a guarantee of victory. Taiwan, possibly assisted by foreign naval forces, could choose to run the blockade, which would put Beijing in the position of making a difficult decision to back down or to fire on the escorts, and thus accept the risk that the conflict would escalate to higher levels of violence.

A benefit of the Joint Island Landing Campaign would be decisively solving the problem – the other two campaigns would leave an adversary regime standing in Taiwan that could organize resistance and appeal for international support. Attempting to seize and occupy the island, however, would entail not only economic and diplomatic costs but also clear military risks that render the chances of success questionable at best. The U.S. Department of Defense's 2023 report on Chinese military power calls amphibious invasions "one of the most complicated and difficult military operations," that would "likely strain [China's] armed forces and invite international intervention."[22] The intricate timing and coordination required to execute a landing campaign would pose challenges even for a battle-tested force, not to mention a military with no recent combat experience and little first-hand exposure to modern joint warfare.

Structural and personnel factors exacerbate these problems. Many of the units that would be involved in the war, including the airborne corps, the marine corps, the Cyberspace Force, the Aerospace Force, the Information Support Force, and the Joint Logistic Support Force do not fall under the command of the Eastern Theater Command, which would oversee the campaign, nor do they regularly conduct joint training. They would have to be resubordinated to the Eastern Theater, creating potential delays and frictions.[23] Moreover, most senior PLA commanders lack experience in leading forces from other services. Careers in the PLA tend to be siloed, meaning that rising officers gain significant experience within their own services, but few serve in a joint billet prior to being elevated to the level of a theater commander. It would be a challenge for someone with limited joint experience to have the confidence or skills necessary to make effective and timely decisions for a joint force struggling through the fog of war.

Other aspects of the PLA's organizational culture could create risks in a full-scale assault. Chapter 1 noted that the PLA has retained an identity as a party–army, and that party control has been strengthened through the centralization of authority in the hands of the party general-secretary (currently Xi Jinping) and by Leninist features, such as party committees and political commissars. It is doubtful, however, that tendencies toward centralized and consensus decision-making would be advantageous in wartime. Faced with unforeseen complications – likely in any major use of force – the slower and more laborious processes through which decisions are reached in the PLA could become a hindrance. Chinese doctrine recognizes this dilemma and asserts that in exigent circumstances commanders have greater latitude to make difficult choices and, in exercises, officers are often rewarded for boldness. Yet, in a fundamentally Leninist system, it is hard to conclude that efficiency will trump control.[24]

A more tangible problem concerns the logistics requirements of an island landing. The PLA assesses that huge amounts of munitions, oil, medical supplies, and other materiel would be expended, due to the scale of the campaign and high levels of attrition.[25] Additional capacity might have to be drawn from other parts of the country to address requirements in the main theater, but this would come at the expense of readiness elsewhere, which is problematic because of longstanding Chinese anxieties that other rivals, such as Vietnam or India, could take advantage of a war to press their own territorial claims or settle scores. The PLA also lacks sufficient sealift and airlift to transport the full complement of amphibious and airborne brigades and resupply them. It is attempting to solve these problems by experimenting with civilian ferries to transport and unload troops and by increasing the production of military transport aircraft.[26] Yet those solutions could prove ineffective unless the PLA can achieve air and sea superiority – a circumstance which may occur if Taiwan can mount an effective defense or if a foreign power were to intervene.

Finally, Taiwan's unique characteristics create additional risks for any invading force. As an island, Taiwan is vulnerable to blockade and would not be as easily resupplied in any conflict as Ukraine has been across its land border with Poland during Russia's invasion. Taiwan is also a narrow stretch of territory – ninety miles across at its widest point – and lacks Ukraine's strategic depth. Yet, in a landing scenario, Taiwan's insularity and other features can provide certain advantages. Well-known problems include typhoon seasons that narrow opportunities to move forces across the strait, too short windows in the fall and spring, limited and predictable landing beaches, the lack of transportation infrastructure that would make it difficult to move large contingents of troops and heavy equipment from the beaches to Taipei, and complicated topography that transitions from beaches to mountains. The PLA is familiar with each challenge it would face in an island landing campaign, and has worked to improve its readiness, but using force remains a risky proposition.

Countering Intervention

Adding to the risks the PLA would face is the probability of foreign intervention, which would inform Beijing's calculus on whether to initiate a conflict in the first place. Politically, the U.S. role in a Taiwan conflict has been the subject of much discussion. The U.S.–Taiwan alliance ended in 1979 and was replaced by a more hands-off approach focused on arms sales. A policy of "strategic ambiguity" was designed to inform both China's calculus (making Beijing worry about the possibility of U.S. intervention without offering provocative security guarantees to its main rival) and Taiwan's (keeping leaders uncertain enough about U.S. intentions that they would not lean too far forward on independence and would have incentives to strengthen their indigenous capabilities).[27] In a crisis, the U.S. leadership would be under pressure to make a quick decision, given the problems of mobilizing and moving forces across the Pacific.

While the United States does not have a formal security commitment to Taiwan, PLA doctrinal writings assume as a matter of military planning that the United States – often euphemistically referred to as the "strong adversary" – would become engaged in any conflict.[28] This is problematic because U.S. intervention would aggravate the air and naval threats to Chinese forces in the strait and reduce the chance of a quick victory. It could also galvanize Taiwan defenders to fight with greater conviction than if they believed they had been abandoned. The problems for the PLA would be compounded if Japan or other U.S. allies were to assist, either in terms of direct military action or in other forms of support. Preventing or defeating foreign intervention is thus critical in any of the campaigns described above. Without U.S. support, Taiwan's military might only survive for a few weeks; indeed, without hope that others would intervene, Taipei might capitulate before the landing phase of a war had even begun.[29]

China has four options for avoiding foreign intervention in a Taiwan conflict, but each involves drawbacks or risks. First is targeting the political support of U.S. allies. While some U.S. operations might be conducted from the sea, or from U.S. territories such as Guam or the Northern Marianas, it would be difficult to respond to Chinese aggression at a scale sufficient to affect the outcome without also mobilizing forces based in Japan, Australia, South Korea, or the Philippines. Those forces would also need to be resupplied from frontline countries and may need to secure overflight rights. China could attempt to use a combination of political, economic, and military coercion to convince those states to remain on the sidelines in any conflict. This option could deprive the United States of vital coalition partners and complicate U.S. planning but would not eliminate the possibility that U.S. submarines or bombers flying from distant bases could inflict unacceptable damage on Chinese forces at critical points in the campaign. Moreover, Washington would likely exert maximum pressure to convince close allies to play a tangible role in the war.

A second option would be a *fait accompli*; that is, attempting to storm the island and establish control before outside help can arrive. In the past, such an option was not feasible because of the extensive mobilization timelines involved in an island landing campaign. The United States would likely have sufficient warning to begin its own preparations. Surveillance satellites, signals intelligence, and other high-tech systems could also alert foreign leaders about China's intentions. The modern battlefield, in other words, is more transparent than it was prior to Japan's attack on Pearl Harbor in 1941. Nevertheless, this option could become more attractive if the PLA believes it can create enough doubts about its intentions to complicate foreign decision-making. This could be pursued by holding progressively larger exercises that begin to mimic the scale and requirements of war until they can serve as the cover for an invasion. Still, there would be a risk that the plan would be exposed, just as U.S. intelligence called out Putin's preparations for a full-scale invasion of Ukraine in early 2022.

The third option is preemptively striking U.S. bases and platforms in the Western Pacific. This would be conducted through long-range strike assets, including the DF-21D anti-ship ballistic missile, engineered to target U.S. aircraft carriers, DF-26 intermediate range ballistic missiles (known as the "Guam killer" due to its extended range), and cruise missiles with ranges approaching 2,000 km launched from H-6K bombers or from destroyers and submarines. The PLA has also begun deploying DF-17 medium-range ballistic missiles fitted with hypersonic glide vehicles (which follow a rapid, difficult-to-predict trajectory and can thus penetrate standard missile defenses) and is developing longer-range hypersonic weapons. Saturation missile attacks could be complemented by cyber-attacks on critical U.S. communications and logistics networks and strikes against U.S. satellites, which would weaken the ability to coordinate U.S. forces across the Pacific.[30] This option could be decisive but, if it fails, would likely guarantee U.S. intervention and more active support from Japan or others, assuming the PLA chooses to preemptively attack U.S. forces based on foreign soil. Figure 7.1 below shows the growth of PLARF conventional missiles that would be instrumental in these strikes. At the same time, the services would perform their air and missile defense functions to reduce the risks of U.S. assets successfully targeting China's long-range strike forces.

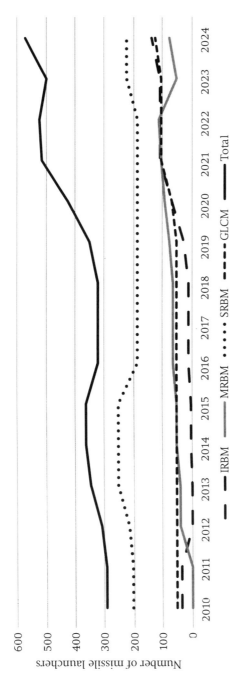

Figure 7.1 PLARF Conventional Ballistic and Cruise Missiles, 2010–2024

Source: Authors' figure based on data from IISS, *Military Balance*, 2010–2024.

The final possibility would be using strategic capabilities to deter Washington. Any war over Taiwan would be conducted under the nuclear shadow. PLA texts such as the 2004 *Science of Second Artillery Campaigns* have argued that China should leverage the threat of nuclear escalation, as well as non-nuclear capabilities, such as cyber-attacks and counter-space weapons, in a way that would have an impact on the lives of ordinary American citizens, to deter U.S. intervention.[31] The logic of "integrated strategic deterrence" is to generate enough risk for U.S. politicians that they would either decide not to intervene or would delay decisions to mobilize U.S. forces and give the PLA an advantage. Such threats might be more credible with the expansion of China's nuclear arsenal and strategic non-nuclear capabilities, as discussed in Chapter 5. Yet those threats might fail. Without preemptive strikes, Washington would have the warning as well as the capabilities it would need to respond.

Lessons from Ukraine

Preparing for combat with Taiwan not only requires the PLA to carefully analyze the military situation across the strait, but also to consider changes in the character of war as reflected in foreign conflicts. Chapter 3 observed that the Gulf War had a strong influence on the development of China's military strategy in the 1990s by demonstrating how a combination of joint operations and long-range precision weapons could promote a quick victory over an otherwise conventionally strong opponent. Russia's February 2022 invasion of Ukraine, however, suggested that the opposite might also be true: a smaller but tenacious opponent could frustrate the plans of a great power trying to execute a *Blitzkrieg*-style assault. The war also witnessed a surprisingly well-orchestrated coalition led by the United States and its European allies that was able to impose severe costs on the Russian economy. Such lessons could encourage Beijing to prepare differently for a conflict that might, at the outset, start to go awry.

At the tactical level, Chinese observers were surprised by the difficulties experienced by Russian forces long considered to rank among the world's finest. The initial phases of the campaign demonstrated several unsettling realities: strategic surprise would be difficult (Western intelligence anticipated Russia's intentions and broadcast them to the world to deprive Moscow of the element of surprise), decapitation strikes against a nimble enemy leadership and key military targets might fail to achieve their objectives, there could be a breakdown in coordination between the different services and branches (for instance, Russian paratroopers failed to coordinate with others in their assaults on Ukrainian airbases), logistics forces might fail to keep up with vanguard units, and unanticipated complications – such as communications vulnerabilities that allowed Ukraine to find and eliminate senior Russian commanders – could reduce the aggressor's morale and cohesiveness. That these challenges afflicted a military with extensive combat experience was of particular concern for a military that had none.

Chinese analysts also paid attention to the novel ways in which Ukrainian defenders kept the Russian side off balance. Much of the focus was on Ukraine's successful targeting of high-value Russian platforms by low-cost but highly lethal defensive weapons, such as Javelin anti-tank missiles, Stinger shoulder-launched anti-air missiles, and Switchblade loitering munitions (sometimes referred to as "kamikaze drones"). Such systems were particularly effective against light Russian ground force columns that lacked protection against concealed enemy missile forces. At sea, Ukraine's success in using anti-ship cruise missiles to sink the Russian Black Sea Fleet flagship *Moskva* in April 2022 was the subject of intense interest in China, given the PLA's obvious reliance on ships in a Taiwan scenario. One expert at China's Academy of Military Sciences remarked that the effectiveness of cheap defensive weapons on the Ukrainian battlefield "has been astonishing, leaving a deep impression on observers."[32]

The proliferation of commercial off-the shelf technology also had troublesome implications for the PLA. Smartphones, drones, and open-source imagery available to anyone with an Internet connection facilitated communications and helped locate Russian targets. There was high Chinese interest in Ukraine's use of the Internet services provided by the Starlink low Earth orbit satellite constellations, supplied by U.S. firm SpaceX and its founder, Elon Musk.[33] Chinese analysts were not only concerned that Taiwan could use similar technologies to oppose an information blackout at the start of the war, but also that the U.S. military could leverage such tools to coordinate its movements across the Pacific. This could complicate PLA efforts to counter U.S. intervention through attacks against critical command, control, and communications systems. In short, Ukraine's successes signaled that the approaches to warfighting pursued by China since the 1990s would be problematic.

Such developments might have reduced Chinese confidence in its own capabilities in the aftermath of the invasion but, over the longer term, the PLA could find ways to adapt. Acknowledging the risks in executing a large campaign against a committed opponent using new systems and operational concepts could lead the PLA to conduct more intricate joint exercises; re-evaluate its organizations (especially army units modeled on the same Russian structure that proved ineffective in Ukraine); increase the value of regular PLA air and naval operations around Taiwan to probe defenses and provide experience for Chinese crews; and instigate efforts to defeat novel systems such as Starlink.[34] China's planners might also devote more attention to contemplating what would happen in a protracted conflict – how many munitions would need to be stockpiled? What preparations should be made if the conflict were to move from the beaches to the cities and mountains? Answering such questions could ultimately put the PLA in a stronger position than if the Ukraine war had never happened.

While Russia's performance might have been generally disillusioning, its success in dissuading an active "boots on the ground" role for the United States and NATO was more inspiring for Beijing. Chinese analysts looked favorably on Russia's use of nuclear threats, including Vladimir Putin's thinly veiled threats to use strategic weapons, allusions to the use of tactical nuclear weapons, strategic bomber exercises, and other signals designed to intimidate Western political leaders. This lesson could increase the attractiveness of leveraging strategic capabilities as an option for avoiding U.S. intervention, especially if Beijing discounts the dissimilarities between the two cases – in particular, that Washington would likely perceive greater national interests at risk in any Chinese aggression toward Taiwan.[35] In addition, because of Taiwan's vulnerability to a blockade, the United States would likely not have available the lesser option of resupplying the island, as it has done with Ukraine.

At the strategic level, the Ukraine conflict provided clues on how the United States would organize a coalition to punish great power aggression. Chinese observers were impressed by the degree to which Washington was able to enlist its European allies in imposing financial and economic sanctions on Russia, including banning Russia from the SWIFT financial transaction processing system and convincing others to agree to sanctions on Russian oil, natural gas, and coal, despite widespread European dependencies on these supplies. The Asian context is, of course, different: most Asian countries are dependent on China as an all-around trade and investment partner, and some might be more reluctant than their European counterparts to agree to heavy and long-lasting sanctions over Taiwan. Nevertheless, Beijing likely had to update its estimates about the economic consequences of a war if Western European and some major Asian players such as Japan were to adopt strong measures.[36]

The worrisome implication is that U.S. alliance solidarity could prompt Beijing to take steps to inoculate itself from punishment. These might include accelerating efforts to promote international transactions in renminbi, finding alternatives to SWIFT, stockpiling critical raw materials that might no longer be available from U.S. coalition partners (such as minerals sourced to Australia), pursuing self-sufficiency in military and high-tech supply chains wherever possible, preventing high-ranking party members from offshoring wealth or establishing extensive foreign ties, and diversifying trade to countries less likely to subscribe to U.S.-led sanctions. A key factor in China's calculus about whether to initiate a war is the degree to which it can avoid similar damage to its national power that Russia has sustained since 2022. To be sure, there are scenarios in which China might not be deterred – such as a declaration of Taiwan independence – but a war of choice would be far less attractive if Beijing remains convinced that it would have to sacrifice its economic prosperity in the process.

Taiwan's Defense

China's increasing military challenge and concerns about its intentions have led to changes in Taiwan's defense posture and in U.S. military preparations for a Taiwan contingency. Rising threats from the mainland, coupled with Taiwan's limited resources, prompted U.S. officials in the 2000s to argue that Taipei should reorient its posture from conventional warfighting – maintaining a large standing army, supplemented by a modern air force and navy – to a more "innovative and asymmetric" approach. This would require Taipei to spend more on survivable defensive weapons, such as mobile coastal defense cruise missiles, man-portable air defense systems, sea mines, and uncrewed aerial vehicles, supplemented by mobilization, organization, doctrinal, and training changes. These ideas found some support in Taiwan's defense establishment, notably advocated by former Chief of the General Staff Lee Hsi-min, who in 2017 proposed an "overall defense concept" that would shift Taiwan's defenses in these directions.[37]

Taiwan has indeed made some steps in line with a more asymmetric posture. Its weapons purchases from the United States in recent years have included Harpoon coastal defense missiles, MQ-9 drones, high-mobility artillery rocket systems (HIMARS), Stingers, portable communications systems, and Volcano mine delivery systems – some of the same kinds of relatively low-cost but highly effective equipment that proved useful for Ukraine. Taiwan's defense industry has also produced asymmetric systems such as the *Hsiung Feng* 2 and 3 antiship missiles and new sea mines. Under Tsai Ing-wen, Taiwan also made other reforms to improve its readiness for an invasion, such as creating a new agency to handle mobilization of reserve personnel, increasing the conscription period from four months to one year, and pledging to increase the defense budget from about two to three percent of GDP. There have also been relevant training changes: the 2023 annual *Hankuang* exercise, for instance, featured an unprecedented drill to protect Taoyuan international airport near Taipei from a Chinese airborne assault.[38]

However, several constraints have limited Taiwan's ability to focus on resisting an invasion. Operationally, the most important consideration is that the military must still be able to respond to PLA intimidation tactics in peacetime. The air force requires fighters that can intercept PLA jets near its airspace and the navy and Coast Guard must be able to patrol around the coast. While these systems are less useful in a high-end combat scenario – they would likely be destroyed in the opening salvos – their peacetime operations require significant financial outlays to recruit and train crews, maintain older systems, and purchase new ones. Among the most expensive U.S. arms sales to Taiwan in recent years, for instance, was the 2019 sale of 66 F-16V fighters. These systems would also be critical in responding to higher levels of coercion such as a Chinese quasi-blockade that would require Taiwan to escort commercial ships. Expenses in these areas are likely only to grow as the intensity of Chinese coercion increases.

Taiwan's defense preparations are also complicated by other realities. Demographically, Taiwan's population has peaked at less than 25 million people and is beginning to decline as the tolls of one of the world's lowest birthrates accumulate. This has already made it difficult to fill the annual recruitment quotas, a problem compounded by lackluster enthusiasm for military service among Taiwan's younger generations. Financially, Taiwan deserves credit for increasing its defense spending, but allocating even three percent of GDP is still poorly aligned with the external threats it faces – Israel, by contrast, spends more than five percent. Bureaucratically, the services have not embraced a shift to an asymmetric approach, preferring continued purchases of high-value systems such as main battle tanks, fighters, and destroyers. There is no credible joint command structure and, even if there were, some analysts worry that an organizational culture that prizes deference to high-level authority would contribute to paralysis if frontline units were cut off from their headquarters in a conflict.

Taiwan can influence China's calculus through necessary acquisitions and defense reforms, but the equation will also depend on third parties. The focus of most U.S. discussions in recent years has been on how to deter Chinese aggression. One school of thought focuses on deterrence by punishment – the idea that the massive economic, military, and diplomatic costs would be sufficient to steer Beijing away from a war of choice. This puts a premium on whole-of-government and international coordination to increase the anticipated costs.[39] Another school argues that deterrence by punishment would fail due to the high rewards of unification and steps that China is likely to take to mitigate the costs. This leads to an emphasis on deterrence by denial; that is, fielding sufficient military strength to convince Beijing that plans to conquer Taiwan by force are untenable.[40] Recent U.S. defense strategies have avoided a choice between these two approaches, pursuing instead the idea of "integrated deterrence" that can both impose costs *and* reduce the chance of a quick military victory.

Pursuing a deterrence strategy creates a dilemma of how best to engage with Taiwan. Practical steps such as selling defensive weapons, assisting Taiwan with doctrinal development, reorganization, or training, and continuing to educate Taiwan officers in U.S. military institutions are likely to continue. The question is whether to expand assistance to areas that may inadvertently push China into a war of necessity, even if Washington officially pledges that it rejects Taiwan independence. Those areas might include shifting from foreign weapons sales to large amounts of foreign military financing (i.e. providing grants that make it far easier for Taipei to procure large volumes of U.S. weapons), authorizing direct talks between the two sides at senior levels, putting large numbers of U.S. troops on Taiwan, inviting Taiwan to participate in U.S.-led exercises, and offering explicit security guarantees. The challenge is that China has not articulated clear red lines, making it hard to know what it will or will not tolerate. Future administrations will have to decide whether such activities are more likely to deter or provoke.

U.S. military planners are also considering options should deterrence fail. China's development of capabilities that can hold U.S. forces in the region at risk has led to a new emphasis on operational concepts that stress mobility, concealment, lethality, and distribution of combat power to a broader range of platforms.[41] There has also been an increasing emphasis on the use of uncrewed systems to hold PLA assets at risk during an invasion; in June 2024, for instance, Indo-Pacific Commander Admiral Samuel Paparo stated that a U.S. operational goal would be to create a "hellscape" of combat drones that could delay PLA operations by up to a month.[42] This came after the Department of Defense announced an ambitious Replicator initiative, whose main focus would be on acquiring large numbers of drones to "swarm the Strait."[43]

Each of the services has developed its own doctrine to explain how they will continue to operate in a contested environment: the air force has prioritized distributed bombing campaigns from standoff distances, the navy has tried to spread combat power to a larger range of vessels, the army has begun to field "multi-domain task forces" composed of long-range artillery, air defenses, and cyber teams, and the marines have explored how to operate from austere locations close to China. Joint doctrine has been rewritten to explain how these pieces can fit together to deter aggression and win wars, with an explicit focus on a Taiwan conflict – the Pentagon's new "pacing scenario."

Taiwan's ability to survive a Chinese assault will also depend on roles played by U.S. allies and partners. Any U.S. intervention would likely be accompanied by a broader coalition. Some members would implement economic and diplomatic sanctions on China with no active military role, others may take on more of the burden in other theaters to free up U.S. forces (for instance, South Korea may increase its readiness to respond to North Korean opportunism, while European nations may pick up more responsibility for Russian aggression), and still others may play a valuable logistics and sustainment role.[44] Many countries will likely find themselves in the middle of intense pressure from Washington and Beijing. Some will have to make choices about basing, access, and overflight for U.S. forces in a conflict. Nevertheless, there remain doubts about whether any ally would participate in direct combat against China. Japan is the most likely given Tokyo's significant military capabilities and its concerns that any conflict could endanger its southwestern islands. Others might be drawn into a conflict only if China preemptively attacked bases on their territory to improve the chances of a successful invasion.

Conclusion

While the U.S. military has begun to refer to a Taiwan contingency as its "pacing scenario," the PLA had a head start. China's military came to regard a cross-strait conflict as its own primary planning scenario when it overhauled its strategy in 1993. This pivotal shift in attention laid the foundation for a new generation of doctrine focused not only on the major campaigns the PLA might need to conduct across the strait, but also on the task of defeating or disrupting U.S. intervention. While tensions rose and abated based on political turnover in Taiwan, the PLA never ceased training for a large amphibious assault. Xi Jinping's major contribution was instituting a joint command structure better able to plan and train for high-end combat scenarios in peacetime, and better postured to transition from a peacetime to a wartime footing. The PLA also gradually expanded its capabilities advantages over Taiwan, which had trouble modernizing its own forces, carrying out needed reforms, and even filling the ranks.

The recent increase in military coercion against Taiwan can be interpreted as a sign of Xi Jinping's bold stance and as a reaction to DPP policies and growing U.S. support. These patterns can also be attributed to a PLA that has more capacity to carry out air, maritime, and missile activities close to Taiwan. A thirty-year focus on the problem has yielded the doctrine, training, capabilities, and structure that China would need to escalate while having some degree of confidence that tensions can be controlled. A stronger military gives Beijing an option to escalate to new levels to express its frustration with external developments, cater to nationalist sentiment at home, and provide real-world training for otherwise untested crews. A "new normal" also complicates Taiwan's defense because it supports the argument that expensive conventional platforms such as fighters and destroyers are needed to resist Chinese pressure. Short of a large increase in defense spending, those requirements could sap energy from the task of reorganizing and rearming for an invasion, when most of that equipment would be irrelevant.

However, Beijing does not yet view the conditions as right for war. A war of necessity cannot be ruled out and might even be a certitude if Taiwan were to declare *de jure* independence, but China has given itself enough flexibility that it does not have to be boxed into a decision that could create enormous political risk for the regime. The strongest evidence that a war of choice is unlikely in the immediate future is Xi's instruction for the PLA to be better able to conduct an invasion by 2027. Why the need to motivate a system already ready to go? Many factors complicate these preparations: lack of experience in modern joint warfare, serious logistics and sustainment challenges, Taiwan's intrinsic geographic advantages, and the possibility that not only the United States but also others could intervene. Russia's stalled invasion of Ukraine broadcast the message that quick victories against smaller neighbors cannot be guaranteed, and that the economic risks of any military adventure could be greater than anticipated.

An alternative perspective worthy of greater consideration is that the risks of an amphibious invasion are low but Taiwan's vulnerability to a blockade is increasing. This option is supported by China's unrivaled naval and Coast Guard capabilities, Taiwan's reliance on seaborne imports, and its inherent vulnerability to blockade. Nevertheless, neither a quasi-blockade designed to exert pressure while avoiding an international response, nor a Joint Blockade Campaign involving the use of lethal force would guarantee success. Rather than convincing Taipei to capitulate, such operations could embolden Taiwan's leaders, enrage the population, and at some point require Beijing to make a choice about whether to escalate or back down. That choice could be forced on them if Taiwan or a foreign power were to resist the blockade. Escalating to an invasion would be difficult in the best of circumstances, but even harder following a blockade because China would have lost the element of surprise.

There has been much speculation about whether China finds itself in a narrowing window of opportunity to achieve unification by force. This appears unlikely because China's leaders have spoken optimistically about their long-term prospects and because it is doubtful that the benefits of unification, which they do not need to guarantee their survival, will outweigh the risks, which could endanger it. Instead, Taiwan itself has a window of opportunity, albeit perhaps a short one, to improve its defenses before China's calculus shifts in response to adaptations from its observations of the Ukraine war, expanded capabilities, efforts to insulate the economy from sanctions, and completion of a nuclear expansion that could spur optimism that foreign powers can be convinced not to join the fight. The question is whether Taipei, and members of a coalition organizing around its defense, can make costly investments to improve its readiness without the catalyst of having been attacked, as Ukraine was in Crimea eight years before Russian tanks rolled toward Kyiv. Such choices should be made in a low-key way, taking care to avoid symbolic political flourishes that might goad Beijing into a war of political necessity.

Further Reading

Cancian, Mark F. et al., *The First Battle of the Next War: Wargaming a Chinese Invasion of Taiwan* (Washington, DC: CSIS, 2023).

Colby, Elbridge, *The Strategy of Denial: American Defense in an Age of Great Power Conflict* (New Haven: Yale University Press, 2021).

Glaser, Bonnie S., Jessica Chen Weiss, and Thomas J. Christensen, "Taiwan and the True Sources of Deterrence," *Foreign Affairs*, November 30, 2023.

Green, Brendan Rittenhouse and Caitlin Talmadge, "Then What? Assessing the Military Implications of Chinese Control of Taiwan," *International Security* 47: 1 (2022): 7–45.

Henley, Lonnie D., *Beyond the First Battle: Overcoming a Protracted Blockade of Taiwan* (U.S. Naval War College China Maritime Studies Institute, March 2023).

Mastro, Oriana S., "The Taiwan Temptation: Why Beijing Might Resort to Force," *Foreign Affairs* (July/August 2021).

Meyers, John Speed, *Planning War with a Nuclear China: US Military Strategy and Mainland Strike* (Amherst, NY: Cambria Press, 2023).

Pottinger, Matt, ed., *The Boiling Moat: Urgent Steps to Defend Taiwan* (Stanford, CA: Hoover Institution, 2024).

Sacks, David, "What Is China Learning from Russia's War in Ukraine?" *Foreign Affairs*, May 16, 2022.

Wuthnow, Joel et al., eds., *Crossing the Strait: China's Military Prepares for War with Taiwan* (Washington, DC: NDU Press, 2022).

8

A Global PLA

Impressions of China as an assertive country muscling its way to greater influence and preparing for war against Taiwan are relevant in Asia but become murkier as the geographic lens widens to other regions. Most countries outside of Asia – and even some within it who are not China's territorial rivals – are acquainted with a different PLA. This is not the menacing actor bent on regional hegemony, but a friendlier and more cooperative presence. This is a military known for its occasional overseas visits in modest numbers, as when the navy's hospital ship *Peace Ark* arrives in a port to treat patients, or when senior Chinese officers arrive in a capital to discuss security cooperation programs, which often complement economic and diplomatic initiatives under the framework of China's strategic partnerships. Such activities are filtered through the lens of a Chinese propaganda machinery that seeks to portray their country in the best possible light, countering narratives of China as exploitative and opportunistic. Nevertheless, this narrative is based on a set of overseas military activities that are not overtly coercive.

Increasing Chinese power projection assets and changes in the global strategic landscape raise concerns that this more benign image might evolve into something more worrisome. Greater Chinese military ambitions are already on display with Beijing's attempts to negotiate basing agreements in many countries. Future deployments could involve not only peacekeepers (Chinese forces wearing the iconic UN "blue helmets"), but also aircraft carriers, nuclear submarines, and long-range bombers, backed by capabilities less tied to terrestrial geography, such as cyber and counter-space forces. In an era of strategic competition, those forces could be used to expand China's security perimeter or even, one day, to pursue the kinds of overseas combat missions that few powers in history have been able to conduct far from their home bases. This would represent a sharp turn from where the PLA has been recently.

This chapter outlines the contours of the global actor the PLA has become and speculates on what its overseas roles might be in the future. The first section documents the overseas missions the PLA has conducted in the last few decades, such as peacekeeping and anti-piracy patrols, and argues that the main drivers include protecting China's global interests when other options are not available, advancing China's diplomatic aims, and gaining experience for PLA soldiers and sailors whose real-world experience is otherwise quite low.

The second section turns to the question of overseas PLA basing and access. It explains the ways in which Chinese forces are transported and sustained in distant theaters, and why the PLA has started to build a network of what Chinese officers call "strategic strongpoints," including civilian ports and an initial base in Djibouti, to support larger and longer-duration operations.

The final section sketches three scenarios for the global roles the PLA might adopt in the next few decades. These include larger contributions as a peacetime force; an expanding ability to conduct strikes and raids, either against foreign powers that wish to project power into Asia or to coerce smaller countries and even non-state actors who cross China's red lines; and a new role as a global power that can conduct larger and more complex joint operations on other continents. The PLA can already project limited power, but evolving into a more combat-capable overseas force would require significant changes to its command and control, logistics, and human capital. The conclusion discusses the implications of these scenarios for the international community and explores how others, including the United States and its allies, are likely to interpret and respond to these developments.

A Light Footprint

At any given time, less than one percent of the PLA's two-million-person active-duty force (roughly 5,000 in total) is deployed overseas. Most are individuals serving for a year in a United Nations (UN) peacekeeping mission in Africa or the Middle East, or are naval personnel taking part in an anti-piracy patrol off the Horn of Africa.[1] The remainder are members of China's defense attaché corps, which maintains offices in more than 110 embassies and consulates worldwide, and small contingents in overseas bases. This limited presence pales in comparison to the U.S. military, which deploys more than 160,000 troops abroad. However, a small expeditionary force has been useful in protecting Chinese citizens and property, augmenting China's diplomacy, and offering real-world experience for a military that has not been tested in combat for decades. It is also consistent with the focus of China's military strategy on warfighting and deterrence within Asia.

On land, most PLA personnel abroad can be found in UN peacekeeping missions. China joined the UN in 1971 but was aloof toward peacekeeping at first: it regularly abstained on peacekeeping resolutions in the Security Council, did not contribute to the peacekeeping budget, and did not send troops. This reflected China's skepticism toward peacekeeping – Mao had fought a war in Korea against U.S. troops operating under a UN mandate and viewed such operations as tools of superpower rivalry. Deng Xiaoping, however, sought to build China's ties with the international community under his "reform and opening" policy, while adhering to the principle that military interventions should be conducted with UN authorization, and by extension with China's consent as a permanent member of the UN Security Council. Beijing thus began voting for new missions, which became more numerous as conflicts sprang up in the developing world, and making financial contributions.[2] Deng also sought to counter the opprobrium China faced after the 1989 Tiananmen crackdown. The following year, Chinese troops made their UN peacekeeping debut, with five PLA soldiers sent to monitor a ceasefire agreement in the Middle East, followed by 400 troops sent to assist in Cambodia's reconstruction in 1992.

Limited participation in the 1990s gave way to a larger presence in the 2000s. Chinese peacekeepers increased to more than 1,000 in 2004 when Beijing sent a contingent to Lebanon and doubled three years later when PLA members arrived in Sudan after the Darfur crisis. In the following two decades, Chinese personnel in UN peacekeeping missions hovered between 2,000 and 2,500, fluctuating as operations started and ended (see Figure 8.1 below). In most cases, China contributed only support elements, such as engineers, logisticians, and medics. Combat units were added with the arrival of an infantry company in Mali in 2013 and an infantry battalion in South Sudan two years later. These forces have guarded UN compounds and occasionally gone on armed patrols. In another qualitative improvement, in 2017 an army helicopter unit deployed to Darfur. In addition to sending units, individual PLA officers have staffed and even led entire UN missions, which are composed of contributors from many nations. A key date was 2007, when a Chinese general for the first time became a mission commander (in the Western Sahara).

The PLA has also prepared additional peacekeeping capacity that it has not yet deployed. In a 2015 speech to the UN General Assembly, Xi Jinping pledged 8,000 troops to the UN Peacekeeping Capability Readiness System. This system consists of a set of capabilities identified by UN member states that can be mobilized in as little as 60 days to address conflicts or respond to natural disasters anywhere around the globe. Xi's pledge did not result in a single large formation, but rather a collection of units at the brigade or smaller level scattered around the country, including infantry, helicopters, medical personnel, and logisticians, that have been handpicked to train to UN standards and undergo inspections by UN staff. The units offer Beijing options to augment its overseas presence but have not yet been called on for service.

At sea, China's overseas presence centers on the anti-piracy patrols. Chinese naval ships have traveled beyond the first island chain since 1980, but typically in small numbers and only for short durations. That changed in 2008. The collapse of the Somali central government in 1991 and the ensuing civil war resulted in a piracy challenge as militants hijacked foreign ships for ransom. These threats precipitated an international response as the United States and the European Union both established task forces. Beijing was initially reluctant to send its own ships but yielded when the George W. Bush

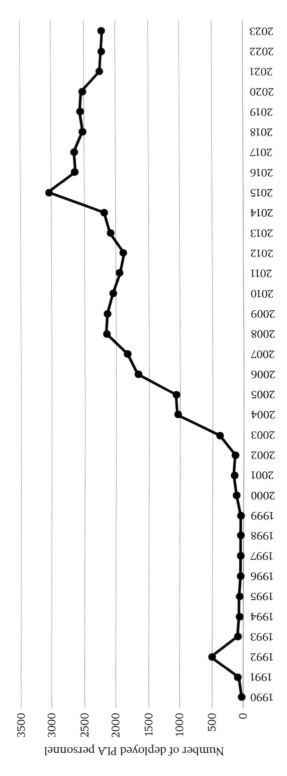

Figure 8.1 Chinese Participants in UN Peacekeeping Missions, 1990–2023

Source: Authors' figure based on data from UN Peacekeeping. Data report year-end totals.

administration encouraged it to do so as a sign that it would be a "responsible stakeholder," and not a free rider, in global security. A PLA navy task force thus arrived in December 2008 with a flotilla of two guided-missile frigates and a replenishment ship. Their role was escorting Chinese commercial ships through dangerous waters, but they were also on call to assist foreigners as needed.[3]

The PLA has maintained its anti-piracy task forces ever since. Task forces are composed of 3–4 ships that stay on station for roughly four months before turning over their responsibilities to the next task force. Between 2008 and 2023, there were 45 such flotillas. In the early years, there were cases in which naval crews and their onboard special operations commandos fired warning shots or prepared to board hijacked ships, but cases became less frequent with the reduction in Somali piracy after 2012. Continued deployments, however, offered other opportunities. This included making port visits along the route, as noted in Chapter 6, often to conduct military diplomacy with strategic partners such as Saudi Arabia or Pakistan. This might involve a small exercise or a friendly sports competition. On a few occasions, including in the civil conflicts in Libya (2011), Yemen (2015), and Sudan (2023), PLA naval ships in the Gulf of Aden have also been used to evacuate Chinese and foreign citizens in distress.

PLA Navy ships also travel beyond Asia for other reasons. Sometimes surface ships travel to distant locations for exercises outside the context of anti-piracy patrols. Usually, these exercises focus on non-combat subjects such as search and rescue, disaster relief, or anti-piracy, though there have been occasional combat-related drills with close partners such as Russia, Iran, and Pakistan. The hospital ship *Peace Ark*, launched in 2007, has circumnavigated the globe several times, providing treatments to locals in countries such as Gabon and Mexico, and in 2013 assisted in the response to Typhoon Haiyan in the Philippines.[4] Other cases were more controversial. Chinese surveillance ships have made uninvited appearances at U.S.-led exercises such as the *Rim of the Pacific* series near Hawaii. In 2014, a Chinese nuclear attack submarine docked at Colombo port, Sri Lanka, ostensibly as part of an anti-piracy task force, raising suspicions from India, which lodged a protest.

Unlike the army and navy, the PLA Air Force does not maintain an overseas presence and the PLA lacks any overseas air bases. Nevertheless, air force planes have flown overseas for various reasons. Chinese pilots have participated in combat-oriented drills with countries such as Pakistan and Thailand, and have taken part in aerial competitions such as Aviadarts with Russia. They have also ferried peacekeepers on both older Il-76 transports and newer Y-20s. Occasionally, the PLA has also sent aircraft to support contingency operations. In the 2011 Libya evacuation, four Il-76s flew from Xinjiang to help evacuate Chinese citizens. The Y-20 made its operational debut during the Covid pandemic in 2020 with the delivery of medical aid to Pakistan and has since been used to transport supplies related to the pandemic or after natural disasters occurred in countries such as Afghanistan, Tonga, and the Solomon Islands.

Other parts of the PLA support overseas goals in more nuanced ways. As discussed in Chapter 5, the Rocket Force maintains intercontinental ballistic missiles to enhance deterrence and operates long-range conventional missiles that could be relevant in a future conflict. The Aerospace Force is responsible for China's space programs, including operating and protecting the communications, navigation, weather monitoring, and surveillance satellites that facilitate traditional overseas operations. As part of its mission, this force operates space tracking stations in Namibia, Pakistan, Argentina, and Kenya. The Cyberspace Force's offensive cyber units project power from the comfort of home by collecting sensitive data from foreign information systems, gaining access to adversary critical infrastructure, and manipulating foreign discourse. PLA attachés, most of whom come from the ground forces, function as human intelligence collectors as well as diplomats responsible for strategic messaging. Even military media such as the *PLA Daily* augment China's messaging through favorable portrayals of PLA actions.

China's foreign military activities are driven by three overlapping goals: defending China's overseas interests, furthering its diplomatic agenda, and providing opportunities for the PLA to enhance its own modernization. First is protecting material interests. Deng's "reform and opening" policy implied increasing connections with the outside world to fuel China's growth. In 1993, China became a net importer of oil, reliance on which increased in the next decades. Jiang Zemin's 1999 "go out" policy led to a rise in the number of Chinese expatriates and businesses operating in far-flung regions. Hu Jintao counted protection of sea lanes and other overseas interests among the "new historic missions" he gave to the PLA in 2004.[5] Under Xi Jinping, there has been deepening foreign engagement through the Belt and Road Initiative. From a security perspective, part of the challenge is protecting the so-called Maritime Silk Road linking Asia with Europe and Africa. Another part is that Chinese infrastructure projects and laborers are often in areas prone to natural disasters or civil strife; some have even been targeted due to anti-Chinese sentiment. Examples includes attacks in places such as the Central African Republic, Afghanistan, and Pakistan.

The clearest military role in defending these interests is sea lane protection. Historically, China had few capabilities to protect distant sea lanes, relying instead on the U.S. Navy and others to underwrite its security. The production of a blue water navy, however, has allowed China to reduce its reliance on others (even though its presence in some maritime choke points, such as the Strait of Hormuz, remains negligible). Chinese crews have become more proficient in skills relevant to sea lane protection through deployments past the first island chain, anti-piracy patrols in the Gulf of Aden, and drills with foreign partners. As discussed below, the opening of the PLA's first overseas base in Djibouti, and the building of dual-use ports across the Indian Ocean, provide infrastructure to sustain deployments in a theater vital to Chinese trade. The 2014 submarine visit to Sri Lanka was a sign that the navy needed not only to combat piracy but also to take steps to prepare for high-end threats to its shipping, such as from India or the United States.

In other cases, military involvement is only one – and typically the last – option for protecting overseas interests. As a starting point, terrorism and other security problems have led companies to be more considerate of risk in their decisions on where to invest in the first place. Risk consultancies have been established to inform those decisions. Another improvement is that Chinese embassies have a better ability to communicate with Chinese travelers and expatriates in emergency situations. When citizens are in danger, the onus is on host governments. In Pakistan, where Chinese construction workers have been subjected to terrorism from militant groups, Islamabad announced in 2015 a special force of 12,000 troops to protect them. Private security companies are also involved. By 2022, there were between 20 and 40 Chinese security firms, many of them staffed by former PLA members, offering services in 40 countries; this was usually sufficient to mitigate risks. Chinese private security companies typically do not carry guns, mostly to prevent deadly incidents that could harm China's image, which limits their utility to small-scale training and protection assignments.[6]

The PLA itself has only played a role in more extreme cases. Between 2006 and 2014, the Chinese government conducted 14 civilian evacuations in places such as the Solomon Islands, Thailand, Egypt, and Syria.[7] Most were limited to the removal of a few hundred or fewer citizens through charter flights. The 2011 Libyan civil war was an exceptional case that required Chinese authorities to evacuate more than 30,000 citizens. The PLA took the lead in orchestrating the response, relying on a combination of civilian charters and military assets. This event prompted more extensive planning in PLA defense attaché offices to prepare for non-combatant evacuations, and top PLA leaders began to discuss such "military operations other than war" more frequently.[8] When several hundred Chinese and foreign citizens were extracted from Yemen four years later, the PLA was better prepared. The navy-led evacuation was dramatized in the 2018 movie *Operation Red Sea* – part of a genre of Chinese films depicting the PLA's greater overseas capabilities.

Nevertheless, there are political and practical limits on how the PLA can be used to protect Chinese interests abroad. Beijing has long adopted a more cautious attitude on direct intervention than Western countries, agreeing to send in troops only with explicit host country approval. Following a stricter interpretation of sovereignty is not merely a matter of principle, but also rooted in the desire to reduce the legitimacy of any foreign intervention aimed at China and to avoid unnecessary damage to its diplomatic relationships. In 2013, Beijing considered using armed drones to kill a wanted drug lord in Myanmar but decided against it.[9] Practically, in many situations, the PLA does not have a credible military option and may also sometimes lack forewarning of threats to its citizens.[10] The Libya and Yemen operations were feasible because they involved ships already in theater picking up civilians at a port, but other operations would have been far riskier or outside the PLA's capabilities, such as rescuing a Chinese citizen captured by ISIS in 2015 or evacuating citizens in Ukraine when Russia invaded in 2022. Military forces have thus been used sparingly.

The second goal is supporting China's larger diplomatic aims. To underscore its strategic messaging, Chinese leaders often note that that Beijing is the top contributor of peacekeeping troops among the five permanent members of the UN Security Council. This draws a favorable contrast with other major powers, though other countries, such as Bangladesh and Nepal, contribute several thousand more troops each year. Chinese media regularly embed with troops, documenting achievements both large and small. A 2019 Xinhua headline, for instance, announced that troops had "rescued a local pickup plunged into [a] roadside gully, helping solve road congestion."[11] Similar headlines appear when naval ships escort civilian vessels through the Gulf of Aden or when hospital ships arrive in a new country. More recently, the use of military aircraft to deliver aid has provided an opportunity to publicize China's contributions and its military capabilities. Since 2023, these kinds of cooperative security ventures have been packaged together under a new label, the Global Security Initiative, which promises to "improve global security governance" and "bring more stability and certainty to a volatile and changing era."[12] This contrasts with portrayals of the United States as supporting bloc confrontation and the continuation of violence from Ukraine to the Middle East.

Overseas military activities also support China's bilateral relations. While China does not maintain military alliances, it does have a wide-ranging network of partnerships (defined by an ascending hierarchy of labels such as "strategic partner" and "comprehensive strategic partner") based on mutual diplomatic and economic interests. There is a strong correlation between Chinese military exercises with foreign partners and countries that rank among China's most cherished strategic partners, such as Russia and Pakistan. As discussed in greater detail in Chapter 6, combined exercises and other forms of military interactions with Russia have been a way to signal solidarity given growing competition with the United States. Other military activities have contributed to larger diplomatic attempts to increase influence in places ranging from the Middle East to the Pacific Islands.

A final purpose of foreign military activities is to enhance PLA modernization. Lack of combat experience has prompted Chinese leaders to consider other ways in which the PLA might improve its general readiness. Alongside other developments, such as more realistic training and a higher tempo of operations within Asia, foreign engagements can assist in closing the gap.

Interactions with more experienced militaries can expose PLA officers and units to those who have been tested in battle or other combat-like circumstances. The PLA certainly seeks to derive operational lessons in its exercises with Russia, which feature advanced weaponry and subjects such as joint operations. Engagements with forces elsewhere can also create learning opportunities. In UN peacekeeping, for instance, the PLA conducts periodic drills with European, Asian, and African militaries, learning best practices in areas such as counterterrorism, military medicine, and de-mining.[13]

Operating abroad is also a practical test for members of the PLA officer corps. Naval commanders who lead anti-piracy task forces gain valuable experience in planning and commanding overseas operations, must be able to interact well with foreigners, and on occasion face unscripted situations, such as facilitating non-combatant evacuations or dealing with broken equipment far from home, that put their skills to the test. Having proven themselves, these officers are better positioned for promotion. Ground force officers likewise have opportunities to lead troops in UN peacekeeping operations at the company or battalion level. There have been cases of PLA officers needing to negotiate with or face-down militant groups, thus validating their own leadership skills. To spread these opportunities across a generation of officers, the PLA rotates involvement in anti-piracy and peacekeeping operations between different naval fleets and group armies, respectively.

The PLA has thus become a global actor, but it has not demonstrated the ability to perform and sustain higher-end combat missions far from home. As mentioned above, only a small fraction of the PLA is overseas at any given time, and most members of the PLA will never deploy. This diminishes the kinds of linguistic, cultural, and geographic acuity needed to operate as an expeditionary force. In terms of capabilities, there are no major combat formations based outside of China, nor are there large stockpiles of equipment or munitions that would be needed for a conflict. Operations are usually carried out by single services, rather than in a joint fashion. A few drills are combat-focused, but most exercises cover non-traditional security subjects, and many involve only small numbers of troops. The repertoire of routine and ad-hoc missions the PLA carries out in the real world is focused on "military operations other than war," such as anti-piracy, peacekeeping, and disaster relief.[14]

Moreover, critical systems are not in place for the PLA to transition into a more combat-credible force. While PLA forces inside China are led by theater commands, there is no equivalent system for joint command and control of troops overseas. A small Joint Staff Department overseas operations office plays a coordinating role, but most operations are led in practice by service headquarters. The lack of robust joint structures would make it difficult for the PLA to plan, organize, and carry out modern combat operations. It is also likely that the PLA lacks the same sophisticated intelligence, surveillance, and reconnaissance apparatus abroad, nor would it have resilient communications of the sort necessary in combat. As discussed below, the PLA's logistics system is designed to support operations short of war. The lack of bases with advanced defenses would create risks for any force seeking shelter in a conflict, and the lack of military alliances makes it questionable that foreign countries would allow the PLA access to their facilities in such cases. In short, the PLA has not built the systems that U.S. forces instituted during the Cold War to be able to fight and win abroad.

Such limitations are not a sign of PLA weakness, but a reflection of its strategy. As discussed in Chapter 3, China's military strategy is intensely focused on preparing for a high-end conflict within Asia, especially across the Taiwan Strait. Other key priorities include responding to domestic emergencies within China, deterring regional rivals, and countering the intervention of U.S. forces in a regional conflict. Protecting overseas interests, using military tools to shore up China's diplomatic partnerships, and gaining operational experience are important, but ultimately secondary interests in the development of military power. Nevertheless, there are already signs that the PLA intends to undertake more ambitious overseas missions in the future, regardless of whether the formal strategy changes to prioritize a global combat capability. Understanding these dynamics requires first a consideration of how the PLA is seeking to sustain forces abroad, followed by discussion of what a more capable expeditionary force could entail in the future.

Bases and Places

Logistics challenges limit China's ability to project combat power into distant theaters. A distinction can be made between the PLA's approaches to logistics at home and abroad. Domestically, Chinese forces rely on internal lines (such as national highways, railways, and airspace) to quickly move personnel and supplies across manageable distances and support them out of garrison. Logistics forces are relatively mature: the Joint Logistic Support Force was created in 2016 as a full-service provider to theater commands, managing general purpose supplies such as oil and food, with the services handling specialized equipment. The PLA has also developed methods for quickly procuring services from the civilian sector and has built information systems that allow logisticians to quickly identify where supplies are located across a nationwide storage and distribution system, and to be able to efficiently mobilize resources. Consistent with the focus of China's military strategy, this system was created to support large-scale operations within China and across its periphery.

Externally, the system is still under development. In the past, Chinese forces deploying abroad lacked an overseas logistics infrastructure. Naval ships traveling beyond the first island chain often brought supplies with them on replenishment ships and tankers. If a critical part were to malfunction, they would need to wait in a port until that part could be found at home and shipped overseas. Peacekeepers had a limited organic logistics capability and relied on the UN system for food, equipment, and other necessities. Moreover, China's military transportation was insufficient to move large numbers of troops across long distances. A small fleet of Il-76s procured from Russia could ferry only about 140 troops each, and the navy lacked large-deck amphibious ships to move larger formations around the globe. Other essential support assets such as refueling tankers and fleet oilers were also limited. The lack of a stronger logistics system not only made it difficult to envision foreign combat operations, but also reduced the extent to which the PLA could handle basic non-traditional security functions such as evacuations.

Recent innovations have provided new options to transport and sustain Chinese forces abroad. The previous shortfall of long-range transport aircraft has been reduced with the serial production of Y-20s, which have a range of nearly 5,000 kilometers and can carry 300 troops. Only 27 of these planes were in the inventory in 2019 but there were more than 70 in 2024. Some of these capabilities are based at a "strategic projection base" located at the Zhengzhou international airport, through which civilian and military support can be provided to service long-haul operations. There has also been an increase in large amphibious ships from five to 11, including three Type-075s, which can each carry 800 troops and 25–30 helicopters. China has also fielded two aircraft carriers and is working on additional units, including a future nuclear-powered version.

To sustain forces overseas, there has been an increasing reliance on terminals in foreign ports owned and operated by Chinese state-owned enterprises. U.S. scholars Isaac Kardon and Wendy Leutert identified 96 ports in 2022 with a Chinese ownership stake.[15] These are generally located astride major shipping routes across the Indian Ocean, through the Middle East, and into the Eastern Mediterranean and Africa, although they can also be found farther afield, including in the United States. Ports such as Gwadar in Pakistan or Hambantota in Sri Lanka typically have stockpiles of critical supplies, repair facilities, and skilled technicians on hand. The utility of these sites, which PLA ships have already begun to visit, has led some Chinese strategists to describe them as "strategic strongpoints," though foreign commentators have sometimes likened them to a "String of Pearls" ringing India's periphery. Relying on these ports thus enables the PLA navy to stay out for longer periods and respond more quickly to crises while managing costs by using commercial facilities. Some of these ports are also likely to play a covert role in collecting intelligence on foreign military movements.

Nevertheless, the PLA has also begun to rely on full-scale military bases.[16] For many years, China's "principled" position was that it would not operate bases in foreign soil, which was too reminiscent of imperial adventurism. That changed in 2017, when the PLA opened its first overseas base, in Djibouti.[17] Strategically located at the southern terminus of the Red Sea, Djibouti's main source of revenue is rents collected from foreign countries operating bases on its territory, including the United States, France, Britain, Saudi Arabia, Turkey, and Japan. The PLA's 90-acre base features underground storage facilities, fuel depots, repair facilities, a heliport, and barracks for a small contingent of marines. In 2021, a new pier opened which was long enough to accommodate all the ships and submarines in the PLA navy, including aircraft carriers. Its location is useful for servicing ships participating in anti-piracy patrols, resupplying peacekeepers throughout the region, non-combatant evacuations, and intelligence collection. It also provides the PLA with experience in how to run a foreign base.

In the future, the PLA will probably open additional bases in other regions. One likely location is the Ream naval base in Cambodia, which Chinese firms have been renovating; commercial satellite imagery suggests facilities designed for PLA naval ships like the ones in Djibouti. A base in Cambodia would allow Beijing to extend its military influence in Southeast Asia and project power into the Indian Ocean. Forces there could also be used in concert with those based in the South China Sea to oppose a blockade of Chinese imports in the maritime chokepoints of Southeast Asia. According to the U.S. Department of Defense, China has also been negotiating with a range of other countries on questions of military access and basing, including Pakistan, Sri Lanka, United Arab Emirates, Equatorial Guinea, Namibia, Vanuatu, and the Solomon Islands. To be sure, the PLA may never gain access to some of these countries, but it is clearly interested in expansion. Compared to civilian facilities, advantages of a base could include weapons storage facilities, permanently deployed units, and better protection from terrorism or sabotage, as well as the political symbolism attached to military presence.

An expanding network of overseas bases does not mean that China intends to replicate the system of large U.S. bases, sometimes called "iron mountains," built during the Cold War. One consideration is whether China's military strategy changes to require the PLA to prepare for combat-focused missions abroad. Continuing to carry out only non-war military operations would mean that small bases such as Djibouti would be sufficient. Another factor is the cost of maintaining permanent bases and whether those are justified given other expenses the PLA will face in the future, especially when civilian ports can provide some of the same benefits at a significantly lower cost. A third issue is whether and under what conditions states, some of which have been reluctant to invite foreign troops onto their territory, will agree to host (or provide temporary access to) the PLA. Unlike the United States, China does not extend mutual defense agreements to its partners. Access could be limited if those states do not perceive the PLA as willing to use its presence to protect their interests. The cost of greater access, even without a formal alliance, could mean an expectation that China would use some of its forward capabilities to assist host nations in the event of domestic emergencies.

A final consideration is how the strategic competition between China and the United States develops. An intensifying contest for influence in strategic regions could prompt Beijing to seek basing and access in places where it otherwise might not have had interest, such as the Atlantic coast of Africa or across the Pacific islands. A potential PLA training facility in Cuba also fits this category.[18] Such locations could be used to create dilemmas for the United States outside China's periphery and could become bargaining chips in negotiations with Washington (for instance, would China agree to scale back its presence in Cuba if U.S. forces do not set foot in Taiwan?). Bases in areas more relevant for China's commercial interests, such as Djibouti or Cambodia, could also more aggressively collect intelligence on U.S. and allied interests or be used to create risks for U.S. forces abroad. China might thus seek to expand those bases beyond their original purpose if host nations consent.

A Global Expeditionary Force

An interest in opening additional bases suggests that China's leaders envision a more ambitious overseas role for the PLA, but what would that entail? The conventional answer would be that the PLA intends to do more of the same. A larger inventory of strategic air and sealift, combined with a network of "strategic strongpoints," whether full-service bases or civilian ports, would allow for an expansion of the range of missions already being conducted: sea-lane protection, peacekeeping, humanitarian assistance and disaster relief, routine military diplomacy such as port visits and exercises, and non-combatant evacuations. This approach would be fully consistent with the tenets of the current military strategy that creates a clear division between combat-focused missions close to home and primarily non-war military operations farther afield.

China has built the capacity to expand its overseas presence without endangering its readiness in Asia. There is no reason why China could not hold additional exercises with foreign partners in more locations, provide security assistance to African or Middle Eastern states,[19] operate training centers similar to one that opened in Tanzania in 2018,[20] use its strategic transport fleet to deliver aid, or sail its surface combatants around the world as a form of influence and prestige, not unlike the 1907–1909 "Great White Fleet" expedition designed to showcase U.S. naval power after the Spanish-American War. Deploying members of the 8,000-person peacekeeping standby force would represent up to a four-fold increase in overseas peacekeepers while still accounting for only a small fraction of the active-duty force. These troops could be used as part of future UN peacekeeping missions to strengthen

China's reputation or even to protect its material interests, while abiding by China's longstanding principle that force should only be used with UN authorization. A precedent was the 2014 UN mission in South Sudan whose mandate Beijing orchestrated to protect the country's oil infrastructure (China being the largest investor).[21] The UN could thus grant resources and legitimacy for Chinese interventions, assuming acquiescence from the United States and other veto players in the Security Council.

A key question in this scenario is China's risk tolerance. While Chinese troops have deployed abroad, they have mostly operated in permissive environments. In peacekeeping, China has typically performed non-combat roles with low casualty risks. Beijing notes that the PLA has lost 25 peacekeepers over three decades, but other countries have paid far greater prices (more than 4300 peacekeepers have lost their lives in UN missions since 1948). At sea, Chinese anti-piracy crews prepared to board ships on a few occasions but there is no record of the navy following through with kinetic operations. Likewise, most non-combatant evacuations have been carried out in low-risk situations. During the 2023 Sudanese civil conflict, U.S. special forces executed an airborne rescue of trapped embassy personnel in Khartoum while China's navy only loaded passengers at a port several hundred kilometers away from the conflict. Such patterns likely reflect a combination of wariness about being more directly engaged in overseas conflicts and a lack of confidence that the PLA could avoid an embarrassing "Black Hawk Down"-like debacle.

Nevertheless, there could be certain benefits for a more risk-acceptant approach. First, exposing troops to danger would be a crucible in which junior commanders prove their skills and overcome what PLA leaders refer to as a "peace disease" infecting the ranks. Second, achieving success under fire would represent a political victory, mirroring the credit U.S. leaders gain following successful counter-terrorism operations. Third, a greater risk tolerance would allow the PLA to protect Chinese lives and property more effectively when no better options are available. For instance, the navy has remained in the Gulf of Aden, where there has been no major piracy threat for more than a decade, but has avoided the Gulf of Guinea on Africa's west coast, where Chinese ships have been recently hijacked.[22] Going there instead would incur risks but also better serve those who need protection. Without accepting greater risks to its own people, the PLA will probably not achieve these rewards.

A second, more ambitious scenario would involve the PLA operating as a strike force with a reach beyond Asia. This is a plausible role for the PLA given the increasing numbers and ranges of its major conventional strike platforms, as discussed in Chapter 4 (see Figure 8.2 below).[23] Between 2019 and 2023, the PLA's most modern destroyers (the *Luyang III*) grew from 10 to 25; eight *Renhai*-class cruisers, each of which possess 112 vertical launch system tubes capable of firing a range of land-attack and anti-ship cruise missiles, were

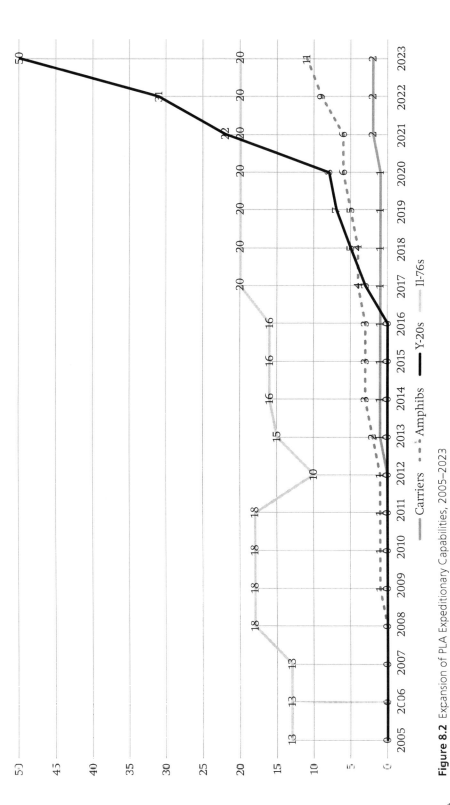

Figure 8.2 Expansion of PLA Expeditionary Capabilities, 2005–2023

Source: Author¹ figure based on data from IISS *Military Balance*, 2005–2024. Amphibs refers to principal amphibious ships, including landing helicopter docks (LHDs) and landing platform docks (LPDs).

commissioned, with another eight planned; and its first indigenously built aircraft carrier entered service. The next decade will see a further increase in large surface combatants, including aircraft carriers, and the introduction of the H-20 bomber, with nearly twice the range of the current H-6Ks (roughly 6,700 vs. 3,700 miles).

One role for these forces would be expanding China's security perimeter past the second island chain. China's long-range bombers and land-based missile forces can already strike targets several thousand kilometers from the mainland. The DF-26 intermediate-range ballistic missile, for instance, has a range of 3,000–4,000 kilometers, sufficient to reach U.S. bases on Guam. Newer missiles with hypersonic glide vehicles, such as the DF-17 and the DF-27, are designed to evade U.S. missile defenses. A mix of air, naval, and missile forces operating from China or its near abroad will allow the PLA to threaten U.S. forces in Hawaii and Alaska. They could also be used to challenge foreign naval presence across the Indian Ocean, and as global warming accelerates, Chinese naval ships could begin to appear in the Arctic sea routes. The 2020 *Science of Military Strategy*, a textbook used to educate senior Chinese officers, referred to a new category of "maritime mobile operations" in distant seas, possibly to counter a foreign blockade or dissuade China's adversaries from attempting one in the first place.[24]

Another role would be to conduct strikes and raids against smaller rivals. China's main forms of overseas influence are currently economic and diplomatic, but ships and aircraft with longer ranges could threaten punitive strikes against countries that cross China's red lines. Failure to submit to China's agenda could result in costly strikes although these would be limited to punishment rather than territorial conquest. Foreign parallels would include U.S. airstrikes against Libya in 1986, Iraq in the 1990s, or Syria in the 2010s. Such strikes could rely on bombers launched from the mainland or from overseas bases (provided access and overflight is possible) or cruise missiles from any of China's large surface combatants or nuclear attack submarines operating in international waters. Inspired by the U.S. Navy SEALs and other elite forces, China's naval special forces are also training for limited raids on hostile territory, such as those against terrorist camps or against more conventional military targets.[25]

This scenario would represent a more aggressive use of military power but would not require a fundamental change in China's military strategy. Enhancing an ability to disrupt the flow of foreign forces into Asia at greater distances would be consistent with a longstanding goal in support of operations in a Taiwan scenario, as would upgrading China's ability to safeguard critical sea lanes and access maritime chokepoints. Conducting limited strikes and raids, without the anticipation that these could escalate into a broader use of force, would represent a major shift in foreign policy but would not require significant reallocation of resources from the primary theater (currently the

Taiwan Strait) – these operations could be conducted with relatively modest numbers of platforms. Moreover, operations conducted at a small scale and primarily by the individual services could also be carried out without a restructuring of China's command and control, intelligence, and logistics architectures.

The main limitations are political, not technological. While there might be operational reasons to target U.S. forces in Hawaii and Alaska, there could be greater perceived escalatory risks to striking the U.S. homeland than U.S. overseas possessions or bases in a foreign country. Outside of Asia, China has been reluctant to consider military force apart from UN-sponsored missions and other non-traditional security missions. Support for more coercive displays by the PLA would require a relaxation of those constraints. Such a shift is not inconceivable – China, after all, abandoned its reluctance to join UN peacekeeping and its previous "principled" opposition to overseas bases – but there remain doubts about the legitimacy and utility of military intervention-ism. Even the deployment of Chinese infantry in UN peacekeeping has been controversial. Authorizing strikes and raids might also simply be unnecessary if Beijing believes it can accomplish its coercive goals through economic and diplomatic statecraft.

A final scenario would involve an ability to conduct medium- or large-scale combat operations abroad. This might include the combination of special operations and conventional forces to seize or retake territory, or to conduct a long-term air and missile campaign against a foreign adversary, either uni-laterally or as a major contributor to an international coalition. Parallels could include late Cold War and post-Cold War campaigns such as the Falkland Islands, Grenada, the Gulf War, or the Kosovo War (which was backed with a credible threat of an ensuring ground campaign). An alternative would involve a protracted counter-insurgency struggle such as the campaigns the Soviets and the United States pursued in Afghanistan. The defining characteristics in this scenario include the dedication of larger combat formations such as army and air force brigades, participation from all the services, heavy logistics burdens, and a possibility for major combat casualties.

The PLA today is far from having the capacity to plan, train for, or conduct such operations. One challenge is the lack of a global joint command structure. The theater commands' responsibility covers domestic and regional contingen-cies; as noted above, there is no joint command with oversight of operations far beyond China's periphery. The PLA, in other words, has no analog to the U.S. global combatant command system or more expeditionary-focused joint structures in the British and French militaries.[26] The services might be able to handle a limited strike campaign, but larger and more complex joint opera-tions would require commanders and staff with the ability to organize and lead joint forces beyond Asia. Any joint headquarters would also need to be responsible for collecting, integrating, and distributing intelligence.

There are several ways in which the PLA could overcome this dilemma. One would be establishing standing joint task forces for overseas operations. The U.S. failure in the 1980 Iran hostage rescue operation ("Desert One") led to significant structural reforms including proposals for permanent joint task forces that would continually strengthen interoperability between disparate forces that would need to coordinate in any complex overseas mission. The PLA could experiment with such a structure in Djibouti, which is currently commanded by the navy, or at a future base elsewhere. Another possibility would be enhancing the overseas role of the Joint Staff Department, giving it a staff and authority like the British Permanent Joint Headquarters (or one of the theater commands could be tasked with this responsibility). The most ambitious option would be to establish one or more overseas combatant commands, which would be predicated on the deployment of larger combat units to the Middle East or elsewhere.

Another challenge is the lack of a more mature global logistics system. Neither civilian ports nor small bases such as Djibouti have the personnel, stockpiles of munitions and other critical resources, or force protection measures, including air and missile defenses, to credibly function as wartime staging areas. The solutions could include upgrading existing bases, opening new bases designed more for combat support than for non-war military operations, or signing deals with foreign countries to provide access to larger bases on their territory (which would be difficult without formal military alliances rooted in mutual defense guarantees). Yet, even these solutions would not address the deeper problem that mobilizing for a large contingency overseas would likely require a reduction in combat capacity available for deterrent and warfighting purposes at home, especially if the PLA needs to rely on its growing but still limited inventory of advanced weapons and equipment, such as fifth generation fighters.

A final challenge concerns the PLA's human capital. As mentioned earlier, only a small percentage of the PLA has any experience with overseas operations, and these are generally in permissive environments. It is also worth noting that senior PLA officers do not serve in foreign assignments, unlike the frequent international experience gained among their U.S. counterparts. Chinese sources have begun discussing the need to expand a cadre of people with experience in areas such as international law, foreign languages and culture, and overseas logistics. Greater peacetime experience would help bridge this gap, but the PLA would lack large numbers of personnel who have been tested in combat or who have been part of a coalition. Reducing risk aversion in peacekeeping and other overseas missions would be one way to cultivate the battle-hardened people it needs. Otherwise, the PLA would face a steep learning curve at the outset of a future conflict.

These changes are unlikely absent a shift in China's military strategy. Non-traditional security, counter-intervention, and limited strikes and raids could all be considered lesser-included cases within a strategy that remains focused on the Asian periphery. Deploying large numbers of troops and materiel to other theaters, building an overseas joint command structure, reforming the logistics system to support wartime requirements, and cultivating a more expeditionary mindset, would represent not only a geographic shift in focus, but also a reconceptualization of the types of conflicts the PLA needs to be prepared to fight – from limited-duration "local wars" against adversaries the PLA has been facing for decades to a more open-ended concept of protracted conflict carried out in remote regions.

Why would such a shift occur and under what circumstances? Chapter 3 argued that changes in the strategic environment could be pivotal. One change would involve an intensification of the Sino–U.S. strategic competition that might not remain confined to Asia. This could involve direct clashes between U.S. and PLA forces, attempts to control territory that one side wants to keep off limits to the other, or proxy conflict. Other changes are also possible. Beijing might conclude that its best option to compete with the United States is to forge its own alliances, which could be useful in geopolitical influence and military access, but also open the possibility of the PLA becoming enmeshed in a foreign conflict. Indeed, some Chinese analysts have already advocated for alliances despite their risks.[27] In a very different future, Chinese troops might have to fill a vacuum in a place like Afghanistan if the United States is not willing to play its traditional role in global security. None of these eventualities appear likely today, but none can be ruled out.

Such changes in the security environment could drive a new strategy, but Beijing would also need adequate resources. A resolution of the Taiwan issue and consolidation of Chinese influence at other points around its borders would free up capacity for a larger overseas role. The more difficult path would be one in which regional contingencies continue to demand attention. Beijing would need to expand military funding to prepare simultaneously for a war in the Asian theater and one or more abroad – a parallel to the "two war" force planning construct adopted by the United States during parts of the Cold War. Much would depend on the status of China's economy and conflicting priorities for the Chinese Communist Party. Accelerating growth could allow for higher military budgets while keeping spending at a modest level of GDP, but the more likely outcome of decelerating growth combined with mounting domestic challenges would create hard choices; even with rising global threats, the party may well choose to keep its focus on what is attainable: preparing for combat closer to home.

Conclusion

The PLA has become a global actor, but it is not yet a global power. Chinese forces can be found outside their base in Asia, most notably in the larger Red Sea arena, which is home to China's anti-piracy patrols, its overseas base in Djibouti, and several of the UN missions in which it participates. They can also be found in defense attaché offices around the world and as visitors through exercises, port visits, and high-level engagements. Yet while China's military is the world's largest and has accumulated tremendous combat potential across Asia, it is only capable of limited missions on other continents and in the global commons. Unlike the U.S. military, the PLA cannot project large-scale combat forces globally to intimidate its rivals or topple regimes and control territory. It would even struggle to execute higher-end non-traditional security operations such as a Bin Laden-type raid. The core reason is that Beijing, pragmatically focused on higher priorities, has not asked its military to be able to conduct such missions.

The changing global strategic landscape, and China's growing power projection capabilities, raise questions about what the future might hold. There is little doubt that, at a minimum, there will be larger numbers of Chinese troops out and about, both as a supporting actor in China's bid to attain greater influence in the developing world, and as the final line of defense when its interests come under threat. It is also likely that long-range missile forces and other capabilities, such as cyber units which have a global reach despite never having to leave the mainland, will play a role in extending China's security perimeter, complicating the tasks for the United States and others who may wish to project power into Asia. It is also possible, though by no means certain, that the PLA will one day make the changes needed to become a credible global power, which would include reforming its command structure, maturing its logistics system, and training its people for new missions.

The trajectory the PLA follows will have consequences for the international community and raise questions about how others will respond. A PLA that does more to contribute to global governance, whether at sea, on land, or by delivering supplies through its larger air transport fleet, could be welcome throughout the world. It would not only provide concrete benefits to those whose own governments cannot provide these services but would also answer U.S. admonitions for China to become a "responsible stakeholder" and not to persistently free ride on U.S. largesse. As U.S.–China competition intensifies, however, it is likely that future administrations will interpret such activities first as a challenge to American influence and only second, if ever, as a positive development that should be encouraged. There have already been extensive U.S. efforts to convince potential host nations not to allow basing or access for the PLA, even when there are doubts that such agreements would support a combat presence. In an era of strategic distrust, the question of ulterior motives looms large.

An expansion of PLA basing has garnered widespread attention, but the most important challenge for the United States may not be access for the PLA, but rather China's ability to deny access for U.S. forces. Foreign access, basing, and overflight are central to a U.S. military strategy that hinges on the ability to conduct military interventions abroad. Conducting the war in Afghanistan in 2001, for instance, required access to air bases in Uzbekistan and Kyrgyzstan. China's prime source of leverage is the political influence it has gained through trade and investments, supported by its voice in regional and international institutions. A worst-case scenario might involve China convincing third parties to close their borders, facilities, and airspace to U.S. forces when access is most needed, such as in a conflict that Beijing opposes. Based on differences in strategy, China's ability to prevent access to the U.S. military (as well as to frustrate coalition-building and deny the imprimatur of the UN) could be more consequential than Washington's success in keeping the PLA out of third countries.

China's marshaling of asymmetric capabilities to complicate foreign intervention in its near abroad has major implications, not only for the United States, but also for other potential members of a coalition, including NATO allies, Australia, and even India. It has been eight decades since Hawaii and Alaska were at risk from conventional strikes from a foreign power, but such possibilities are reemerging with the advent of a Chinese blue water navy, next generation bombers, and innovative capabilities such as long-range missiles fitted with hypersonic glide vehicles or a space-based fractional orbital bombardment system that could deliver nuclear or conventional payloads globally. Such threats will prompt greater U.S. and allied consideration of hardening key sites, dispersal of forces, new doctrine, and the production of similar assets that can strike the Chinese mainland. In this light, it is not surprising that areas of focus for the Australia–U.K.–U.S. (AUKUS) strategic partnership launched in 2021 include nuclear-powered submarines, hypersonics, and counter-hypersonic technology.

The transformation of the PLA into a global power would also have implications for the international community and China itself. One scenario would involve a strategic competition with the United States that mutates into armed rivalry. Avoiding a slide into direct or proxy conflict is one rationale for both sides to pursue greater stability in their bilateral relations. A different scenario would involve more proactive employment of the PLA in regional conflicts outside of Asia. Such a role appears unlikely from today's perspective, but a change in the strategic landscape – such as a resolution of the Taiwan issue on China's terms – could open new possibilities and create new temptations. Some in China have already advocated for the PLA to conduct drone strikes against non-state actors operating on foreign soil; others believe that China should renounce its avoidance of formal military alliances. Entangling itself on foreign battlefields, because its interests demand it and its capabilities allow it, would be the reverse image of how some Chinese officials saw U.S. involvement in Afghanistan and Iraq after 9/11 – a strategic blunder for a rival too confident in its quest for military supremacy.

Further Reading

Duchatel, Mathieu, Oliver Brauner, and Zhou Hang, *Protecting China's Overseas Interests: The Slow Shift Away from Non-Interference* (Stockholm: SIPRI, 2014).

Erickson, Andrew S. and Austin M. Strange, *Six Years at Sea . . . And Counting: Gulf of Aden Anti-Piracy and China's Maritime Commons Presence* (Washington, DC: Brookings Institution Press, 2016).

Fung, Courtney J., *China and Intervention at the UN Security Council: Reconciling Status* (Oxford: Oxford University Press, 2019).

Ghiselli, Andrea, *Protecting China's Interests Overseas: Securitization and Foreign Policy Status* (Oxford: Oxford University Press, 2021).

Kamphausen, Roy and David Lai, eds., *The Chinese People's Liberation Army in 2025* (Carlisle, PA: Strategic Studies Institute, 2014).

Wuthnow, Joel et al., eds., *The PLA Beyond Borders: Chinese Military Operations in Regional and Global Context* (Washington, DC: NDU Press, 2021).

Notes

ACKNOWLEDGMENTS

1 The products of many of these conferences can be found online, most of them for free. Recent offerings include Joel Wuthnow et al., eds., *Crossing the Strait: China's Military Prepares for War with Taiwan* (Washington, DC: NDU Press, 2022); Joel Wuthnow et al., eds., *The PLA Beyond Borders: China's Military in Regional and Global Context* (Washington, DC: NDU Press, 2021); and Phillip C. Saunders et al., eds., *Chairman Xi Remakes the PLA: Assessing Chinese Military Reforms* (Washington, DC: NDU Press, 2019).

INTRODUCTION

1 Shin Kawashima, "The Development of the Debate Over 'Hiding One's Talents and Biding One's Time' (*taoguang yanghui*)," *Asia–Pacific Review* 18: 2 (2011): 17–19.

2 These include Harlan Jencks's *From Muskets to Missiles: Politics and Professionalization in the Chinese Army, 1945–1981* (London: Routledge, 1982), which explained how the PLA developed under Mao; Ellis Joffe's *The Chinese Army After Mao* (Cambridge, MA: Harvard University Press, 1987), which took stock of the PLA's initial reforms under Deng; David Shambaugh's *Modernizing China's Military: Progress, Problems, and Prospects* (Berkeley: University of California Press, 2003), which surveyed the PLA's advances in the 1990s; and Roger Cliff's *China's Military Power: Assessing Current and Future Capabilities* (Cambridge: Cambridge University Press, 2015), which documented PLA modernization into the early 2010s.

3 Andrew Chubb, "Propaganda, Not Policy: Explaining the PLA's 'Hawkish Faction,'" *China Brief*, July 25, 2013. https://jamestown.org/program/propaganda-not-policy-explaining-the-plas-hawkish-faction-part-one/.

4 The China Aerospace Studies Institute's "In Their Own Words" series is an excellent starting point. https://www.airuniversity.af.edu/CASI/In-Their-Own-Words/.

5 See Ian Burns McCaslin and Andrew S. Erickson, "The People's Liberation Army (PLA)," *Oxford Bibliography* (Oxford, UK: Oxford University Press, 2021).

6 These conferences include a series sponsored by the U.S. National Defense University, the RAND Corporation, the Council on Advanced Policy Studies

(Taipei), and most recently the U.S. Institute of Peace. Recent conference volumes, all from NDU Press, include *Crossing the Strait: China's Military Prepares for War with Taiwan* (2022), *The PLA Beyond Borders: China's Military in Regional and Global Context* (2021), and *Chairman Xi Remakes the PLA: Assessing Chinese Military Reforms* (2019). See also James Char, ed., *Modernising the People's Liberation Army: Aspiring to be a Global Military Power* (London: Routledge, 2024).

7 The label "assertive" has often been applied to Xi. See, e.g., Robert D. Blackwill and Kurt M. Campbell, *Xi Jinping on the Global Stage* (New York: Council on Foreign Relations, 2016). Yet there is also a strong academic debate about whether China under his leadership has actually become more assertive. See Alastair Iain Johnston, "How New and Assertive Is China's New Assertiveness?" *International Security* 37:4 (2013), 7–48.

8 Oriana Skylar Mastro, *Upstart: How China Became a Great Power* (Oxford: Oxford University Press, 2024).

9 *Mission Command White Paper*, Joint Chiefs of Staff, April 3, 2012.

1 THE PARTY'S ARMY

1 Peter D. Feaver, "The Civil–Military Problematique: Huntington, Janowitz, and the Question of Civilian Control," *Armed Forces & Society* 23: 2 (1996): 149–178.

2 Mao Zedong, "Problems of War and Strategy," November 6, 1938.

3 Roger R. Reese, *Red Commanders: A Social History of the Soviet Army Officer Corps, 1918–1991* (Lawrence, KS: University Press of Kansas, 2005), 12–86.

4 Mark Stokes, *The People's Liberation Army General Political Department: Political Warfare with Chinese Characteristics* (Arlington, VA: Project 2049 Institute, 2013).

5 Alison A. Kaufman and Peter W. Mackenzie, *Field Guide: The Culture of the Chinese People's Liberation Army* (Arlington, VA: CNA, 2009), 4.

6 "PLA Ideological and Political Education Outline" [中国人民解放军思想政治教育大纲], *PLA Daily* [解放军报], August 4, 2015. http://www.81.cn/jwzl/2015-08/04/content_6614424_5.htm.

7 Combined-arms operations involve multiple army branches such as infantry, artillery, and armor working together in a carefully synchronized fashion. Navies and air forces refer to such operations as "multi-branch operations." These differ from joint operations that involve multiple services and combined operations that involve multiple countries. Confusingly, the PLA usually uses the same term (*lianhe*, 联合) to refer all three types of operations.

8 The PLA's poor performance in the 1979 Sino–Vietnam war highlighted the costs of greater PLA involvement in civilian governance.

9 Phillip C. Saunders and Andrew Scobell, eds., *PLA Influence on China's National Security Policymaking* (Stanford: Stanford University Press, 2015). For further

discussion on the PLA's role in foreign policy, see Yali Chen, *The PLA in China's Foreign and Security Policymaking: Drivers, Mechanism, and Interactions*, Ph.D. dissertation, Johns Hopkins University, 2015.

10 This was also true for other professions in the PRC, including doctors, lawyers, and scientists. When professional ethics and values came into conflict with political obligations as party members, Chinese professionals were expected to place their political identity first and obey CCP orders.

11 James Mulvenon, "China: Conditional Compliance," in M. Alagappa, ed., *Coercion and Governance: The Declining Political Role of the Military in Asia* (Stanford: Stanford University Press, 2001), 317–335.

12 It is worth noting that the CMC vice chairmen hold ex officio seats on the Politburo and several senior PLA officers are represented on the Party Central Committee, though there is little evidence that these Party organs have played a significant role in military affairs.

13 James Mulvenon, "The King Is Dead! Long Live the King! The CMC Leadership Transition from Jiang to Hu," *China Leadership Monitor* 13 (2005): 1–8.

14 General Zhang Yang, who served as Director of the General Political Department and its successor organization the CMC Political Work Department from 2012 to 2017, committed suicide on November 23, 2017, while under investigation for discipline violations and bribery.

15 Robert M. Gates, *Duty: Memoirs of a Secretary at War* (New York: Knopf, 2015), 527–528.

16 Andrew Scobell, "The J-20 Episode and Civil–Military Relations in China," Testimony for the U.S.–China Economic and Security Review Commission, March 2011.

17 Cited in Ken Allen et al., *Institutional Reforms of the Chinese People's Liberation Army: Overview and Challenges* (Alexandria, VA: CNA Corporation, 2002), 67–68.

18 Harlan W. Jencks, "Civil–Military Relations in China: Tiananmen and After," *Problems of Communism* 40: 3 (1991): 14–29.

19 Yali Chen, *The PLA in China's Foreign and Security Policy-making: Drivers, Mechanism and Interactions*, Ph.D. Dissertation, Johns Hopkins University, 2015.

20 Yu Guang, "Looking at Casting the Military Soul from the Modern Values of the Gutian Conference," *Qiushi*, July 31, 2014.

21 Elizabeth Hague, "PLA Career Progressions and Policies," in Roy Kamphausen et al., eds., *The "People" in the PLA: Recruitment, Training, and Education in China's Military* (Carlisle, PA: U.S. Army War College Press, 2008), 233–290.

22 Yu Guang, "Looking at Casting the Military Soul from the Modern Values of the Gutian Conference," *Qiushi*, July 31, 2014.

23 "It is Urgently Required to Settle Apparent Problems in Political Work," *PLA Daily*, November 5, 2014. http://cpc.people.com.cn/pinglun/n/2014/1105 /c78779-25978483.html.

24 Wang Xiaoyi [王晓易], "Effectively Use the 'Sharp Sword' of Auditing to Build a Defense Line of Supervision" [用好审计"利剑" 筑牢监督防线], *PLA Daily*, March 7, 2015.

25 "Push Forward the Innovative Development of Army Audit Work from a New Starting Point," *PLA Daily*, January, 29, 2015. http://cpc.people.com.cn /n/2015/0129/c83083-26471805-2.html.

26 Quoted in Susan Finder, "Shoring Up the 'Rule of Law' in China's Military," *The Diplomat*, February 4, 2015.

27 A reshuffling of the Central Military Commission at the 19th Party Congress in October 2017 reduced the organization's size from eleven to seven. Aside from Xi himself, other members remain uniformed officers. Previously, the designated (civilian) successor to the CCP general-secretary has also served as a CMC member. However, Xi has not designated such an individual.

28 At the Sixth Plenum of the 18th Central Committee in October 2016, the Central Committee apparently voted down a proposal for an "assets-disclosure sunshine regulation" that would have required Central Committee members, their spouses, and their children to disclose their assets.

29 Elliot Ji, "Rocket-Powered Corruption: Why the Missile Industry Became the Target of Xi's Purge," *War on the Rocks*, January 23, 2024. https://waron therocks.com/2024/01/rocket-powered-corruption-why-the-missile-industry -became-the-target-of-xis-purge/.

30 Thomas J. Christensen, "Posing Problems Without Catching Up: China's Rise and Challenges for U.S. Security Policy," *International Security* 25: 4 (2001): 15.

2 THREAT PERCEPTIONS

1 Rush Doshi, *The Long Game: China's Grand Strategy to Displace American Order* (New York: Oxford University Press, 2021).

2 Chalmers A. Johnson, *Peasant Nationalism and Communist Power* (Stanford: Stanford University Press, 1962).

3 Mao Zedong, "Report on an Investigation of the Peasant Movement in Hunan," March 1927.

4 The "Five Principles of Peaceful Coexistence" include mutual respect for sovereignty and territorial integrity, mutual non-aggression, non-interference in internal affairs, equality and mutual benefit, and peaceful coexistence. These "principles" have remained a staple of Chinese diplomatic rhetoric since the 1950s.

5 Ezra F. Vogel, *Deng Xiaoping and the Transformation of China* (Cambridge, MA: Harvard University Press, 2013).

6 Benjamin Schwartz, *In Search of Wealth and Power: Yen Fu and the West* (Cambridge, MA: Harvard University Press, 1964).

7 Rush Doshi, "Hu's to Blame for China's Foreign Assertiveness" in Tarun Chhabra et al., eds., *Global China: Assessing China's Growing Role in the World* (Washington, DC: Brookings Institution Press, 2021), 25–32.

8 "Full Text of the Report to the 20th National Congress of the Communist Party of China," State Council, October 25, 2022. http://english.www.gov .cn/news/topnews/202210/25/content_WS6357df20c6d0a757729e1bfc.html

9 Doshi, *The Long Game*, 159–182.

10 Thomas J. Christensen, *Useful Adversaries: Grand Strategy, Domestic Politics, and Sino-American Conflict, 1947–1958* (Princeton, NJ: Princeton University Press, 1996).

11 The other "modernizations" included agriculture, industry, and science and technology.

12 Jiang Zemin introduced the phrase "period of strategic opportunity" in his work report to the 16th Party Congress in 2002.

13 Naval War College professor Andrew Erickson has compiled English versions of every defense white paper online. These can be found here: https:// www.andrewerickson.com/2019/07/china-defense-white-papers-1995-2019- download-complete-set-read-highlights-here/.

14 "National Security Commission Holds First Meeting, Xi Jinping Delivers Important Speech" [中央国家安全委员会第一次会议召开习近平发表重要讲话滚动], Xinhua, April 15, 2014, https://www.gov.cn/xinwen/2014-04/15/con tent_2659641.htm.

15 Sheena Chestnut Greitens, "Xi's Security Obsession," *Foreign Affairs*, July 28, 2023.

16 "Full Text of the Report to the 20th National Congress of the Communist Party of China," Foreign Ministry, October 25, 2022. https://www.fmprc .gov.cn/mfa_eng/zxxx_662805/202210/t20221025_10791908.html. "Black swans" refers to sudden, unexpected disasters, while "gray rhinos" implies foreseeable problems that are not correctly addressed.

17 For other analyses using the same heuristics, see Andrew J. Nathan and Robert S. Ross, *The Great Wall and the Empty Fortress* (New York: W.W. Norton & Company, 1998), and Kevin Rudd, "Understanding China's Rise Under Xi Jinping," Address to Cadets at West Point, New York, March 5, 2018.

18 Sheena Greitens, Myunghee Lee, and Emir Yazici, "Counterterrorism and Preventive Repression: China's Changing Strategy in Xinjiang," *International Security* 44: 3 (2019): 9–47.

19 Kevin J. O'Brien and Lianjiang Li, *Rightful Resistance in Rural China* (Cambridge: Cambridge University Press, 2006).

20 For extensive background, see Andrew J. Nathan and Andrew Scobell, *China's Search for Security* (New York: Columbia University Press, 2015).

21 From the 1960s through the 1990s, China settled several other boundary disputes, including with Russia, Mongolia, and several former Soviet republics. See M. Taylor Fravel, *Strong Borders, Secure Nation: Cooperation and Conflict in China's Territorial Disputes* (Princeton: Princeton University Press, 2009).

22 Carla Freeman, ed., *China and North Korea: Strategic and Policy Perspectives from a Changing China* (New York: Palgrave Macmillan, 2015).

23 Jessica Chen Weiss, *Powerful Patriots: Nationalist Protest in China's Foreign Relations* (New York: Oxford University Press, 2014).

24 Bill Hayton, *The South China Sea and the Struggle for Power in Asia* (New Haven, CT: Yale University Press, 2015).

25 Michael McDevitt, *Becoming a Great "Maritime Power": A Chinese Dream* (Arlington, VA: CNA, 2016).

26 John Garver, *Protracted Contest: Sino–Indian Rivalry in the Twentieth Century* (Seattle: University of Washington Press, 2011).

27 Dennis J. Blasko, "A Baseline Assessment of the PLA Army's Border Reinforcement Operations in the Aksai Chin in 2020 and 2021," China Landpower Studies Center, April 9, 2024.

28 Gerry Shih, "In Central Asia's Forbidding Highlands, A Quiet Newcomer: Chinese Troops," *Washington Post*, February 18, 2019. https://www.washingtonpost.com/world/asia_pacific/in-central-asias-forbidding-highlands-a-quiet-newcomer-chinese-troops/2019/02/18/78d4a8d0-1e62-11e9-a759-2b8541bbbe20_story.html.

29 Robert Sutter, *China–Russia Relations: Strategic Implications and U.S. Policy Options* (Washington, DC: National Bureau of Asian Research, 2018).

30 Jeffrey A. Bader, *Obama and China's Rise: An Insider's Account of America's Asia Strategy* (Washington, DC: Brookings Institution Press, 2012).

31 *United States Strategic Approach To the People's Republic of China* (Washington, DC: The White House, 2020).

32 M. Taylor Fravel et al., "China Is Not an Enemy," *Washington Post*, July 3, 2019. https://www.washingtonpost.com/opinions/making-china-a-us-enemy-is-counterproductive/2019/07/02/647d49d0-9bfa-11e9-b27f-ed2942f73d70_story.html.

33 *National Security Strategy* (Washington, DC: The White House, 2022), 8.

34 Joel Wuthnow and Elliot Ji, "Bolder Gambits, Same Challenges: Chinese Strategists Assess the Biden Admin's Indo-Pacific Strategy," *China Leadership Monitor* 77 (2023): 1–15.

35 Keith Bradsher, "China's Leader, With Rare Bluntness, Blames U.S. Containment for Troubles," *New York Times*, March 8, 2023. https://www.nytimes.com/2023/03/07/world/asia/china-us-xi-jinping.html.

36 Scott W. Harold, "Expanding Contacts to Enhance Durability: A Strategy for Improving U.S.–China Military-to-Military Relations," *Asia Policy* 16 (2013): 103–138.

37 James P. Nolan, "Why Can't We Be Friends? Assessing the Operational Value of Engaging PLA Leadership," *Asia Policy* 20 (2015): 45–80.

38 Marc Lanteigne, "China's Maritime Security and the 'Malacca Dilemma,'" *Asian Security* 4: 2 (2008): 143–144.

39 Jonathan E. Hillman, *The Emperor's New Road: China and the Project of the Century* (New Haven, CT: Yale University Press, 2020).

40 Nadège Rolland, *China's Eurasian Century? Political and Strategic Implications of the Belt and Road Initiative* (Washington, DC: National Bureau of Asian Research, 2017).

41 Wang Weixing, "'One Belt, One Road' Under Global Vision: Risks and Challenges" [全球视野下的'一带一路': 风险与挑战], *Frontiers* [学术前沿] No. 5 (2015): 10.

42 Joel Wuthnow, *Chinese Perspectives on the Belt and Road Initiative*, China Strategic Perspectives 12 (October 2017).

43 For an earlier discussion, see Linda Jakobson and Dean Knox, *New Foreign Policy Actors in China* (Stockholm: SIPRI, 2010).

3 STRATEGY, ORGANIZATION, AND RESOURCES

1 Alastair Iain Johnston, *Cultural Realism: Strategic Culture and Grand Strategy in Chinese History* (Princeton: Princeton University Press, 1998).

2 Mao Zedong, "Problems of Strategy in China's Revolutionary War," December 1936, trans. https://www.marxists.org/reference/archive/mao/selected-works/volume-1/mswv1_12.htm.

3 Andrew Scobell, *China's Use of Military Force: Beyond the Great Wall and the Long March* (Cambridge: Cambridge University Press, 2003).

4 Larry Wortzel, "Concentrating Forces and Audacious Action: PLA Lessons from the Sino–Indian War," in Laurie Burkitt et al., eds., *Chinese Lessons from Other People's Wars* (Carlise, PA: Army War College, 2003), 327–352.

5 Edward C. O'Dowd, *Chinese Military Strategy in the Third Indochina War: The Last Maoist War* (New York: Routledge, 2007).

6 David M. Finkelstein, "China's National Military Strategy: An Overview of the 'Military Strategic Guidelines,'" *Asia Policy* 4: 1 (2007): 67–72.

7 David M. Finkelstein, *China Reconsiders Its National Security: "The Great Peace and Development Debate of 1999"* (Arlington, VA: CNA, 2000).

8 *Memoirs of Liu Huaqing* [刘华清回忆录] (Beijing: PLA Press, 2004), 608.

9 Jeffrey Engstrom, *Systems Confrontation and System Destruction Warfare* (Santa Monica, CA: RAND, 2018).

10 *China's National Defense in the New Era* (Beijing: State Council Information Office, 2019).

11 While the PLA played a coordinating role, most Chinese citizens were evacuated through commercial aircraft. See Jonas Parello-Plesner and Mathieu Duchâtel, "International Rescue: Beijing's Mass Evacuation from Libya," *Adelphi Papers* 54: 451 (2014): 107–124.

12 Michael S. Chase and Arthur Chan, *China's Evolving Approach to 'Integrated Strategic Deterrence'* (Santa Monica, CA: RAND, 2016).

13 Lonnie Henley, "PLA Logistics and Doctrine Reform, 1999–2009," in Susan Puska, ed., *People's Liberation Army After Next* (Carlise, PA: Army War College Press, 2000), 55–78.

14 For a more extensive discussion, see Joel Wuthnow and Phillip C. Saunders, *Chinese Military Reforms in the Age of Xi Jinping: Drivers, Challenges, and Implications* (Washington, DC: NDU Press, 2017).

15 Dennis J. Blasko, "The Biggest Loser in Chinese Military Reforms: The PLA Army," in Phillip C. Saunders et al., eds., *Chairman Xi Remakes the PLA: Assessing Chinese Military Reforms* (Washington, DC: NDU Press, 2019), 345–392.

16 Elsa Kania and Ian Burns McCaslin, *People's Warfare Against Covid-19: Testing China's Military Medical and Defense Mobilization Capabilities* (Washington, DC: Institute for the Study of War, 2020).

17 Within the CMC Joint Staff Department, there is a small Overseas Operations Office, but this is designed to play a minor coordinating role. Most of the planning and execution is carried out by the services.

18 Liu Xuanzun, "J-20 Fighter Jet Active in All Five PLA Theater Commands: Delegate," *Global Times*, October 20, 2022, https://www.globaltimes.cn/page /202210/1277527.shtml; Joel Wuthnow, *System Overload: Can China's Military Be Distracted in a War over Taiwan?* China Strategic Perspectives 15 (2020): 16–19.

19 Joel Wuthnow, *Gray Dragons: Assessing China's Senior Military Leadership*, China Strategic Perspectives 16 (2022).

20 James Mulvenon, *Soldiers of Fortune: The Rise and Fall of the Chinese Military–Business Complex, 1978–1998* (Armonk, NY: M.E. Sharpe, 2001).

21 Nan Tian and Fei Su, *A New Estimate of China's Military Expenditure* (Stockholm: SIPRI, 2021). Thanks to Tai Ming Cheung for the observation of increasing R&D spending.

22 Kenneth W. Allen et al., *Personnel of the People's Liberation Army* (Washington, DC: BluePath Labs, 2022). Thanks to Dennis Blasko for the clarification on active duty numbers.

23 Allen et al., *Personnel of the People's Liberation Army*, 24.

24 Ibid., 28–29.

25 Ibid., 46–47.

26 Marcus Clay and Dennis J. Blasko, "People Win Wars: The PLA Enlisted Force, And Other Related Matters," *War on the Rocks*, July 31, 2020. https://warontherocks.com/2020/07/people-win-wars-the-pla-enlisted-force-and-other-related-matters/.

27 For an overview of China's military educational system, see Kenneth W. Allen and Mingzhi Chen, *The People's Liberation Army's Academic Institutions* (Washington, DC: China Aerospace Studies Institute, 2020).

28 Jie Gao and Kenneth Allen, "PLA Officer Cadet Recruitment: Part 1," *China Brief,* November 20, 2023. https://jamestown.org/program/pla-officer-cadet -recruitment-part-1/.

29 PLA officers are assigned to one of 10 ranks and one of 15 grades. For a discussion, see Allen et al., *Personnel of the People's Liberation Army,* 53–54.

30 The "two incompatibles" refer to the PLA's inability to fight wars and officers' inability to lead in wars. The "five incapables" refer to officers who cannot judge situations, understand commanders' intentions, make decisions, deploy troops, and deal with unexpected programs. See Dennis J. Blasko, "The Chinese Military Speaks to Itself, Revealing Doubts," *War on the Rocks,* February 18, 2019. https://warontherocks.com/2019/02/the-chinese -military-speaks-to-itself-revealing-doubts/.

31 It is also the case that the degree of "jointness" in the U.S. system is questionable and many officers do not serve in joint billets. But the institutionalization of the joint duty assignment system following the 1986 Goldwater–Nichols Act probably means that more U.S. officers have exposure to joint billets than their PLA counterparts. The differences are likely to be most pronounced at the very senior levels, where PLA commanders can reach the equivalent of 4-star rank without much (or in some cases any) joint experience, which contrasts unfavorably with their U.S. equivalents, who have typically served in several joint assignments. Wuthnow, *Gray Dragons.*

32 Tai Ming Cheung, *Innovate to Dominate: The Rise of the Chinese Techno-Security State* (Ithaca, NY: Cornell University Press, 2022).

33 Alex Stone and Peter Wood, *China's Military–Civil Fusion Strategy* (Washington, DC: China Aerospace Studies Institute, 2020). Thanks to Tai Ming Cheung for the clarification on terminology.

34 Elsa B. Kania, *Battlefield Singularity: Artificial Intelligence, Military Revolution, and China's Future Military Power* (Washington, DC: Center for a New American Security, 2017).

4 CONVENTIONAL FORCES

1 Mark Peattie et al., eds., *The Battle for China: Essays on the Military History of the Sino–Japanese War of 1937–1945* (Stanford, CA: Stanford University Press, 2011).

2 Odd Arne Westad, *Decisive Encounters: The Chinese Civil War, 1946–1950* (Stanford, CA: Stanford University Press, 2003).

3 Chen Jian, *China's Road to the Korean War: The Making of Sino–American Confrontation* (New York: Columbia University Press, 1994).

4 Bertil Lintner, *China's India War* (New York: Oxford University Press, 2018).

5 Edward C. O'Dowd, *Chinese Military Strategy in the Third Indochina War: The Last Maoist War* (New York: Routledge, 2007).

6 Harry Gelman, *The Soviet Far East Buildup and Soviet Risk-Taking Against China* (Santa Monica, CA: RAND, 1982).

7 For details, see Dennis J. Blasko, "The Biggest Loser in Chinese Military Reforms: The PLA Army," in Phillip C. Saunders et al., eds., *Chairman Xi Remakes the PLA: Assessing Chinese Military Reforms* (Washington, DC: NDU Press, 2019), 345–392.

8 Joshua Arostegui, *The PCH191 Modular Long-Range Rocket Launcher: Reshaping the PLA Army's Role in a Cross-Strait Campaign* (Newport, RI: Naval War College China Maritime Studies Institute, 2023).

9 Dennis J. Blasko, "China's Contributions to Peacekeeping Operations: Understanding the Numbers," *China Brief*, December 5, 2016. https://jamestown.org/program/chinas-contribution-peacekeeping-operation-understanding-numbers/.

10 Kyle Mizokami, "How Do Chinese Tanks Compare to Russia's and America's?" *The National Interest*, November 5, 2021. https://nationalinterest.org/blog/reboot/how-do-chinese-tanks-compare-russias-and-americas-195633.

11 Teddy Ng, "China's New Light Tank for Mountainous Areas Goes Into Service," *South China Morning Post*, December 28, 2018. https://www.scmp.com/news/china/military/article/2179892/chinas-new-light-tank-mountainous-areas-goes-service.

12 Elsa B. Kania and Ian Burns McCaslin, *Learning Warfare from the Laboratory – China's Progression in Wargaming and Opposing Force Training* (Washington, DC: Institute for the Study of War, 2021).

13 Other military districts, based on provincial boundaries, are supervised by the CMC National Defense Mobilization Department.

14 Thanks to Dennis Blasko for this clarification.

15 Michael Kofman and Rob Lee, "Not Built for Purpose: The Russian Military's Ill-Fated Force Design," *War on the Rocks*, June 2, 2022. https://warontherocks.com/2022/06/not-built-for-purpose-the-russian-militarys-ill-fated-force-design/; "The U.S. Army Turns Focus to the Division Level," Signal, May 26, 2023. https://www.afcea.org/signal-media/defense-operations/us-army-turns-focus-division-level.

16 Joel Wuthnow, *China's Other Army: The People's Armed Police in an Era of Reform*, China Strategic Perspectives 14 (2019).

17 Sue-Lin Wong, "China Masses Troops in Stadium Near Hong Kong," *Financial Times*, August 15, 2019. https://www.ft.com/content/f52c298c-bf23-11e9-b350-db00d509634e.

18 Xiaoming Zhang, *Red Wings Over the Yalu: China, the Soviet Union, and the Air War in Korea* (College Station, TX: Texas A&M University Press, 2022).

19 Kevin McCauley, "PLA Yijiangshan Joint Amphibious Operation: Past Is Prologue," *China Brief*, September 13, 2016. https://jamestown.org/program/pla-yijiangshan-joint-amphibious-operation-past-is-prologue/.

20 Kenneth Allen and Cristina Garafola, *70 Years of the PLA Air Force* (Washington, DC: China Aerospace Studies Institute, 2021), 81–2.

21 Phillip C. Saunders and Joshua K. Wiseman, *Buy, Build, or Steal: China's Quest for Advanced Military Aviation Technologies,* China Strategic Perspectives 4 (2011).

22 Michael S. Chase and Cristina Garafola, "China's Search for a 'Strategic Air Force,'" *Journal of Strategic Studies* 39: 1 (2016): 4–28.

23 Allen and Garafola note that "command of the air" (制空权) refers to the "control of a given air space over a given period of time," and is less extensive than "air superiority" or "air supremacy." Allen and Garafola, *70 Years of the PLA Air Force*, 73.

24 Based on the Soviet model, the Airborne Corps resides within the air force and not the ground forces, as in some Western militaries.

25 "China's Air Force Conducts Combat Air Patrol in South China Sea," Xinhua, July 18, 2016. http://www.xinhuanet.com//english/2016-07/18/c_13 5522387.htm.

26 Mark R. Cozad and Nathan Beauchamp-Mustafaga, *People's Liberation Army Air Force Operations Over Water* (Santa Monica, CA: RAND, 2017), 30. However, Beijing did not declare an air defense identification zone for the South China Sea, which would have been difficult to enforce on a regular basis given its vast size and was perhaps more useful as a threat to be leveraged in negotiations with Southeast Asian countries.

27 Confusingly, PLA writings use "third generation" for what foreign analysts typically call fourth generation fighters, and "fourth generation" for what are usually called fifth generation fighters. The reason is that the PLAAF's first generation of fighters were second-generation Soviet aircraft.

28 Sam Lagrone, "Report: China Hacked Two Dozen U.S. Weapon Designs," USNI News, May 28, 2013. https://news.usni.org/2013/05/28/report-china -hacked-two-dozen-u-s-weapon-designs.

29 Minnie Chan, "China Puts Advanced WS-15 Engines Through J-20 Stealth Fighter Paces," *South China Morning Post*, July 5, 2023. https://www. scmp.com/news/china/military/article/3226562/china-puts-advanced-ws-15- engines-through-j-20-stealth-fighter-paces.

30 Andrea Gilli and Mauro Gilli, "Why China Has Not Caught Up Yet: Military–Technological Superiority and the Limits of Imitation, Reverse Engineering, and Cyber Espionage," *International Security* 43: 3 (2018): 141–189.

31 Joslyn Fleming et al., *Kicking the Tires? The People's Liberation Army's Approach to Maintenance Management* (Santa Monica, CA: RAND, 2023), 85–86.

32 Andreas Rupprecht and Gabriel Dominguez, "PLAAF's New H-6N Bomber Seen Carrying Large Missile," Jane's, October 19, 2020. https://www.janes .com/defence-news/news-detail/plaafs-new-h-6n-bomber-seen-carrying-large -missile.

33 Michael S. Chase, Kenneth W. Allen, and Benjamin S. Purser III, *Overview of People's Liberation Army Air Force "Elite Pilots"* (Santa Monica, CA: RAND, 2016).

34 "Former Armed Forces Personnel Training Foreign Militaries Could Be Prosecuted Under National Security Act," United Kingdom Ministry of Defence, September 17, 2023. https://www.gov.uk/government/news/former-armed-forces-personnel-training-foreign-militaries-could-be-prosecuted-under-national-security-act#:~:text=It%20comes%20after%20the%20Ministry,and%20attracted%20by%20high%20salaries.

35 Thanks to Ken Allen for this clarification.

36 Rod Lee, "PLA Naval Aviation Reorganization 2023," China Aerospace Studies Institute, July 31, 2023.

37 Toshi Yoshihara, *Mao's Army Goes to Sea: The Island Campaigns and the Founding of China's Navy* (Washington, DC: Georgetown University Press, 2023).

38 Michael McDevitt, "The PLA Navy's Antiaccess Role in a Taiwan Contingency," in Phillip C. Saunders et al., eds, *The Chinese Navy: Expanding Capabilities, Evolving Roles* (Washington, DC: NDU Press, 2011), 191–214.

39 Robert Zoellick, "Whither China: From Membership to Responsibility?" Remarks to the National Committee on U.S.–China Relations, September 21, 2005. https://2001-2009.state.gov/s/d/former/zoellick/rem/53682.htm.

40 PLA Navy ships did not transport evacuees, but did play a role in providing security for ferries and monitoring the security situation. Parello-Plesner and Duchâtel, "International Rescue," 113.

41 Jennifer Rice and Erik Robb, *The Origins of "Near Seas Defense" and "Far Seas Protection"* (Newport, RI: Naval War College, China Maritime Studies Institute, 2021).

42 Peter A. Dutton and Ryan Martinson, eds., *China's Evolving Surface Fleet* (Newport, RI: Naval War College Press, 2017).

43 Katherine Si, "China Cements Position as World's Top Shipbuilder in 2023," Seatrade Maritime News, January 16, 2024. https://www.seatrade-maritime.com/shipyards/china-cements-position-worlds-top-shipbuilder-2023.

44 Liu Huaqing, *Memoirs of Liu Huaqing* [刘华清回忆录] (Beijing: PLA Press, 2004), 477.

45 Hayley Wong, "China's Aircraft Carrier No 4 on Track with 'No Technical Bottleneck,' Admiral Reveals in First Official Confirmation," *South China Morning Post*, March 6, 2024. https://www.scmp.com/news/china/military/article/3254415/chinas-aircraft-carrier-no-4-track-no-technical-bottleneck-admiral-reveals-first-official.

46 Thanks to Michael McDevitt for this observation.

47 This assumes that the submarines are traveling at relatively slow speeds, which would not be the case in combat. At higher speeds, their battery life would diminish. Thanks to Bud Cole for this insight.

48 Tong Zhao, *Tides of Change: China's Nuclear Ballistic Missile Submarines and Strategic Stability* (Washington, DC: Carnegie Endowment for International Peace, 2018).

49 Conor Kennedy, "The New Chinese Marine Corps: A 'Strategic Dagger' in a Cross-Strait Invasion," China Maritime Report No. 15, China Maritime Studies Institute, October 2021.

50 Joshua Arostegui, "PLA Army and Marine Corps Amphibious Brigades in a Post-Reform Military," in Joel Wuthnow et al., eds., *Crossing the Strait: China's Military Prepares for War with Taiwan* (Washington, DC: NDU Press, 2022), 161–194.

51 *Annual Threat Assessment of the U.S. Intelligence Community*, Office of the Director of National Intelligence (February 2024), 10.

52 According to one report, "low-frequency transmitters allows contact" between land-based headquarters and SSBNs on patrol in the South China Sea. Peter Wood, Alex Stone, and Thomas Corbett, *Chinese Nuclear Command, Control, and Communications* (Washington, DC: CASI, 2024), 59.

53 Lyle J. Goldstein, *Five Dragons Stirring Up the Sea: Challenge and Opportunity in China's Improving Maritime Enforcement Capabilities* (Newport, RI: Naval War College Press, 2010).

54 Ryan Martinson, "Getting Synergized? PLAN-CCG Cooperation in the Maritime Gray Zone," *Asian Security* 18: 2 (2022): 159–171.

55 Aside from the maritime militias, there are also local ground force militias based in provincial military districts; both can be mobilized for large-scale contingencies through the CMC National Defense Mobilization Department.

56 Conor M. Kennedy and Andrew S. Erickson, "China's Third Sea Force, the People's Armed Forces Maritime Militia: Tethered to the PLA," China Maritime Report No. 1, China Maritime Studies Institute, March 2017.

57 Derek Solen, "Chinese Views of All-Domain Operations," China Aerospace Studies Institute, June 30, 2020.

58 Ian Burns McCaslin and Andrew S. Erickson, *Selling a Maritime Air Force: The PLAAF's Campaign for a Bigger Maritime Role* (Washington, DC: China Aerospace Studies Institute, 2019).

59 Kenneth W. Allen, *Overview of the PLA Air Force's Kongtian Yiti Strategy* (Washington, DC: China Aerospace Studies Institute, 2019).

60 Robert Ross, "China's Naval Nationalism: Sources, Prospects, and the U.S. Response," *International Security* 34: 2 (2009): 46–81.

61 However, in practice many of China's non-combatant evacuations have been carried out through chartered aircraft, not the Air Force. Thanks to Cristina Garafola for this observation.

5 NUCLEAR, SPACE, AND CYBER FORCES

1 *Science of Military Strategy* [战略学] (Beijing: Academy of Military Sciences, 2013), 160.

2 U.S. Department of Defense, *Military and Security Developments Involving the People's Republic of China, 2023* (Washington, DC: Office of Secretary of Defense, 2023), 95–96. https://media.defense.gov/2023/oct/19/2003323409/ -1/-1/1/2023-military-and-security-developments-involving-the-peoples-repub lic-of-china.pdf.

3 Engstrom, *Systems Confrontation and System Destruction Warfare.*

4 John Costello and Joe McReynolds, *China's Strategic Support Force: A Force for a New Era*, China Strategic Perspectives 13 (2018). https://inss.ndu.edu/ Media/News/Article/1651882/chinas-strategic-support-force-a-force-for-a-new -era/.

5 Wu Qiao, Ministry of National Defense News Conference, April 19, 2004. http://eng.mod.gov.cn/xb/News_213114/TopStories/16302051.html.

6 Xinhua, "PLA Information Support Force Founding Meeting Held in Beijing" [中国人民解放军信息支援部队成立大会在京举行], April 19, 2024. https://www.gov.cn/yaowen/liebiao/202404/content_6946295.htm.

7 John Chen, Joe McReynolds, and Kieran Green, "The PLA Strategic Support Force: A 'Joint' Force for Information Operations," in *The PLA Beyond Borders*, 151–179.

8 Xiao Tianliang, ed., *Science of Military Strategy* [战略学] (Beijing: National Defense University Press, 2020).

9 *China's National Defense in the New Era* (Beijing: State Council Information Office, 2019).

10 For a discussion of the evolution of Chinese perspectives on the space and cyberspace domains, see Fiona S. Cunningham, "Strategic Substitution: China's Search for Coercive Leverage in the Information Age," *International Security* 47 (1) (2022): 46–92.

11 Costello and McReynolds, *China's Strategic Support Force*, 25, 53.

12 James Mulvenon, "PLA Computer Network Operations: Scenarios, Doctrine, Organizations, and Capability," in Roy Kamphausen et al., eds., *Beyond the Strait: PLA Missions other than Taiwan* (Carlisle, PA: Strategic Studies Institute, April 2009), 277.

13 Joint Cyber Security Advisory, "People's Republic of China State-Sponsored Cyber Actor Living off the Land to Evade Detection," June 2023. https://media.defense.gov/2023/May/24/2003229517/-1/-1/0/CSA_PRC_ State_Sponsored_Cyber_Living_off_the_Land_v1.1.PDF. For a regularly up-dated technical assessment of PRC cyberspace capabilities, see Cybersecurity and Infrastructure Security Agency, "China Cyber Threat Overview and Advisories." https://www.cisa.gov/topics/cyber-threats-and-advisories/advan ced-persistent-threats/china.

14 *Military and Security Developments Involving the People's Republic of China, 2023*, 95.

15 Josh Fruhlinger, "The OPM hack explained: Bad security practices meet China's Captain America," February 2020. https://www.csoonline.com/

article/566509/the-opm-hack-explained-bad-security-practices-meet-chinas-captain-america.html.

16 This paragraph draws on Mulvenon, "PLA Computer Network Operations," 253–86; and Bryan Krekel, "Capability of the People's Republic of China to Conduct Cyber Warfare and Computer Network Exploitation," report prepared by Northrup Grumman for the U.S.–China Economic and Security Review Commission, October 2009.

17 Joe McReynolds, "China's Military Strategy for Network Warfare," in Joe McReynolds, ed., *China's Evolving Military Strategy* (Washington, DC: Jamestown Foundation, 2016), 229.

18 *China's Military Strategy* (Beijing: State Council Information Office, May 2015).

19 *Science of Military Strategy* [战略学] (Beijing: NDU Press, 2020), 143.

20 This paragraph draws on Dean Cheng, "Space and Chinese National Security: China's Continuing Great Leap Upwards," in Joel Wuthnow et al., eds., *The PLA Beyond Borders: Chinese Military Operations in Regional and Global Context* (Washington, DC: NDU Press, 2021), 324–327.

21 U.S. Department of Defense, *Military and Security Developments Involving the People's Republic of China, 2023* (Washington, DC: Office of Secretary of Defense, 2023), 99.

22 Cheng, "Prospects for China's Military Space Efforts," 231–34.

23 Pollpeter, "The Chinese View of Military Space Operations"; Kevin Pollpeter and Jonathan Ray, "The Conceptual Evolution of China's Military Space Operations and Strategy," in *China's Evolving Military Strategy*, 265–307.

24 U.S. Department of Defense, *Military and Security Developments Involving the People's Republic of China, 2023* (Washington, DC: Office of Secretary of Defense, 2023), 66.

25 U.S. Department of Defense, *Military and Security Developments Involving the People's Republic of China, 2023* (Washington, DC: Office of Secretary of Defense, 2023), 56.

26 National Security Commission on Artificial Intelligence, *Interim Report* (Washington, DC: National Security Commission on Artificial Intelligence, 2019), 7.

27 National Security Commission on Artificial Intelligence, *Interim Report*, 53–55.

28 Paul Mozur, "Beijing Wants A.I. to Be Made in China by 2030," *New York Times*, July 20, 2017.

29 For an overview of PLA thinking and research lines of effort, see Elsa B. Kania, "Chinese Military Innovation in Artificial Intelligence," testimony before the US–China Economic and Security Review Commission Hearing on Trade, Technology, and Military–Civil Fusion, Washington, DC, June 7, 2019. https://www.uscc.gov/sites/default/files/June%207%20Hearing_Panel%201_Elsa%20Kania_Chinese%20Military%20Innovation%20in%20Artificial%20Intelligence_0.pdf.

30 Alexi Mostrous, Joe White, and Serena Cesareo, "The Global Artificial Intelligence Index," Tortoise Media, June 28, 2023. https://www.tortoisemedia.com/2023/06/28/the-global-artificial-intelligence-index/ and Nestor Maslej et al., "The AI Index 2024 Annual Report," AI Index Steering Committee, Institute for Human-Centered AI, Stanford University, Stanford, CA, April 2024.

31 Paul Scharre, *Four Battlegrounds: Power in the Age of Artificial Intelligence* (New York: W.W. Norton & Company, 2023).

32 Helen Toner, Jenny Xiao, and Jeffrey Ding, "The Illusion of China's AI Prowess," *Foreign Affairs*, June 2, 2023.

33 Ma Xiu, *PLA Rocket Force Organization* (Washington, DC: China Aerospace Studies Institute, 2022), 2; Decker Eveleth, *People's Liberation Army Rocket Force Order of Battle 2023* (Monterey, CA: James Martine Center for Nonproliferation Studies, 2023).

34 U.S. Department of Defense, *Military and Security Developments Involving the People's Republic of China, 2023* (Washington, DC: Office of Secretary of Defense, 2023), 66–67.

35 See Jeffrey Lewis, *Paper Tigers: China's Nuclear Posture* (New York: Routledge, 2014), 13–23.

36 For a Chinese analysis, see Xu Weidi, "China's Security Environment and the Role of Nuclear Weapons," in Li Bin and Tong Zhao, eds., *Understanding China's Nuclear Thinking* (Washington, DC: Carnegie Endowment for International Peace, 2016), 19–50.

37 M. Taylor Fravel and Evan S. Medeiros, "China's Search for Assured Retaliation: The Evolution of Chinese Nuclear Strategy and Force Posture," *International Security* 35: 2 (2010): 48–87; Wu Riqiang, "Certainty of Uncertainty: Nuclear Strategy with Chinese Characteristics," *Journal of Strategic Studies* 36: 4 (2013): 579–614.

38 The DF-21 MRBM, a solid-fuel mobile missile initially deployed in 1991, is the main exception.

39 China's initial nuclear weapons were air-deliverable on A-5 fighter-bombers and B-6 bombers, but these aircraft could not reliably penetrate air defenses. The advent of ground-based ICBMs in the 1970s allowed China's deterrent to become operational.

40 See, for example, Li Bin, "China and Nuclear Transparency," in Nicholas Zarimpas, ed., *Transparency in Nuclear Warheads and Materials: The Political and Technical Dimensions* (New York: Oxford University Press, 2003), 51–53; "A Brigade of the Rocket Army Refined and Improved the Synthetic Training Evaluation System: An Innovative Mechanism to Test the Battalion's Independent Combat Capability" [火箭军某旅细化完善合成训练考评体系创新机制检验营独立作战能力], *PLA Daily* [解放军报], April 14, 2019, http://www.81.cn/jfjbmap/content/2019-04/14/content_231587.htm. On China's nuclear command and control, see Fiona Cunningham, *Nuclear Command,*

Control, and Communications Systems of the People's Republic of China, NAPSNet Special Report (Berkeley, CA: Nautilus Institute for Security and Sustainability, July 18, 2019). https://nautilus.org/napsnet/napsnet-special-reports/nuclear-command-control-and-communications-systems-of-the-peo ples-republic-of-china/. On China's nuclear-warhead-handling practices see Mark Stokes, *China's Nuclear Warhead Storage and Handling System* (Arlington, VA: Project 2049 Institute, March 12, 2010. https://project2049.net/wp-con tent/uploads/2018/05/chinas_nuclear_warhead_storage_and_handling_sys tem.pdf.

41 *Military and Security Developments Involving China, 2021,* 90–92; Michael S. Chase, "Nuclear Bomber Could Boost PLAAF Strategic Role, Create Credible Triad," *China Brief* (July 6, 2017), 5–9; and Tong Zhao, *Tides of Change: China's Nuclear Ballistic Missile Submarines and Strategic Stability* (Washington, D.C.: Carnegie Endowment for International Peace, 2018).

42 For an example, see Hans M. Kristensen, "China's Strategic Systems and Programs," in *China's Strategic Arsenal,* 93–124.

43 Joby Warrick, "China Is Building More Than 100 New Missile Silos in Its Western Desert, Analysts Say," *Washington Post*, June 30, 2021. https://www .washingtonpost.com/national-security/china-nuclear-missile-silos/2021/06 /30/0fa8debc-d9c2-11eb-bb9e-70fda8c37057_story.html; William J. Broad and David E. Sanger, "A 2nd New Nuclear Missile Base for China, and Many Questions About Strategy," *New York Times*, July 26, 2021. https://www.ny times.com/2021/07/26/us/politics/china-nuclear-weapons.html; and Rod Lee, "PLA Likely Begins Construction of an Intercontinental Ballistic Missile Silo Site near Hanggin Banner," *China Aerospace Studies Institute*, August 12, 2021. https://www.airuniversity.af.edu/CASI/Display/Article/2729781/pla-likely-be gins-construction-of-an-intercontinental-ballistic-missile-silo-si/.

44 See, for example, Jeffrey Lewis, "China Is Radically Expanding Its Nuclear Missile Silos," *Foreign Policy*, June 30, 2021. https://foreignpolicy.com/2021/06 /30/china-nuclear-weapons-silos-arms-control/; Sean O'Connor, "Questions Remain Over Identification of China's Missile Silos," *Jane's Intelligence Review*, August 6, 2021; Matthew Kroenig, "China's Nuclear Silos and the Arms Control Fantasy," *The Wall Street Journal*, July 7, 2021. https://www.wsj. com/articles/chinas-nuclear-silos-and-the-arms-control-fantasy-11625696243; and James Cameron, "China's Silos: New Intelligence, Old Problems," *War on the Rocks*, August 12, 2021. https://warontherocks.com/2021/08/ beijings-silos-new-intelligence-old-problems/.

45 The DF-26 was first fielded in 2016. See Charles A. Richard, "Statement before the Senate Committee on Armed Services," February 13, 2020, 4. See also Kristin Huang, "China's Hypersonic DF-17 Missile Threatens Regional Stability, Analyst Warns," *South China Morning Post*, August 23, 2019. https:// www.scmp.com/news/china/military/article/3023972/chinas-hypersonic-df -17-missile-threatens-regional-stability.

46 David E. Sanger and William J. Broad, "China's Weapon Tests Close to a 'Sputnik Moment,' U.S. General Says," *New York Times*, October 27, 2021. https://www.nytimes.com/2021/10/27/us/politics/china-hypersonic-missile.html.

47 *Military and Security Developments Involving the People's Republic of China, 2021*, 91, 93–94.

48 *Annual Report to Congress: Military and Security Developments Involving the People's Republic of China 2022* (Washington, DC: Office of the Secretary of Defense, 2023), 59.

49 *Annual Report to Congress 2023*, 59; Tong Zhao, *Tides of Change: Nuclear Ballistic Missile Submarines and Strategic Stability* (Washington, DC: Carnegie Endowment for International Peace, 2018).

50 *Annual Report to Congress 2022*, 94; Anthony J. Cotton, Testimony before the Subcommittee on Strategic Forces, Committee on Armed Services, U.S. House of Representatives, March 8, 2023; Minnie Chan, "China's New Nuclear Submarine Missiles Expand Range in US: Analysts," *South China Morning Post*, May 2, 2021. https://www.scmp.com/news/china/military/article/3131873/chinas-new-nuclear-submarine-missiles-expand-range-us-analysts; Hans M. Kristensen, Matt Korda, and Eliana Reynolds, "Chinese Nuclear Weapons, 2023," *Bulletin of the Atomic Scientists* 79: 2 (2023): 125.

51 Michael S. Chase, "Nuclear Bomber Could Boost PLAAF Strategic Role, Create Credible Triad"; *Annual Report to Congress 2021*, 91–92.

52 *Military and Security Developments Involving the People's Republic of China, 2023*, 111.

53 *Military and Security Developments Involving the People's Republic of China, 2021* and Hans M. Kristensen and Matt Korda, "Chinese Nuclear Weapons, 2021," *Bulletin of the Atomic Scientists*, 77:6 (2021), 318–336. doi: 10.1080/00963402.2021.1989208. These sources are supplemented by *Ballistic and Cruise Missile Threat 2020* and Office of the Deputy Assistant Secretary of Defense for Nuclear Matters, *Nuclear Matters Handbook 2020* (Washington, DC: DOD, 2020).

54 See Jeffrey A. Larsen and M. Shane Smith, eds., *Arms Control at a Crossroads: Renewal or Demise?* (Boulder, CO: Lynne Rienner, 2024).

55 For analysis of these alternative explanations, see David C. Logan and Phillip C. Saunders, *Discerning the Drivers of China's Nuclear Force Development: Models, Indicators, and Data*, China Strategic Perspectives 18 (2023).

56 For examples of past debates, see Alastair Iain Johnston, "China's New 'Old Thinking': The Concept of Limited Deterrence," *International Security* 20: 3 (1995–1996): 5–42; Gregory Kulacki, *China's Military Calls for Putting Its Nuclear Forces on Alert* (Cambridge, MA: Union of Concerned Scientists, January 2016).

57 For a survey of views on the implications for the United States, see Caitlin Talmadge and Joshua Rovner, "The meaning of China's nuclear moderniza-

tion," *Journal of Strategic Studies* 46: 6–7, 1116–1148. https//doi.org/10.1080/014 02390.2023.2212871.

58 Michael S. Chase and Arthur Chan, *China's Evolving Approach to Integrated Strategic Deterrence* (Arlington, VA: RAND, 2016). https://www.rand.org/pubs /research_reports/RR1366.html.

59 Chris Buckley, "Fear and Ambition Propel Xi's Nuclear Acceleration," *New York Times*, February 4, 2024. https://www.nytimes.com/2024/02/04/world /asia/china-nuclear-missiles.html.

60 Xiao Tianliang, ed., *Science of Military Strategy* [战略学] (Beijing: National Defence University Press, 2020), 387.

61 David C. Logan and Phillip C. Saunders, *Discerning the Drivers of China's Nuclear Force Development: Models, Indicators, and Data*, China Strategic Perspectives 18 (July 2023) (2023). https://ndupress.ndu.edu/Media/News/News-Article-View/Article/3471053/discerning-the-drivers-of-chinas-nuclear-force-develop ment-models-indicators-an/.

6 SHAPING THE NEW SECURITY ENVIRONMENT

1 Deng Bibo, "Major Achievements and Basic Experience in China's Military Diplomacy in the New Era" [新时代中国军事外交的重大成就及基本经验], *China Military Science* [国军科学] 182 (April 2022): 54–63.

2 U.S. Energy Information Administration, *China Country Analysis Brief*, November 2023, 13.

3 See Dawn C. Murphy, *China's Rise in the Global South: The Middle East, Africa, and Beijing's Alternative World Order* (Stanford, CA: Stanford University Press, 2022).

4 Ministry of Foreign Affairs of the People's Republic of China, "The Global Security Initiative Concept Paper," February 21, 2023. https://www.mfa.gov .cn/eng/wjbxw/202302/t20230221_11028348.html and Carla P. Freeman, "Xi's Global Campaign for Chinese Security," *Asian Perspective* 47: 2 (2023): 313–322. https://doi.org/10.1353/apr.2023.0016.

5 Michael Schuman, Jonathan Fulton, and Tuvia Gering, "How Beijing's newest global initiatives seek to remake the world order," *Atlantic Council Issue Brief*, June 21, 2023. https://www.atlanticcouncil.org/in-depth-research-reports/issue-brief/how-beijings-newest-global-initiatives-seek-to-remake-the-world-order/.

6 Kenneth Allen, Phillip C. Saunders, and John Chen, *Chinese Military Diplomacy, 2003–2016: Trends and Implications*, China Strategic Perspectives 11 (2017): 22.

7 James Sicbens and Ryan Lucas, *Military Operations Other Than War in China's Foreign Policy* (Washington, DC: Stimson Center, 2022).

8 The two N/A entries in Figure 6.2 are meetings with the United Nations on peacekeeping.

9 For details, see Andrew S. Erickson and Austin M. Strange, *Six Years at Sea and Counting: Gulf of Aden Anti-Piracy and China's Maritime Commons Presence* (Washington, DC: Brookings Institution Press, 2016).

10 Of note, replenishment visits in the Covid period involve almost no interactions with host country nationals. According to PLA media, supplies are shipped from China via a COSCO ship and are transferred to the PLAN replenishment ship via forklift with minimal human interaction.

11 Deng, "Major Achievements and Basic Experience in China's Military Diplomacy in the New Era."

12 Deng, "Major Achievements and Basic Experience in China's Military Diplomacy in the New Era."

13 James Siebens and Ryan Lucas, *Military Operations Other Than War in China's Foreign Policy* (Washington, DC: The Stimson Center, 2022), 23.

14 Dr. Andrew Taffer contributed to the analysis of Sino–Russian military relations in this section.

15 Office of the Director of National Intelligence, *Support Provided by the People's Republic of China to Russia*, July 2023.

16 Frank G. Hoffman, "Examining Complex Forms of Conflict: Gray Zone and Hybrid Challenges," PRISM 7: 4 (2018): 36.

17 Ketian Zhang, "Explaining China's Large-Scale Land Reclamation in the South China Sea: Timing and Ratonale," *Journal of Strategic Studies* 46 (6–7) (2023): 1185–1214.

18 Jeff M. Smith, "High Noon in the Himalayas: Behind the China–India Standoff at Doka La," *War on the Rocks*, July 13, 2017. https://waronthe rocks.com/2017/07/high-noon-in-the-himalayas-behind-the-china-india-stand off-at-doka-la/.

19 Joel Wuthnow, Satu Limaye, and Nilanthi Samaranayake, "Doklam, One Year Later: China's Long Game in the Himalayas," *War on the Rocks*, June 7, 2018. https://warontherocks.com/2018/06/doklam-one-year-later-chinas-long-game-in-the-himalayas/.

20 M. Taylor Fravel and Alastair Iain Johnston, "Chinese Signaling in the East China Sea?" *Washington Post*, April 12, 2014. https://www.washingtonpost .com/news/monkey-cage/wp/2014/04/12/chinese-signaling-in-the-east-china -sea/.

21 Aaron-Matthew Lariosa, "4 Philippine Sailors Injured, 2 Vessels Damaged in Chinese Attempt to Block Second Thomas Shoal Resupply," USNI News, March 5, 2024. https://news.usni.org/2024/03/05/4-philippine-sailors-in jured-2-vessels-damaged-in-chinese-attempt-to-block-second-thomas-shoal-resupply.

22 *Thin Ice in the Himalayas: Handling the India–China Border Dispute* (New York: International Crisis Group, 2023).

23 Sun Yun, "China's Strategic Assessment of the Ladakh Clash," *War on the Rocks*, June 19, 2020. https://warontherocks.com/2020/06/chinas-strategic-as sessment-of-the-ladakh-clash/.

24 Raul Pedrozo, "Preserving Navigational Rights and Freedoms: The Right to Conduct Military Activities in China's Exclusive Economic Zone," *Chinese Journal of International Law* 9: 1 (2010): 9–29.

25 "Department of Defense Releases Declassified Images, Videos of Coercive and Risky PLA Operational Behavior," U.S. Department of Defense, October 17, 2023. https://www.defense.gov/News/Releases/Release/Article/3559903 /department-of-defense-releases-declassified-images-videos-of-coercive-and -risky/.

26 "Chinese Propaganda Campaign Demands More Awareness," Taiwan FactCheck Center, September 15, 2022. https://tfc-taiwan.org.tw/articles /8169.

27 Scott W. Harold, Nathan Beauchamp-Mustafaga, and Jeffrey Hornung, *Chinese Disinformation Efforts on Social Media* (Santa Monica: RAND, 2021), 59–62.

28 Joel Wuthnow, "China's Military Claims to Be Virus-Free," *Foreign Policy*, March 20, 2020. https://foreignpolicy.com/2020/03/20/pla-coronavirus-inva sion-chinas-military-claims-to-be-virus-free/.

29 Michael D. Swaine, "Xi Jinping's Speech to the Central Conference on Work Relating to Foreign Affairs: Assessing and Advancing Major-Power Diplomacy with Chinese Characteristics," *China Leadership Monitor* 46 (2013): 1–19.

30 Andrew D. Taffer and David Wallsh, "China's Indo-Pacific Folly," *Foreign Affairs*, January 31, 2023. https://www.foreignaffairs.com/asia/china-indo-pacific-folly.

31 "China's Approach to Foreign Policy Gets Largely Negative Reviews in 24-Country Survey," Pew Research Center, July 27, 2023.

32 James Siebens, "Keep Calm and Carry On: China's Armed Coercion Isn't Working," Stimson Center, December 19, 2023. https://www.stimson.org /2023/keep-calm-and-carry-on-chinas-armed-coercion-isnt-working/.

7 PREPARING FOR WAR WITH TAIWAN

1 "Colin Kahl on America's Defense Strategy," *Foreign Policy*, April 17, 2023. https://foreignpolicy.com/live/colin-kahl-on-americas-defense-strategy/.

2 Robert S. Ross, "The 1995–1996 Taiwan Strait Confrontation: Coercion, Credibility, and the Use of Force," *International Security* 25: 2 (2000): 87–123.

3 Taiwan's formal name, the Republic of China, dates back to when the Nationalist Party ruled all of China before 1949. Changing the name would break Taiwan's symbolic ties to China.

4 "Taiwan Says 5 China Coast Guard Ships Entered Waters Near Frontline Islands," Reuters, February 26, 2024. https://www.reuters.com/world/asia -pacific/taiwan-minister-says-5-china-coast-guard-ships-entered-waters- around-kinmen-2024-02-27/.

5 "Taiwan Independence v. Unification with the Mainland," National Chengchi University Election Study Center, February 22, 2024. https://esc .nccu.edu.tw/PageDoc/Detail?fid=7801&id=6963.

6 Li Yuan, "Perils of Preaching Nationalism Play Out on Chinese Social Media," *New York Times*, August 4, 2022. https://www.nytimes.com/2022/08 /04/business/new-world-nancy-pelosi-taiwan-social-media.html.

7 Yu-Jie Chen and Jerome A. Cohen, "China–Taiwan Relations Re-Examined: The '1992 Consensus' and Cross-Strait Agreements," *University of Pennsylvnia Asian Law Review* (2019): 1–40.

8 "Full Text of the Report to the 20th National Congress of the Communist Party of China," Ministry of Foreign Affairs, October 25, 2022. https://www .fmprc.gov.cn/eng/wjdt_665385/zyjh_665391/202210/t20221025_10791908 .html.

9 "CIA Chief: China Has Some Doubt on Ability to Invade Taiwan," AP, February 26, 2023. https://apnews.com/article/russia-ukraine-taiwan-poli tics-united-states-government-eaf869eb617c6c356b2708607ed15759.

10 Brian Hart, Bonnie S. Glaser, and Matthew P. Funaiole, "China's 2027 Goal Marks the PLA's Centennial, Not an Expedited Military Modernization," *China Brief*, March 26, 2021. https://jamestown.org/program/chinas- 2027-goal-marks-the-plas-centennial-not-an-expedited-military-moderniza tion/.

11 "Anti-Secession Law Adopted by NPC (Full Text)," *China Daily*, March 14, 2005. http://www.chinadaily.com.cn/english/doc/2005-03/14/content_4246 43.htm.

12 Brendan Rittenhouse Green and Caitlin Talmadge, "Then What? Assessing the Military Implications of Chinese Control of Taiwan," *International Security* 47: 1 (2022): 7–45.

13 Agatha Kratz and Charlie Vest, "Sanctioning China in a Taiwan Crisis: Scenarios and Risks," Rhodium Group, June 22, 2023.

14 "Full Text of Xi Jinping's Report at the 19th CPC National Congress," Xinhua, November 3, 2017. http://www.xinhuanet.com/english/special/ 2017-11/03/c_136725942.htm.

15 Cai Xia, "The Party That Failed," *Foreign Affairs* 100 (2021): 78–96.

16 Andrew Scobell, "China's Calculus on the Use of Force: Futures, Costs, Benefits, Risks, and Goals," in Wuthnow et al., eds., *Crossing the Strait*, 65–86. However, this is likely only in extreme circumstances. In cases of instability where there is no existential risk to the regime, Chinese history and political science literature suggests that "diversionary wars" are uncommon. See M. Taylor Fravel, "The Myth of Chinese Diversionary

War," *Foreign Affairs*, September 15, 2023. https://www.foreignaffairs.com/china/myth-chinese-diversionary-war.

17 Hal Brands and Michael Beckley, *Danger Zone: The Coming Conflict with China* (New York: W.W. Norton & Company, 2022).

18 Oriana Skylar Mastro and Derek Scissors, "China Hasn't Reached the Peak of Its Power," *Foreign Affairs*, August 22, 2022. https://www.foreignaffairs.com/china/china-hasnt-reached-peak-its-power.

19 In 2020, the PLA started the process of updating the joint doctrine with the release of a new Joint Operations Outline. New doctrine will take into consideration the revised PLA organizational structure (see Chapter 3 for details). See David M. Finkelstein, *The PLA's New Joint Doctrine: The Capstone of the New Era Operations Regulations System* (Arlington, VA: CNA, 2021).

20 Michael Casey, "Firepower Strike, Blockade, Landing: PLA Campaigns for a Cross-Strait Conflict," in Wuthnow et al., eds., *Crossing the Strait*, 113–138.

21 Lonnie Henley, *Beyond the First Battle: Overcoming a Protracted Blockade of Taiwan* (Newport, RI: Naval War College China Maritime Studies Institute, 2023).

22 *Military and Security Developments Involving the People's Republic of China* (Washington, DC: Department of Defense, 2023), 127.

23 Joel Wuthnow, "Who Does What? Chinese Command and Control in a Taiwan Scenario," in Wuthnow et al., eds., *Crossing the Strait*, 277–306.

24 Larry Worzel, "The PLA and Mission Command: Is the Party Control System Too Rigid for its Adaptation by China?" Association of the United States Army, Land Warfare Paper 159, March 2024.

25 Chieh Chung, "PLA Logistics and Mobilization Capacity in a Taiwan Invasion," in Wuthnow, *Crossing the Strait*, 253–276.

26 J. Michael Dahm, *More Chinese Ferry Tales: China's Use of Civilian Shipping in Military Activities, 2021–2022* (Newport, RI: Naval War College China Maritime Studies Institute, 2023).

27 Nancy Bernkopf Tucker, "Strategic Ambiguity or Strategic Clarity?" in Nancy Bernkopf Tucker, ed., *Dangerous Strait: The U.S.–Taiwan–China Crisis* (New York: Columbia University Press, 2005), 186–212.

28 Mark Cozad et al., *Gaining Victory in Systems Warfare* (Santa Monica, CA: RAND, 2023), 84.

29 Mark F. Cancian, Matthew Cancian, and Eric Heginbotham, *The First Battle of the Next War: Wargaming a Chinese Invasion of Taiwan* (Washington, DC: CSIS, 2023), 96–97.

30 Engstrom, *Systems Confrontation and System Destruction Warfare*.

31 Eric Heginbotham et al., *China's Evolving Nuclear Deterrent* (Santa Monica, CA: RAND, 2017), 28–31.

32 Zhao Xiaozhuo, "Evolving Forms of War: A Perspective from the Ukraine Crisis" [从乌克兰危机看战争形态演变], *China Security Studies* [国家安全研究], February 2023.

33 Chris Buckley, "China Draws Lessons from Russia's Losses in Ukraine, and Its Gains," *New York Times*, April 1, 2023. https://www.nytimes.com/2023/04/01/world/asia/china-russia-ukraine-war.html.

34 Joel Wuthnow, "Rightsizing Chinese Military Lessons from Ukraine," *INSS Strategic Forum* 311 (September 2022).

35 Chris Buckley, "Fear and Ambition Propel Xi's Nuclear Acceleration," *New York Times*, February 4, 2024. https://www.nytimes.com/2024/02/04/world/asia/china-nuclear-missiles.html.

36 Evan A. Feigenbaum and Adam Szubin, "What China Has Learned From the Ukraine War," *Foreign Affairs*, February 14, 2023. https://www.foreignaffairs.com/china/what-china-has-learned-ukraine-war.

37 Lee expands on his ideas in a 2022 book, *How Taiwan Can Win* [臺灣的勝算] (Taipei: Linking Publishing Co. Ltd., 2022).

38 "Military Conducts First Anti-Takeover Drills at Taoyuan," *Taipei Times*, July 27, 2023. https://www.taipeitimes.com/News/front/archives/2023/07/27/2003803809.

39 George J. Gilboy and Eric Heginbotham, "America Needs a Single Integrated Operational Plan for Economic Conflict with China," *Lawfare*, December 17, 2023. https://cis.mit.edu/publications/analysis-opinion/2023/america-needs-single-integrated-operational-plan-economic.

40 Elbridge A. Colby, *The Strategy of Denial: American Defense in an Age of Great Power Conflict* (New Haven: Yale University Press, 2021).

41 Mark A. Milley, "Strategic Inflection Point: The Most Historically Significant and Fundamental Change in the Character of War Is Happening Now," *Joint Force Quarterly* 110 (2023): 6–15.

42 Josh Rogin, "The U.S. Military Plans a 'Hellscape' to Deter China From Attacking Taiwan," *Washington Post*, June 10, 2024, https://www.washingtonpost.com/opinions/2024/06/10/taiwan-china-hellscape-military-plan/.

43 Stacie Pettyjohn, Hannah Dennis, and Molly Campbell, *Swarms Over the Strait: Drone Warfare in a Future Fight to Defend Taiwan* (Washington, DC: CNAS, 2024).

44 Arzan Tarapore, *Deterring an Attack on Taiwan: Policy Options for India and Other Non-Belligerent States* (Washington, DC: Australian Strategic Policy Institute, 2024).

8 A GLOBAL PLA

1 Joel Wuthnow, "The PLA Beyond Asia: China's Growing Military Presence in the Red Sea Region," *INSS Strategic Forum* 303 (January 2020).

2 M. Taylor Fravel, "China's Attitude Toward UN Peacekeeping Operations Since 1989," *Asian Survey* 36: 11 (1996): 1102–1121.

3 Andrew S. Erickson and Austin Strange, *Six Years at Sea . . . and Counting: Gulf of Aden Anti-Piracy and China's Maritime Commons Presence* (Washington, DC: Brookings Institution Press, 2015).

4 Peter W. Mackenzie, *Red Crosses, Blue Water: Hospital Ships and China's Expanding Naval Presence* (Arlington, VA: CNA, 2011).

5 Daniel M. Hartnett, "The 'New Historic Missions': Reflections on Hu Jintao's Military Legacy," in Roy Kamphausen et al., eds., *Assessing the People's Liberation Army in the Hu Jintao Era* (Carlisle, PA: U.S. Army War College Press, 2014), pp. 31–80.

6 Andrea Ghiselli, "Market Opportunities and Political Responsibilities: The Difficult Development of Chinese Private Security Companies Abroad," *Armed Forces & Society* 46: 1 (2020): 25–45.

7 Mathieu Duchâtel, Oliver Bräuner, and Zhou Hang, *Protecting China's Overseas Interests* (Stockholm: SIPRI, 2014).

8 Andrea Ghiselli, "Civil-Military Relations and Organizational Preferences Regarding the Use of the Military in Chinese Foreign Policy: Insights from the Debate on MOOTW," *Journal of Strategic Studies* 43:3 (2020), 421–442.

9 Jane Perlez, "Chinese Plan to Kill Drug Lord With Drone Highlights Military Advances," *New York Times*, February 20, 2013. https://www.nytimes.com/20 13/02/21/world/asia/chinese-plan-to-use-drone-highlights-military-advances .html.

10 This appears to have been the case when China was caught off guard by Russia's February 2022 invasion of Ukraine.

11 "Chinese Peacekeepers in Sudan Rescue Trapped Vehicle," Xinhua, November 7, 2019. http://www.xinhuanet.com/english/2019-11/07/c_138536 485.htm.

12 *The Global Security Initiative Concept Paper* (Beijing: Ministry of Foreign Affairs, February 21, 2023).

13 Joel Wuthnow, "PLA Operational Lessons from UN Peacekeeping," in Joel Wuthnow et al., eds., *The PLA Beyond Borders: Chinese Military Operations in Regional and Global Context* (Washington, DC: NDU Press, 2021), 235–262.

14 Joel Wuthnow, Phillip C. Saunders, and Ian Burns McCaslin, "PLA Overseas Operations in 2035: Inching Toward a Global Combat Capability," *INSS Strategic Forum* 309, May 2021.

15 Isaac B. Kardon and Wendy Leutert, "Pier Competitor: China's Power Position in Global Ports," *International Security* 46: 4 (2022): 9–47.

16 In addition to Djibouti, there is a People's Armed Police outpost in Tajikistan, which focuses on counter-terrorism missions. The Aerospace Force operates several satellite tracking stations around the world.

17 Peter Dutton, Isaac B. Kardon, and Conor Kennedy, *Djibouti: China's First Overseas Strategic Strongpoint* (Newport, RI: Naval War College China Maritime Studies Institute, 2020).

18 Warren P. Strobel et al., "Beijing Plans a New Training Facility in Cuba, Raising Prospect of Chinese Troops on America's Doorstep," *Wall Street*

Journal, June 20, 2023. https://www.wsj.com/articles/beijing-plans-a-new-training-facility-in-cuba-raising-prospect-of-chinese-troops-on-americas-doorstep-e17fd5d1.

19 Paul Nantulya, "Chinese Professional Military Education for Africa: Key Influence and Strategy," U.S. Institute of Peace, July 5, 2023.

20 "Chinese-Built Military Training Centre Opens in Tanzania," defenceWeb, February 13, 2018. https://www.defenceweb.co.za/land/land-land/chinese-built-military-training-centre-opens-in-tanzania/.

21 Colum Lynch, "U.S. Peacekeepers to Protect China's Oil Interests in Sudan," *Foreign Policy*, June 16, 2014.

22 "Risk Firm: Pirates Board Chinese-Run Ship in Gulf of Guinea," AP, April 11, 2023. https://apnews.com/article/pirates-board-ship-gulf-of-guinea-chinese-9f22a5038eb7c38d9e675113f771e151.

23 See also Kristen Gunness, "The PLA's Expeditionary Force: Current Capabilities and Future Trends," in Joel Wuthnow et al., eds., *The PLA Beyond Borders: China's Military in Regional and Global Context* (Washington, DC: NDU Press, 2021), 23–50.

24 *Science of Military Strategy* [战略学] (Beijing: NDU Press, 2020), 232–233.

25 John Chen and Joel Wuthnow, "Sea Dragons: Special Operations and China's Maritime Strategy," China Maritime Report 18, China Maritime Studies Institute, January 2022.

26 Phillip C. Saunders, "Beyond Borders: PLA Command and Control of Overseas Operations," *INSS Strategic Forum* 306, July 2020.

27 Li Ruonan and Liu Feng, "Contending Ideas on China's Non-Alliance Strategy," *Chinese Journal of International Politics* 10: 2 (2017): 151–171.

Index